A Guide for
Social Workers and
Other Human Service
Professionals

Values-Based Coaching

By Marilyn Edelson

NASW PRESS

National Association of Social Workers
Washington, DC

James J. Kelly, PhD, ACSW, LCSW, President
Elizabeth J. Clark, PhD, ACSW, MPH, Executive Director

Cheryl Y. Bradley, *Publisher*
Lisa M. O'Hearn, *Managing Editor*
John Cassels, *Project Manager and Staff Editor*
Marla Bonner, *Copyeditor*
Lori J. Holtzinger, *Proofreader and Indexer*

Cover by Naylor Design, Inc.
Interior design by Electronic Quill
Printed and bound by Victor Graphics

© 2010 by the NASW Press

Library of Congress Cataloging-in-Publication Data

Edelson, Marilyn.
Values-based coaching: a guide for social workers and other human service professionals / by Marilyn Edelson.
    p.   cm.
Includes bibliographical references and index.
ISBN 978-0-87101-398-9
1. Personal coaching. 2. Life skills. I. Title.
BF637.P36E34 2010
361.3'2—dc22

2009018845

Printed in the United States of America

A coach is someone who tells you what you don't want to hear, who has you see what you don't want to see, so you can be who you have always known you could be.

—Tom Landry

Table of Contents

Foreword

My two lovely daughters, Sara and Jessica, are and have always been my main inspiration. They have been wonderful coaches to me over the years—gently admonishing me, often late at night while I am still at my computer, not to "work too hard" and to keep balance (something we coaches talk about a lot) in my own life.

I am grateful to both my friends—particularly Pam Narahara and Kris Lasker—and staff—particularly Forum leaders Roger Smith, David Cunningham, and Joe DiMaggio—at Landmark Education, where, as a result of my experience participating in the Landmark Forum and other courses, I learned to live life from a place of new possibilities, to bring possibility to others, and to expand my world into a space larger than I ever would have imagined.

I also want to thank Mimi Sohn Licht, Patience Sampson, and the late Bonnie Jaffe, my trusted "peer group." We came together over 18 years ago to discuss cases but have ended up "doing life" together—marriage, divorce, raising children, grandchildren, illness, job transition, and career reinvention. Carol Trust, Executive Director of the Massachusetts Chapter of NASW, has been my main champion. It was she who had the courage to promote my conferences both locally and regionally, produced home education tapes that have been widely distributed, and encouraged me to spread the word on this new and somewhat controversial area. I salute her for her groundbreaking approach to social work in her column in NASW Massachusetts' *Focus* newsletter, "Possibilities."

Thanks also to Mike Harris, a corporate client who trusted me enough to actually go into business with me, and to David Herron, a respected senior IT consultant who welcomed me into that world.

I also have been fortunate enough to be mentored by Roz Zander, who was instrumental in pointing me to Landmark Education, where I experienced a significant personal transformation that led me toward coaching; the late Laura Whitworth, an original founder of the Coaches Training Institute, who was one of my initial trainers in co-active coaching; Frederic Hudson, whose workshop I audited with friends at Fielding Institute in the 1980s; and Carl Kaestner, good friend and neighbor, who I met while he was teaching an executive coaching course on Cape Cod and with whom I have had the pleasure of brainstorming and collaborating since. Also an inspiration, as well as the person responsible for my sticking with my game plan over the past 10 years, is Jinny Ditzler, creator of the Best Year Yet planning process. Jinny was coaching long before there was even a word for it.

I am grateful to Carl, Marita Frijohn, David Cunningham of Landmark Education, Virginia Kellogg, Randy Nathan, Phil Sandahl, Ruth Hegarty, and others—some well-known in the field and some not—for sharing their experiences of coaching with me.

Finally, I thank my cousins, Natalie and Arthur Schatz, for their support and kindness over the years. Special thanks go to Arthur, who helped with the painstaking editing process of my initial homegrown publication, and to my good friend Joyce Levine, author of *Breakthrough Astrology*, who gave me the real push to submit my proposal to the publisher. Finally, I thank Daniel Dreyfuss, whose persistent challenges to help him understand how coaching is distinguished from psychotherapy and wise commentary on my manuscript helped me refine my thoughts and clarify my message.

Introduction

When I began my journey as a coach, I had no idea what a roller coaster ride it would be. I only knew I loved to witness the joy of people transforming their lives. As a therapist, I enjoyed deep, long, intimate relationships and many profoundly moving moments; yet something was missing. The ethical guidelines of my profession often prevented me from saying everything I felt ought to be said. They also prevented me from giving needed hugs (which, I confess, I often did anyway) and from addressing my clients' whole lives, including their businesses, their finances (except when they didn't pay and the "transference" needed to be addressed), and their spirituality. But, most of all, I would hesitate to ask powerful questions or suggest that they might be responsible for their own happiness. Instead, I indulged their stories, many of which were, in fact, extremely painful, and I participated unwittingly in reinforcing their notions of themselves as victims. I had tools for helping clients get in touch with denied anger toward their families, but none to help them successfully move through to the other side of that anger. Of course, I too felt like a victim in my own life, despite years of my own personal, successful, life-altering psychotherapy. Therapy had helped me heal my childhood pain sufficiently to function successfully in my work, to marry, and to have children. However, it took much too long and still did not leave me feeling fully in the driver's seat of my life. I enjoyed my work and did well at it, but . . . something was missing.

In 1981, I participated in a one-day workshop in adult development with Frederic Hudson, author of *Adult Development, LifeMaps,* and *The Coaching Handbook* and founder of the Hudson Institute. During the workshop, Frederic drew a simple wheel representing various areas of our lives—work, family, friendship, money, personal growth, and so forth. He asked us to rate our level of satisfaction in those areas. He then had us write our goals in each area for the next three months, six months, one year, two years, five years, and 10 years on index cards, and he instructed us not to look at them for at least a year. I actually forgot about the cards altogether until a number of years later, when they literally fell out of a book I was taking off the shelf. Amazingly, almost 75 percent of what I had written had come to pass! When I wrote them down, many of those goals seemed unimaginable, yet I achieved them. What I didn't realize then was that my workshop with Frederic had been my first experience of coaching.

I had left my job of 15 years as chief social worker on a general hospital in-patient psychiatry unit in the Boston area and spent a transition year selling residential real estate. I felt burnt out after 17 years of in-patient psychiatry. When I started my private practice, it filled quickly. Other

1

practitioners began to call me and ask me my "secret." I told them I had none, but when asked to speak with the private practice committee of the Massachusetts Chapter of NASW, I sat down to think about it and realized I had integrated some valuable lessons from real estate. I realized I was not afraid of marketing or self-promotion—concepts that many therapists find distasteful. I also had integrated the possibility of selling as a service that could make a difference.

Around 1992, I began to think about new career options. Managed care was looming large in Massachusetts, and although I was doing well and enjoyed my practice, I had a strong wish to expand beyond the safe four walls of my office. I wanted to make a bigger difference than I could one-on-one, with families, or small groups. Many of my consultations with other therapists supported or inspired interesting and valuable directions and projects. I saw that I could make a difference with them. I was also curious about and drawn to the world of business. Some "coaching" I had offered a client resulted in a large windfall for him. Around that time, I discovered the growing profession of coaching and knew that coaching was what I wanted to do.

This book is a product of the transformation I have made from therapist to coach. Unlike many coach/therapists who have completely given up their therapy practices, I continue to practice both. My perspective is that coaching is both a set of new skills and a new career path. You can choose for yourself. Hopefully, the following pages will give you some direction. I provide the basic framework for understanding the developing field of personal and professional coaching, exercises to help you directly experience coaching and understand its potential in working with clients, and some tips on developing and marketing a coaching practice.

What I describe as "values-based coaching" is more than the expression of the basic value of collaborating and partnering with (as opposed to managing or controlling) others to help them achieve their goals. I am speaking of coaching that is informed by the core values of social work—serving underprivileged and underserved populations and taking on big problems with small dollars.

The primary mission of the social work profession is to enhance human well-being and to help meet the basic human needs of all people, with particular attention paid to the needs and empowerment of people who are vulnerable, oppressed, and living in poverty. A historic and defining feature of social work is the profession's focus on individual well-being in a social context and the well-being of society. Fundamental to social work is attention to the environmental forces that create, contribute to, and address problems in living.

Social workers promote social justice and social change with and on behalf of clients. "Clients" is used inclusively to refer to individuals, families, groups, organizations, and communities. Social workers are sensitive to cultural and ethnic diversity and strive to end discrimination, oppression, poverty, and other forms of social injustice. These activities may take the forms of direct practice, community organization, supervision, consultation administration, advocacy, social and political action, policy development and implementation, education, or research and evaluation. Social workers seek to enhance the capacity of people to address their own needs. Social workers also seek to promote the responsiveness of organizations, communities, and other social institutions to individuals' needs and social problems.

The mission of the social work profession is rooted in a set of core values. These core values, embraced by social workers throughout the profession's history, are the foundation of social work's unique purpose and perspective:

- service,
- social justice,
- dignity and worth of the person,
- importance of human relationships,
- integrity, and
- competence.

This constellation of core values reflects what is unique to the social work profession. Core values, and the principles that flow from them, must be balanced within the context and complexity of the human experience.

Coaching, which began as a somewhat elite service (much as psychoanalysis once was for well-heeled individuals and corporate entities), can and increasingly does have a place inside of social agencies, grants, and organizations being designed and brought into existence by creative coaches from both the social work profession and other backgrounds. Social entrepreneurship, a relatively new phenomenon, is also using coaching to increase effectiveness and build business skills in a new generation of social change agents—the nonprofit leaders who understand the importance of knowing how to obtain and grow an organization's financial reserves to thrive and make a difference.

The International Coach Federation (2009) *Code of Ethics* does not place value on serving needy populations. What *is* stated is the following: "Coaching is partnering with clients in a thought-provoking and creative process that inspires them to maximize their personal and professional potential" (Part One, Section 1).

My goal is to share the basic principles of coaching, highlight the current trends in the field, present a number of case examples, and finally share with you some inspiring applications of coaching. Ultimately, my goal is to leave you touched, moved, and inspired by what coaching has to offer and open to creative ways to bring coaching into your work—be it in an agency or with special populations. Please read this book with the filter of what is important to *you*—in your work and in your own life and career.

I want to hear from you and learn about *your* ideas. Please write to me at book@ ontrackcoaching.com, or go to my blog: http://www.ontrackcoaching.com/blog.

1

The Practice of Coaching

Kindness is the language which the deaf can hear and the blind can see.
—Mark Twain

Coaching might be best described as much as a form of consulting as a subset of therapy and counseling. It, in fact, combines aspects of both. It is a *distinct field* as well as a *methodology* as well as a *set of specific skills* that can be incorporated into one's existing work as a social worker, psychotherapist, physician, nurse, mental health practitioner, consultant, or manager.

One need not become a coach to incorporate coaching into one's work. Physicians and nurse practitioners can benefit from learning how to coach patients to take their medications and follow their diets and exercise regimes; collaborative lawyers need coaches to help guide couples through the divorce process and prevent relationships from deteriorating into chaos; and even prisoners can benefit from being coached to think about their situations from new perspectives so they can become productive citizens when they are released.

Coaching is strengths based. It emphasizes that people are *whole, complete, and resourceful* as they are. The role of the coach (or of "coaching," if one is serving in another capacity such as social worker, doctor, or nurse) is to help bring an individual's strengths to the foreground and move the individual to engage in the right actions to improve his or her personal and/or work lives. The coach is at once teacher, mentor, guide, cheerleader, "nag" (D. White, 1998), visionary, keeper of the vision, and process agent, facilitating meaningful linkages between inner and outer work in the lives of clients. "Whole" refers to the whole self, for which career, family and friends, health, spirituality, finances, and physical environment all matter. "Complete and resourceful" are the qualities we uncover when we mine for gold and find the strengths each individual or system already has within.

Coaching begins with the identification of the core values, sense of purpose, and vision of client and coach. A client works from the inside out, from examining his or her own passions, goals, and abilities to clarifying a more fulfilling life or work path. The coach facilitates the journey by asking wise questions, providing empathy, probing and confronting, sometimes training, and usually extracting from the client a vision and a plan for taking action toward realizing a new future.

The coach works primarily in the present, helping people separate fact and interpretation so that they can be clear and focused on doing what they need to do to get where they want to go. Similar to a sports coach,

5

the life or business coach wants his or her client to experience "wins." Many wins—even small ones—over time can transform the client's outlook as well as produce concrete results in major, lasting, and generalizable ways. Coaching, above all, is truly inspiring. It gives as much to the practitioner as to the client because it moves both into the realm of what is really possible for people—individually, in families, in groups, and in communities. One has only to use one's imagination to see a myriad of possibilities for individuals and potential applications beyond those I describe in the pages that follow.

Laura

Dear Marilyn,

I wanted to send greetings to you. It's been just about one year since I took your intro to coaching course. I wanted to let you know the powerful and positive impact your work has had on my personal and professional life. It was through my brush with coaching that I gave myself permission to put myself out there and expect success.

Over the past year, I advocated for our local daily paper to do a feature story on my work as an art therapist and trainer (printed in January), and I will be involved in another story in an arts paper next November. I also began advertising my private practice and workshops and am slowly building my business. Now when people see me on the street, they greet me by saying "There's the famous Laura Seftel." I asked one client where she saw my name, and she said "everywhere." I would never have had the nerve without your workshop. My brother has also been an incredible role model—he's a documentary filmmaker who needs to be brazen in his self-promotion. He sent 19 press packs to the *Boston Globe;* after the 20th they interviewed him.

I'm also still getting mileage out of the concept of "extreme self-care" and in turn teach this powerful tool to my workshop participants. One of my goals is to offer more workshops. Rather than compete with the approximately 500 therapists in the Northampton area, I decided to make them my clients! I offer various trainings for therapists, in the realm of art and healing. Several of the participants have gone on to become private clients.

The last accomplishment I want to share with you is a small local arts grant I won to coordinate a show called "The Secret Club: an exhibit about miscarriage." Curating the show is part of an overall effort to develop expertise in this area. In addition to writing about this topic, I also plan to offer weekend retreats for women who have experienced miscarriage.

I am grateful that I found your workshop at a pivotal time in my life. Hope things are going well for you. Your spirit has helped me ride out the risks and the occasional loneliness of starting my own business. Thank you.

—Laura Seftel, Northampton, MA

Roughly one-third of coaches are therapists or even have psychologically oriented training; however, social workers, therapists, and other human service and health care providers who take a holistic view can make the best coaches, because they understand human nature, already take a whole-person view, and generally have good listening skills.

Just as there are over 125 types of therapy ("List of Therapies," n.d.), there are many types and schools of coaching. At the time of this writing, 45 accredited coach training programs (programs that provide all 125 hours of coach-specific training required for certification) were listed on the International Coach Federation (ICF) Web site, and six were pending approval. A number of others, including a growing number offered by academic institutions (most of which focus on business coaching), were listed as offering a minimum of 30 hours of approved coach-specific training hours.

The flexibility of the coaching discipline does not lend itself to fitting into neat categories, but there are some key areas in which coaching can be both critical and empowering to human service professionals—in private practice, agency work, and community work. Listed here are five areas in which coaching is relevant to social work and human services:

Personal and Professional or "Life" Coaching

Life coaching is a practice focused on helping clients determine and achieve personal goals. Life coaches use multiple methods to help clients with the process of setting and reaching goals. Coaching is not targeted at psychological illness, and coaches are not trained as therapists, although there are overlapping skills. Coaching is unlike therapy in that it does not focus on examining the past or diagnosing mental dysfunctions. Instead, coaching focuses on effecting change in a client's current and future behavior.

According to a 1998 survey of coaching clients, "sounding board" and "motivator" were the top roles selected for a coach. Clients are looking for a coach "to really listen to them and give honest feedback."

Coaching provides an alternate means of making a difference in the lives of individuals who do not have a psychiatric diagnosis but do have life issues, concerns, needs, wishes, and desires to address. Some of these needs might not be viewed as "critical" services, but to the individuals concerned, they are. Examples from my students' coaching niches include helping breast cancer survivors find inspiration to reengage fully in life and helping returning expatriot's families successfully reengage and find new purpose in their communities. Coaching is also increasingly being used as an adjunct to healthcare treatment—for example, with patients with diabetes and teenagers who are HIV positive—and it has been used with challenging populations such as incarcerated prisoners.

In my own practice, career dissatisfaction is the primary issue for which clients seek services. These clients vary from those who are suffering job displacement in a changing global economy, are looking to escape the stresses of corporate America, or are underearning or want to improve their careers to those experiencing severe distress in the workplace who do not wish to use traditional employee assistance program (EAP) services. Although they are aware that EAP is confidential, they may wish to keep coaching separate, particularly if they are considering a job change.

Social workers and other professionals can and do provide coaching, usually for executives, as part of EAP services when client companies include it in their contract. Social workers are the predominant providers of EAP services. Additional knowledge and awareness of coaching can equip these providers with new tools and techniques to help any employee with distress related to job-specific issues.

As an example, here is one coaching request I received:

> Single successful professional leading a life that feels incomplete! Trapped in a routine, and losing prospective on what I really want in life. Have been working alone on some internal and external conflicts for years with no resolution. Need a coach with an open mind who understands cultural diversity and has experience dealing with highly educated clients.

Another client sought coaching because she was dissatisfied with her job of 15 years in her ex-in-law's company. A friend had forwarded an issue of my newsletter to her. She saw a quote I used from Napoleon Hill, author of *Think and Grow Rich*—the very same quote she had used in an article she wrote for a trade magazine— and she knew it was time for her to move herself forward. Her complaint was, "I always do things that make others succeed. . . . It's time to do it for myself!"

Business Coaching

Business coaching is the practice of providing support and advice to an individual or group to help them recognize ways in which they can improve the effectiveness of their business and leadership skills. Business coaches often specialize in different practice areas such as executive coaching, corporate coaching, and leadership coaching or small business coaching.

A business coach need not have specific business expertise or experience in the same field as the person receiving the coaching to provide quality business coaching services, but some of the most successful executive coaches have been executives themselves, and some of the best entrepreneur coaches have been entrepreneurs. The most important thing is to have good interpersonal skills and values that match the client's needs. I have personally enjoyed, for instance, coaching family businesses and government executives because their dedication to service is very similar to that of nonprofit leaders (case examples are provided later).

Nonprofit Coaching

Coaching in the nonprofit world is a perfect fit for social worker coaches and other human service professionals.

Impact on Agencies and Services

Coaching can bring new energy and creativity to some of our most frustrating social issues. For instance, an agency in Philadelphia that worked with teenagers who are HIV positive converted from a casework approach to a coaching approach. Clients were asked what they wanted to do with their lives. After initial responses of anger or confusion, the youths started to think differently about their future—about having futures at all, in fact. A key unforeseen consequence was a dramatic increase in drug compliance. A pediatric social worker brought coaching to a children's diabetes unit to encourage patients' compliance with their diabetes regimens, and the findings were similar. Other venues where I have presented coaching or in which coaching has been used include the following:

- a Veteran's Administration outpatient service;
- a coaching and mindfulness class in a school-to-work program in the Boston public school system;
- a teen drug and alcohol state conference;
- Epilepsy Foundation of Massachusetts and Rhode Island jobs programs and education of corporate employers; and
- a (pending) National Institutes of Health grant to measure the effectiveness of training nurse–practitioners to coach diabetic patients.

Coaching skills and techniques can be used successfully to launch and develop new nonprofit organizations. Two case studies (Birthday Wishes and Women's Empowerment for Cape Area Networking) are discussed in chapter 15.

Coaching Nonprofit Leaders and Organizations

Nonprofit leaders are often torn between the enormous demands of providing for their organizations and their personal lives. Coaching is an obvious choice to help these leaders to successfully prioritize and balance demands on their time and personal and organizational resources and become more effective at delegating and focusing on what is most important.

I have personally coached leaders of several nonprofits. Not all were social workers or human service professionals, but all were making significant contributions in their communities, collaborating successfully with existing social service agencies, and the successful growth of their organizations would provide prospective employment for social workers.

Health and Wellness Coaching

Staggering health costs associated with the rise of diseases like cancer and AIDS as well as the epidemics of childhood obesity and diabetes all speak to a tremendous need for coaching around health-related issues. Just as coaches have been recognized for their skills in helping athletes, teams, and executives to be their best, coaches are now beginning to help individuals create lasting improvement in their health and well-being. If two-thirds of our health status is related to our personal choices, learning new life skills so that we engage in healthy behaviors—diet, exercise, moderate drinking, nonsmoking, and relaxation—can make a huge difference.

Companies such as Wellcoaches Corporation (http://www.wellcoaches.com) are setting the trend in this new field of coaching, offering a range of services for both wellness and sports medicine, including "laser coaching"—sessions lasting just 10 to 15 minutes, provided in person or by phone. Some insurance companies and health management organizations have already incorporated health coaching into their programs, and I predict that this trend will explode in years to come.

Supervision and Management

Coaching skills add knowledge and best practices to supervision and management. In clinical settings, clinical supervision can be distinguished from administrative supervision or management.

As a supervisory model, coaching offers the opportunity to draw the learning from the supervisee. Questions like the following are all possible lines of inquiry: What is the learning here? About this patient (or client)? About their illness? About yourself? What might you have done differently if you knew what the outcome would be? How would you need to be different or have more success with this kind of case in the future?

The coaching manager (Hunt & Weintraub, 2002) focuses on helping his or her supervisees or employees learn and grow. Coaching managers are developers of talent and achievers of results. A coaching context encourages learning and takes mistakes, questions, and concerns and turns them into learning opportunities. Employees are encouraged to be open with their questions and concerns. If people are punished for making honest mistakes, coaching will not mean much. If you want to encourage learning, you have to cope with the frustration you may feel knowing that you could have done a job better,

---

Profile of Coaching Industry (ICF, 2008)

- Estimated 30,000 coaches globally
- 67 percent female
- 38.8 percent between ages 46 and 55
- 60.8 percent part time, the majority being female; 39.2 percent full time
- 86.4 percent coaching 10 years or fewer
- 53 percent have advanced degrees—master's or doctorate degree
- 71 percent received training through an ICF-accredited program
- Annual incomes averaged $82,671 for full time and $26,150 for part time

faster, or cheaper yourself. If you are coaching, you must try and stay on the sidelines. You cannot say "What did you learn from that?" one minute and chew an employee out the next. People are more receptive to learning new skills and using both positive and negative feedback if they feel engaged in the process and see the value for themselves.

Some good manager coaching questions are simple:

- What were you trying to do?
- What were you hoping to accomplish?
- What did you actually accomplish?
- Where do you see gaps?
- How do you understand the gaps?
- What, if anything, do you need to start doing, keep doing, or stop doing?

A coaching manager also looks out for the career development of his or her employees. What is their potential? How can their overall career development needs be met while helping them be successful at the job at hand? How can coaching/supervision meetings be used to help employees move in the desired direction?

2

What Coaching Is

The psychotherapist learns little or nothing from his successes. They mainly confirm him in his mistakes, while his failures, on the other hand, are priceless experiences in that they not only open up the way to a deeper truth, but force him to change his views and methods.

—Carl Gustav Jung

Coaching Defined

According to the International Coach Federation (ICF) (n.d.) definition,

> coaching is an ongoing relationship which focuses on clients taking action toward the realization of their visions, goals or desires. Coaching uses a process of inquiry and personal discovery to build the client's level of awareness and responsibility and provides the client with structure, support and feedback. The coaching process helps clients both define and achieve professional and personal goals faster and with more ease than would be possible otherwise.

The Coaches Training Institute (n.d.) stated that coaching is a "powerful alliance designed to forward and enhance the lifelong process of human learning, effectiveness, and fulfillment," whereas Robert Hargrove (1995) described transformational coaching as "unleashing the human spirit" and "helping people learn powerful lessons in personal change as well as expand their capacity for action" (p. 6).

The following historical definitions are also of interest:

- 16th century: "transporting a high-ranking person from place A to place B."
- 19th century: "helping a team win."
- 21st century: "the new positive psychology."

Another way to look at coaching is to look at why people seek it. The vast majority of individuals who seek coaching are looking for career, business, or some form of achievement help. They want to change jobs; advance in their current company; start a business; take a business to the next level; deal with a difficult situation at work; or, perhaps, write a book, start a nonprofit, or pursue their life's dream. A smaller but growing percentage seek coaching

13

for personal issues—for example, relationship maintenance or specific health issues such as attention-deficit hyperactivity disorder (ADHD) or Asperger's syndrome. Looked at from this perspective, coaching is simply a set of skills to help people do better and be better.

Still, many coaches have difficulty explaining what coaching is and how it differs from therapy. The best way, many coaches believe, to help someone understand what coaching is to allow him or her to experience it directly. Therefore, a common practice among coaches is a brief (usually 30-minute) "sample" session.

Coaching is active. You *move with* the client. Ed Nevis (1987) has referred to the position of the therapist with the metaphor "working by sitting down." In contrast, he described the consultant role as more active, calling it "working by standing up," which captures nicely the different presences that therapists and coaches bring to their practices. Others refer to it, using a sports analogy, as "being on the court" versus "in the stands" with clients.

Like mediation, coaching is an *unregulated profession*. Its standards and ethics are established by its primary professional organization, the ICF. The ICF has established a credentialing program according to a list of "Coaching Core Competencies" (see Appendix B) and guidelines regarding professional ethics (see Appendix A). Only in its second decade of existence, the ICF credentialing program provides three levels of credentialing for professional coaches: associate certified coach (ACC), professional certified coach (PCC), and master certified coach (MCC). A team coaching certification is in the process of being approved. Each credential requires a specific set of hours of coach-specific training and coaching experience of the applicant.

According to the ICF (2008) Global Coaching Study, 52 percent of coaches report that their clients expect the coach they hire to be credentialed. Today, more than 4,000 coaches worldwide hold an ICF credential—approximately 1,200 at the PCC level and fewer than 1,000 at the MCC level. The number of coaches practicing worldwide is somewhat more difficult to determine and is roughly estimated to be about 35,000, including coaches not identified by the ICF. A coach in Israel told me that in Israel alone (a country of only a few million), for instance, although few are ICF certified, there are 5,000 practicing coaches. Coaching is, in fact, growing in other parts of the world, whereas it may be temporarily stabilizing in the United States. It is my belief, however, that coaching will grow in the future as more and more people need to invent or reinvent their careers, start their own businesses, take charge of their health, and manage nonprofit and philanthropic organizations with less and less government funding.

Approximately one-third of coaches are trained therapists or human service professionals. At least one-third of all coaches come from various forms of corporate life. Many have been managers, executives, or organizational development specialists in large corporations. A number of the key players in the coaching field come from accounting backgrounds, and a few come from the theater. The blend of backgrounds provides an interesting array of expertise, ranging from the concrete (interest tests and style assessments) to a process orientation.

Coaches work in remedial, developmental, or transformational modes, depending on the client's agenda. A corporation might want coaching for a difficult but valuable employee, such as an executive with a bad temper (remedial coaching), a valued employee who needs to develop leadership skills (developmental coaching), or a team that needs to become more creative (transformational coaching). Individuals might seek coaching to succeed in a new position in which they failed before (remedial/potentially developmental), to take on a big challenge (developmental), or to make a life transition to live a life they love (transformational).

To better understand coaching, it is helpful to look at its history.

The History of Coaching

Coaching is a relatively new discipline—at least in its present form. The current coaching field is a result of the convergence of several developmental strands dating back as far as the ancient Greek philosophers, who recognized the need to offer to their followers ways to achieve fulfillment in their lives. Socrates's open-ended questions are the earliest form of coaching as we know it today.

Life coaching has roots that go back to 1950s, to executive coaching, which itself drew on techniques developed in management consulting, leadership training, and organizational psychology. Life coaching also draws inspiration from disciplines including sociology, psychology, positive adult development, career counseling, mentoring, and other types of counseling. Coaches may apply mentoring, values assessment, behavior modification, behavior modeling, goal setting, and other techniques in helping their clients.

Coaching as a profession may have started in the 1960s, growing out of sports (performance) coaching. In the 1970s, the Neuro-Linguistic Programming (NLP) school proposed the first set of techniques to use one's inner resources to reach one's life goals. The development of the personal growth movement included Erhard Seminars Training (est), which used NLP techniques and drew on Eastern philosophy, and W. Timothy Gallwey's (1974) book *The Inner Game of Tennis* —both considered milestones in the development of coaching as a profession. Coaching also stemmed from the work of the major therapy schools, particularly behavioral approaches, the person-centered approach, cognitive psychology, family therapy, and Eriksonian hypnosis.

In the 1980s, Frederic Hudson—psychologist, educator, and founder of the Fielding Institute—established the Hudson Coaching Institute and brought executives from large corporations such as AT&T and IBM to Santa Barbara, California, for a week to explore their lives and careers. In the 1990s, Thomas Leonard, Laura Whitworth, Henry Kimsey-House, and Phil Sandahl compiled the body of coaching theories and techniques that led to coaching's being recognized as a largely cohesive set of principles, knowledge, and skills. Leonard, who is rumored to have worked in a key position within the est organization at one time, began training coaches through teleclasses—a new format that would enable coaches to be "portable" (Leonard & Larson, 1998) and coach from anywhere. (Leonard himself, although a wealthy man, apparently chose to live in a mobile home!) He founded Coach University (Coach U) in 1992. Around the same time, Whitworth, Kimsey-House, and Sandahl founded the Coaches Training Institute, still the second largest coaching program, which differed from Coach U in offering in-person training.

Bestselling books such as Cheryl Richardson's (1998) *Take Time for Your Life* popularized coaching, which was simultaneously spreading in other parts of the world. Richardson, one of the first coaches to be trained by Leonard, talked about how, although not an accountant herself, she kept her father's accounting business going after he died because clients had come to rely on her for her good, instinctive advice. She soon began going into the community, offering sessions at local churches and libraries, where she did laser coaching with people in the audience. *Take Time for Your Life* was an instant success, and Richardson is probably the person most responsible for the overnight popularity of life coaching.

Other influences have been the "existential" or "ontological" coaches, such as Argentineans Julio Olalla and Fernando Flores, who brought new distinctions regarding the use of language to the field and are represented by the Newfield Group. Others, including Frederic Hudson, brought the adult development field to coaching. Hudson now focuses

---

Client Example

Kristen was a 19-year-old high school graduate who, when I met her, was waitressing and had no ambitions to go to college. Her parents had been through a difficult divorce. She had lived for a time with each and was unhappy and directionless in each home. A relative who was a successful businessman and felt she had more "potential" offered her the opportunity to move to the city and pay for coaching. She had rejected the idea of therapy because it was "my parents who have the problem."

At first, Kristen was reluctant to engage in coaching. She complained that her relative wanted her to work *and* go to school. Reluctantly, she decided to take two courses in an extension school summer program. She was so sure she had failed both that she didn't even bother to look up her grades at the end of the semester, but when she learned she received Bs, she perked up. By the following year, she was accepted into a state university. Her relative recommended her to a friend who was a partner in a law firm, and she began to work there part time. When the firm asked her to help organize their annual holiday party, she did it so successfully that she received public acknowledgment at the event. She is now in law school.

Had she been in therapy, I might have focused on her relationship with her parents, the sources of her low self-esteem, or her social anxieties. Instead, I focused directly on what actions she could take to improve her situation. Because she resented her relative's "intrusion" into her life, the "compelling" reason for her to succeed was achieving independence. Once she could see that creating a new future for herself—one that totally broke with what she and everyone expected of her—would provide that, she became very motivated, and each success led to the next one.

on "Third Age" issues for later life adults looking for alternatives to their parents' retirement. At one point, there were two professional coaching organizations; these merged in 1995 to form the ICF. A number of years ago, Leonard (now deceased) sold Coach U and began an Internet-based organization called CoachVille. The CoachVille Web site (http://www.coachville.com/home/indcx) contains an overwhelming amount of information. An inexpensive lifetime membership offers access to forms, lists, and even a free referral service.

So, what do coaches actually do?

The Primary Distinctions of Coaching

The primary distinctions of coaching (versus therapy) are the following:

- future orientation versus past orientation;
- client is whole, complete, and resourceful versus hurt and needy;
- creating/generating new paradigms and possibilities versus fixing or getting rid of an existing problem;
- finding creative solutions versus healing pain;
- collegial versus hierarchical relationship between coach and client; and
- freedom from versus being tied to third-party payors and the professional constraints that limit the ways in which practitioners get referrals.

A complete chart of comparisons can be found in Appendix D. Many forms of therapy practiced today are collaborative, so the contrasts you will see are drawn to show what distinctions there *might* be and may not apply to all types of therapy. There is one primary difference between coaching and all therapies, however, and that is the absence of a diagnosis or third-party payor. When new clients wonder whether they can use their insurance to pay for coaching, I explain that coaching is not designated "medically necessary" by insurance companies, and therefore it is an out-of-pocket expense. If a client has a bona fide diagnosis, an assessment must be made about whether therapy is needed as an adjunct to coaching. Some potential coaching clients will already have a therapist. In other cases, it is clear that therapy would better meet their needs. The major distinction I use here is the client's willingness to be "100 percent responsible" for the result of our work together.

Disciplines from Which Coaching Has Dawn

A look at the disciplines from which coaching has drawn will help clarify that other approaches have skillfully been woven into coaching (see Rock, 2006).

Coaching and Adult Learning Theory

Some of the first-known life coaching sessions grew out of adult learning programs run in New York in the 1960s. At that time, the commonly held belief was that most learning occurred in childhood and that only people such as academics continued to learn in any significant way into adulthood. A number of researchers in the 1960s and 1970s, of whom the best known was Malcolm Knowles, began to explore the ways in which adults learned. In 1973, Knowles came up with a range of adult learning principles designed to inform the way courses or classes for adults should be structured (Knowles, 1990). His work, building on earlier ideas gained from being a program director at the YMCA, was a significant factor in reorienting adult educators from "educating people" to "helping them learn" (Knowles, 1950), and it informed coaching as a field.

Clinical Psychology/Therapy

Cognitive–behavior therapy (CBT) became widely accepted as a cornerstone of clinical psychology in the 1960s. In *The Feeling Good Handbook*, David Burns (1989) put CBT techniques into everyday language for the layperson to use, promoting the idea of self-healing through adherence to a set of practices.

Beginning in the late 1970s, Stephen de Shazer—cofounder along with his wife and long-time collaborator, Insoo Kim Berg, of the Milwaukee Brief Family Therapy Center—began developing and consistently refining the solution-focused brief therapy (SFBT) approach. SFBT represents a paradigm shift from the traditional psychotherapy focus on problem formation and problem resolution that was seen as underlying almost all psychotherapeutic approaches since Freud. Instead, SFBT focuses on client strengths and resiliencies, examining previous solutions and exceptions to a problem and then, through a series of interventions, encouraging clients to engage in more of those behaviors. SFBT also offers a future-focused, goal-directed approach, using questions designed to identify exceptions and solutions and scales to measure a client's current level of progress toward a solution and identify the behaviors needed to achieve or maintain further progress. The approach is characterized by the following:

- clear and specific goal setting,
- strategic planning with the client,
- an expectation of change in a short period of time,
- emphasis on what will happen (future orientation), and
- recognition of the client's resources and experience for producing change.

All of these characteristics are hallmarks of coaching today.

In the 1970s, psychologists began to work increasingly with normally functioning clients to improve their performance. The most notable exemplar of this trend is Martin E. P. Seligman's (1994) work on optimism. It was Seligman's research that first indicated that pessimism and optimism could be learned or unlearned. Seligman was one of the first psychologists to research how highly functioning people become so successful. He is also regarded as the father of "positive psychology" (Seligman, 2002) and actually used his recently past position as president of the American Psychological Association as an opportunity to challenge psychologists to adopt this new way of thinking. There is presently a merging of positive psychology and coaching in psychology, particularly in academic circles.

Adult Development

Frederic Hudson is widely respected as an expert in adult change. As the founding president in 1973 of the Fielding Institute, the most innovative doctoral studies graduate school in America, he is highly regarded for his contributions to adult training in management, organizational developmental, and education. Believing that existing graduate schools and professions were unable devote themselves to the endless swirl of change to prepare people adequately for the future, Hudson left Fielding in 1986 to establish the Hudson Institute of Santa Barbara, a training center for professionals focusing on renewal and resilience at work and at home. Per Hudson's (n.d.) core beliefs, the central tasks of the coach are

- to facilitate continuity and change in the lives/systems of clients;
- to clarify core values, beliefs, and sense of purpose;
- to identify and define key social roles and activities and their balance;
- to tap the emergent developmental challenges of the person/system within a visionary consciousness; and
- to invent a vital, continuous learning agenda.

Hudson was referred to as "Dr. Midlife" by the *Los Angeles Times* and as "The Dr. Spock of the Adult Years" by a reviewer of his first book, *The Adult Years: Mastering the Art of Self-Renewal* (Hudson, 1991). He subsequently wrote or cowrote *The Joy of Old: A Guide To Successful Elderhood* (Murphy & Hudson, 1995); with his wife, Pamela McLean, *Life Launch: A Passionate Guide to the Rest of Your Life* (Hudson & McLean, 1995), a book used as a text in college and university courses of adult life and career planning; and *The Handbook of Coaching* (Hudson, 1999). "Having spent a lifetime immersed in studying and understanding the ways that people get 'off-track' from their inner purpose, Hudson sensed and implemented the undiluted role of 'coach' long before it became a buzzword" (Hudson Institute, n.d.-a).

Sports Psychology

Achievement on the sporting field has long been a source of inspiration to many, which is why we enjoy being spectators—particularly of winning teams. At times, we all have wanted to understand how we might tap into the "special something" that produces a Lance Armstrong or a Tiger Woods. Winning on the playing field has increasingly found its way into boardrooms, classrooms, workshops, and coaching outside of sports (Blanchard, & Shula, 1995; Gallwey, 1974; Garfield, 1984). Some of the notions borrowed from sports coaching—working together as teams to accomplish something, individual peak performance, and striving to be one's best—lend themselves to use of a coach who provides perspective, direction, encouragement, and structure.

Personal Development

Believed to have begun with Napoleon Hill's (1982) seminal *Think and Grow Rich* (first published in 1937) and Norman Vincent Peale's (1952) classic *The Power of Positive*

Thinking, which drew intense criticism from the mental health community, the personal development movement began to proliferate in the 1980s. Peale has been credited with the tagline "change your thinking and change your life" and the expression "possibility thinking."

The key principles of the personal development movement have been the following:

- a move toward increasing self-awareness, including work on the "filters" through which we see the world, which fuel our expectations and assumptions;
- a focus on accepting responsibility for one's actions;
- the idea of people having choice in their lives; and
- possibility thinking.

The personal development movement has created an optimal environment for the acceptance of coaching in the wider community. Individualized coaching is a logical next step from mass participation in personal development and life skills training programs (Chopra, 1994; Hay, 1984; Peale, 1952; Peck, 1978).

Existential Philosophy

Drawn from contemporary applied psychology and philosophy, an existential perspective bases its approach on the central assumption that life is uncertain and that, paradoxically, uncertainty is the one thing that we can rely on at any point throughout our journey. The existential perspective takes the position that anxiety is not necessarily a "bad" thing that must be reduced or removed. Rather, the feeling of anxiety can be stimulating, can put us in touch with our sense of being alive, and is the source of all creative and original insight and decision making.

Unlike other coaching perspectives that focus on broadly positive, self-actualizing qualities and possibilities for each client, the existential approach recognizes and gives equal emphasis to the divided stances, aims, and aspirations that may well exist as competing values and beliefs held by each client. The approach helps clients to clarify and reconsider the meanings and values given to the various interrelations that make up their personal and professional lives. Through this exploration, clients can be empowered to assess more honestly and accurately how the relational stances that they adopt are affecting the quality of—and their ability to enjoy—their lives.

In an existential approach, basic concepts of existentialism—including isolation, freedom of choice, meaninglessness, and death—are examined. These concepts are integrated in existential psychology, as presented in logotherapy and humanistic psychology (Frankl, 1984; Maslow, 1968; May, 1981; Spinelli, 2005), in a way that is consistent with coaching:

- Life has meaning under all circumstances, even the most miserable ones.
- Our main motivation for living is our will to find meaning in life.
- We have freedom to find meaning in what we do and what we experience, or at least in the stand we take when faced with a situation of unchangeable suffering.

NLP

Originally developed by Richard Bandler and John Grinder in 1975, NLP represents one of the most practical applications of psychological concepts and techniques. NLP is used in both professional and personal domains, including management, sales and performance, interpersonal and communication skills, personal development, motivation, and effective learning techniques.

Bandler and Grinder (1979) began by modeling and duplicating the patterns of a few top communicators and therapists, including hypnotherapist Milton Erickson, Gestalt therapist Fritz Perls, and family therapist Virginia Satir. Coaching uses NLP techniques as well as related techniques such as "focusing" (Gendlin, 1982), and many coaches have additional training in NLP.

Motivation

The motivational area has been an enormous contributor to contemporary culture. Millions of people worldwide have read the top motivational books by Napoleon Hill (1982), Tony Robbins (1991), Zig Ziglar, Tom Peters, Brian Tracy, and others, and millions worldwide have seen motivational speakers and writers like Wayne Dyer (1976, 2005) on educational television or attended their workshops. The motivational world has also had a strong influence in the development of all types of coaching. Changes in the economic outlook, the increased cost of living, erosion of the public safety net, the speeding up of modern life, and the need to produce more with less have increased the need for individuals to seek more ways to motivate themselves to increase their income, send their children to college, and afford to retire. These many social changes have contributed to the rise in coaching as a source of motivation for individuals and corporations to effect desired change.

Management and Leadership Development

A key strand that has contributed to coaching is the move toward improved work performance through management development techniques. Coaching concepts have been pivotal in business literature, and more recently, increasing numbers of individuals who are starting their own businesses for either primary or secondary income are turning to these resources (Blanchard & Johnson, 1983; Covey, 1989; Gerber, 1995).

Robert Greenleaf's (2002) idea of the servant as leader, which was born out of reading Hermann Hesse's (1932/1956) *Journey to the East*, was adopted by many top management and leadership development thinkers, including Peter Senge of the MIT Organizational Learning Center and Margaret Wheatley (2002).Unlike leadership approaches with a top-down hierarchical style, servant leadership emphasizes collaboration, trust, empathy, and the ethical use of power. At heart, the individual is a servant first, making the conscious decision to lead in order to better serve others, not to increase his or her own power. The objective is to enhance the growth of individuals in the organization and increase teamwork and personal involvement. The characteristics are listening, empathy, healing, awareness, persuasion, conceptualization, foresight, stewardship, commitment to the growth of others, and building community. Other concepts, such as "communities of commitment" (Kofman & Senge, 1995) and Ben & Jerry's ice cream's once revolutionary idea of bringing one's "whole self" to work, have had a major influence on coaching.

Creativity

The last 10 to 15 years have seen a surge of interest in how the brain works. Emotional intelligence, multiple intelligences, the left brain/right brain distinction, and Edward De Bono's (1990) insights on lateral thinking have all contributed to our understanding of the many pathways to creativity and productivity. Gardner's (1993) work on the various types of intelligence—including musical, spatial, and emotional—opened the way for new distinctions within these types of intelligence, most notably emotional intelligence. There have been many other works (for example, Fritz, 1984) that have broken new ground and opened the way for improving individual performance through thinking tools and new ways of modeling aspects of our thoughts, actions, or worlds. It is probably no accident that some of the best coaches come from theater and performing arts and that artists such as Benjamin Zander, coauthor of *The Art of Possibility* (Zander & Zander, 2000), have made such a major contribution to the understanding of what really helps people perform at their best.

Emotional Intelligence

In the past 10 years, there has been a growing recognition that the intelligence quotient (IQ), the historically accepted measurement of future success, is *not* the best indicator of that success. Technology has allowed scientists to map the architecture of the human brain with great accuracy, and although there is still much to be learned, we know more about the brain every day. Daniel Goleman (1995, 2000, 2006), who coined the term *emotional intelligence*, has written most extensively on the subject. He has emphasized that self-awareness, self-discipline, persistence, altruism, personal motivation, empathy, and the ability to love and be loved by friends, partners, and family members have a far more important role to play in human success than IQ. This emotional quotient enables people to succeed in work as well as play, building thriving careers and healthy relationships. Goleman's model of what it means to be "intelligent" puts emotions at the center of aptitudes for living.

Research has also indicated that emotions play a significant role in our physical health. Toxic emotions put our health at risk in the same way that exposure to pollutants can harm us. A poor emotional life also exposes us to a whole range of risks, including depression, eating disorders, and alcohol and drug abuse. In his research, Goleman has discovered that social isolation seems to be nearly twice as dangerous to personal health as smoking.

Although not advertised as such, the emotional journey that underlies good coaching is often the most significant thing that comes out of the entire process. The prospective achievement of certain goals in a client's life may be the initial reason why he or she signs on for coaching, yet a large part of what makes coaching so powerful is the emotional journey and the resultant shifts—in beliefs, attitudes, aptitudes, and habits—that can literally be life changing that occur in the client.

Linguistic Theory

Coaching is, in part, grounded in a branch of philosophy that emerged in the second half of the 20th century called the *philosophy of language*. The new claim of the philosophy of language was that when we speak, not only do we describe existing reality, but we also act. Language, in fact, is action. This perspective contrasted the previous view of language as a way of accounting for what already existed. Drawing on the work of his Chilean countryman Humberto Maturana, from whose work family systems therapists derived key concepts regarding entropy and change, Fernando Flores introduced a "biology of language" (Flores & Winograd, 1989). Flores saw that communication, truth, and trust are at the heart of power (Rubin, 2007). He said, "I made my own assessment of my life, and I began to live it. That was freedom" and began his lectures saying,

> In language we build our own identities, our relationships with others, the countries we live in, the companies we have, and the values we hold dear. With language we generate life. Without language we are mostly chimpanzees. (Budd & Rothstein, 2000, p. 25)

The biology of language has five key components:

1. When we speak, we act. Language is generative.
2. Listening does not necessarily result in receiving the accurate transmission of what is spoken but, rather, always involves an act of interpretation.
3. If we change the language we use to describe our experience, we can change our interpretation and alter our experience—even regarding traumatic events.
4. Language spoken into a future that is open creates the possibility of something new; language that is past-referenced will give us "more of the same" of what we've already had.
5. In language, we have choice; our choices determine our actions. Therefore, the language we choose to use can alter history—personally, socially, and globally.

Friedman and Fanger (1991) expanded on these ideas in relation to brief therapy, and Roz and Ben Zander (2000) took the concepts to a new level in their seminal work, *The Art of Possibility*. (See chapter 5 for a more in-depth discussion of these issues.)

Mentoring

Worldwide, mentoring (Peddy, 2002) has grown significantly as a discipline in the last decade, both within corporations, as a form of knowledge sharing and development, and externally to support career development and small business. There are many formal mentoring programs now supported by governments around the world to help small businesspeople and independent organizations that connect mentors with their mentees.

Neuropsychology and Evidence-Based Coaching

Stober and Grant (2006) have evaluated single-theory and integrative approaches to coaching in a handbook that looks at measurable results in coaching. The former approach includes humanistic, behavior-based, and psychoanalytically informed coaching; the latter includes adult learning, positive psychology, and adventure-based frameworks.

Coach David Rock (2006) and neuroscientist Jeffrey Schwartz (Rock & Schwartz, 2006; Schwartz, Stapp, & Beauregard, 2005) have studied specifically why coaching has such a positive impact. They emphasized the study of attention, reflection, insight, and action. Scientists studying these domains often do not communicate with one another, as neuroscience is such a vast field. Schwartz has done major work on the science of attention and how it changes the brain, which provides strong evidence for how a self-directed, solutions-focused approach to coaching works.

Corporations began to apply coaching techniques as a way to enhance the learning process of their key executives in the 1980s. Since then, coaching has spread at all levels in organizations.

Contrasting Coaching and Psychotherapy

Although coaching as a profession is both distinct from and similar to other professions, it includes aspects of many professions, including sports coaching, training, consulting, and counseling. The most obvious comparison is to psychotherapy, but this area can be a little murky because therapy is not just one thing. In their book, *Therapist as Life Coach,* Patrick Williams (founder of Therapist University) and Deborah Davis (2002) contrasted traditional psychoanalytic therapy with coaching, describing the SFBTs as "transitional." Although the solution-focused model created by Insoo Kim Berg, Steven de Shazer, and Bill O'Hanlon creates a new paradigm of solutions, moving away from pathology, it still reflects the medical model of diagnosis and treatment. Dialectic behavioral therapy (DBT) and, in the field of alcoholism, motivational interviewing also have some interesting parallels to coaching. Coaching is unique in its focus on solutions as opposed to problems.

The primary distinction between personal or life coaching and therapy or counseling is the absence of a problem defined by medical-model necessity. Coaching deemphasizes the "problem" to be solved, focusing instead on alternative futures, or futures that would otherwise not be possible. When the HIV-positive teenagers mentioned in chapter 1 were asked what they wanted to do with their lives, the focus was not on coping with HIV but on their hopes and dreams for the future. By moving from a casework to a coaching approach in overall agency philosophy, staff began asking questions that they had not previously viewed as relevant to even ask!

Both therapy and coaching may bring about behavioral change and help people to understand how their thoughts and emotions can interfere with personal effectiveness, performance, and well-being. Both approaches are based on building a strong foundation of trust with clients. Some of the core skills, such as deep listening and the ability to ask questions that raise awareness, are the same. There are also similarities in some of the underlying philosophies behind coaching and therapy. Like coaching, a variety of therapy practices rely on a client-centered, collaborative partnership that encourages clients to find their own unique solutions.

So, what are the key differences between coaching and therapy?

Coaching Focuses on the Present and Future, Whereas Therapy Deals With the Past

Some therapy does focus on the future, and competent coaches also may focus on the past when there is a need to do so. The difference is in *the degree and the type of therapy being discussed*. Short-term, solution-focused therapy has much in common with coaching, whereas long-term psychoanalysis is fundamentally different.

Coaching Is Geared to Highly Functioning People, Whereas Therapy Is for People Who Have Experienced Trauma or Who Have Some Form of Psychopathology

This distinction is somewhat artificial. Although there are some very high-functioning and successful people who enter coaching, there are many who seek coaching because they've "done therapy and it didn't make a difference," and the idea is that perhaps coaching will help. And for some health-related issues such as ADHD and Asperger's, both of which are discussed later, coaching may even be an intervention of choice.

It is also true that successful managers can have psychological problems. Issues of stress, addiction, depression, and family crisis are increasingly surfacing in corporate life. Anyone who coaches people in business will be ill-prepared if they are not aware of and attuned to these potential client challenges. People enter therapy for many reasons, including self-exploration, self-knowledge, professional development, and better self-management.

The Intentions of Coaching and Therapy Are Different

This is where there is clear daylight between the two disciplines: The primary goal of coaching is to improve a person's effectiveness, usually in business or at work, in ways linked to improved productivity and overall business success. A coach will sometimes guide an individual toward increased awareness of how his or her thoughts and emotional reactions lead to problematic behaviors in the workplace and how changing views can improve performance. Therapy may share coaching's goals of improved functioning in the workplace, but it also addresses nonwork aspects of an individual's life and frequently involves in-depth explorations of the client's history, relationships with parents and other family members, and self-esteem. Therapy may also lead to intense emotional experiences that demand skillful guidance from an experienced practitioner. Although emotions are legitimate in coaching, they are usually the focus only if they pose a challenge to the coaching process. When there is unfinished emotional business from the past, the coach should refer the client to a competent therapist.

The Training, Skill Sets, and Experience of Coaches and Therapists Are Different

Therapists are required to have extensive training, typically far in excess of what is required to become a coach. Psychotherapy and counseling training can last many years, during which time therapists themselves are often involved in personal therapy. Coach training typically lasts from a few days to a full year. Only recently have new coaching models, such as organization and relationship systems coaching, begun helping trainees to develop more sophisticated psychological knowledge. Executive and business coaches, however, generally have a great deal of other training along with extensive corporate experience, but rarely have they undertaken the lengthy training required of a therapist.

Coaches and Therapists Bring a Different "Presence"

The therapist's presence tends to be more composed, thoughtful, and pondering. The coach uses his or her energy differently to create a more action-, motivation-, and results-focused atmosphere. Intuition is used in place of analysis and interpretation. Even in relation to managed care, the pace in coaching is also generally quicker.

Other Differences

- Coaching is more results- and action-focused than therapy.
- Therapy typically involves greater privacy, acknowledging two-way confidentiality and Health Insurance Portability and Accountability Act laws. Although life coaching respects the same confidentiality standards, it is not protected by law. In business coaching, it is not uncommon for a coachee's line manager or human resource manager to be in the feedback loop.
- The delivery of coaching may also involve processes very rarely used in therapy, such as structured feedback from bosses, peers, and subordinates (known as "360 feedback") in a corporate setting; use of assessments, such as the DiSC Universal Assessment and Myers–Briggs Type Indicator; and written plans.
- Therapy is often conducted within a 50-minute time frame. Coaching sessions tend to last longer and to be spaced at longer intervals.
- Therapy tends to take place in the therapist's consulting rooms, whereas coaching can occur, for example, at Starbucks, in a manager's office, or over the telephone.
- Therapists do not have contact with clients socially and are very careful about boundary issues. Coaches regularly accept invitations from clients to attend corporate hospitality events and may invite clients to their own events.
- Coaching is faster paced, and many therapists who do corporate coaching find they have to learn new life skills themselves and quicken their own game.
- Therapists who are also coaches may find their personal values to be in conflict with a world that is primarily profit oriented and in which highly competitive and driven individuals are the norm.
- Fee rates can vary enormously between coaching and therapy. Typically, fees for coaching can be as much as quadruple those for therapy.

Summary

Coaching and therapy have some similarities, but the differences are significant. Typically, the intention is different, with coaching strongly grounded in work effectiveness and performance rather than in broader life issues. Certain skill sets are similar, but the therapist is trained to work at a deeper level, particularly where psychological and emotional issues exist. Experienced executive coaches will often have a higher level of competence in corporate issues.

Operational procedures of coaches and therapists also vary in terms of contracting (that is, the issue of who is the client in the coaching situation) and practical considerations, such as location, session length, pricing, and boundaries. Professional supervision is stressed as a vital aspect of good practice for coaches, just as it has been for many years in therapy.

Coaching Compared With Consulting, Development, and Training

Coaching also has similarities with other disciplines such as organizational or management consulting, leadership development, and training (Bluckert, 2004). Some consultants and trainers play the expert role, whereas others adopt a facilitative role not unlike that of a coach. Because many therapists, psychologists, and management trainers have entered consulting and coaching with their specific understandings, skill sets, and professional norms, new models of coaching have been constructed on the proposition that coaching is an amalgam of these different disciplines.

According to Bluckert (2008), Jane Greene—along with Anthony Grant, a pioneer of evidence-based coaching (see Greene & Grant, 2003)—presented a model incorporating consulting, training, and mentoring, viewing the coach's role as that of a "personal management consultant" who understands both business and strategy and psychology and human behavior in order "to facilitate content improvement via process improvement." Others, Bluckert noted, refer to organizational development thinker Edgar Schein (2006), who said

> the coach should have the ability to move easily among the roles of process consultant, content expert and diagnostician/prescriber. The ultimate skill of the coach, then, is to assess the moment-to-moment reality that will enable him to be in the appropriate role. (p. 24)

Other differences are described in Appendix E.

Coaching and Solution-Focused Therapy

SFBT therapists help people identify the things that they wish to change in their life and to construct a concrete vision of a preferred future by means of a commonly used method of questioning known as "the miracle question." An SFBT therapist then helps a client to identify times in his or her current life that most closely resemble this future and to examine the differences between these occasions. By bringing these small successes to the client's awareness, and helping him or her repeat these successes during less challenging times, the therapist helps the client move toward the preferred future he or she has identified.

Personal coaches use a broader array of questions, referred to as "inquiries," frequently emphasizing "what" questions. The focus is always on moving to a more compelling future—a passion or purpose consistent with the individual's core values—rather than on moving away from the problem.

Coaching and DBT

DBT is a psychological method and subset of cognitive therapy developed by Marsha Linehan to treat borderline personality disorder (BPD). DBT combines standard cognitive–behavioral techniques for emotion regulation and reality testing with concepts of mindful awareness, distress tolerance, and acceptance largely derived from Buddhist meditative practice. DBT is the first therapy that has been experimentally demonstrated to be effective for treating BPD. Built on key elements of behaviorist theory, dialectics, cognitive therapy (and its central component, mindfulness), DBT can be seen as incorporating aspects of coaching.

All DBT therapy involves two components. In individual sessions with the DBT therapist, the patient discusses issues that come up during the week, recorded in a diary, and follows a treatment-target hierarchy. Self-injurious and suicidal behaviors are focused on first, followed by behaviors that interfere with therapy. The therapist then gently moves into quality-of-life issues, with the goal of the patient's life improving generally. In the DBT group component, usually meeting once a week for two to two and a half hours, the individual learns to use specific skills that are broken down into four modules:

1. core mindfulness skills,
2. interpersonal effectiveness skills,
3. emotion regulation skills, and
4. distress tolerance skills.

Although the group sessions teach the skills unique to DBT, they also provide opportunities to practice regulating emotions and behavior in a social context.

The structured and focused nature of DBT makes it a coaching-like model, but the explicit focus of DBT on BPD, with the hallmark of treating uncontrolled emotional issues and management of suicidal urges, provides the differentiation. *Coaching deals with emotional distress when it arises but does not aim to address emotional distress.* BPD would contraindicate coaching. Guidelines for assessing coachability are clearly outlined later in this chapter.

Coaching and Motivational Interviewing

Motivational interviewing (MI) (see http://motivationalinterview.org) refers to a counseling approach developed by clinical psychologists William R. Miller and Stephen Rollnick (2002) and is a client-centered method of engaging intrinsic motivation to change behavior. MI recognizes and accepts the fact that clients who need to make changes in their lives approach counseling at different levels of readiness to change their behavior. MI is nonjudgmental, nonconfrontational, and nonadversarial. The approach attempts to increase the client's awareness of the potential problems caused, consequences experienced, and risks faced as a result of the behavior in question. MI therapists help clients envision a better future and become increasingly motivated to achieve it. Although best known as an effective intervention for alcoholism, MI has also been used with drug abusers, pregnant mothers (for smoking cessation), adolescents and men who are HIV positive, people with eating disorders, and clients in correctional settings.

MI departs from traditional Rogerian client-centered therapy through its use of direction, in which therapists attempt to influence clients to consider making changes rather than explore themselves nondirectively. The main goals of MI are to establish rapport, elicit change talk, and establish commitment language from the client, based on four principles:

1. express empathy—guides therapists to share with clients their understanding of clients' perspectives;
2. develop discrepancy—guides therapists to help clients appreciate the value of change by exploring the discrepancy between how clients want their lives to be and how their lives currently are (or between their deeply held values and their day-to-day behavior);
3. roll with resistance—guides therapists to accept client reluctance to change as natural rather than as pathological; and
4. support self-efficacy—guides therapists to embrace client autonomy explicitly (even when clients choose to not change) and help clients move toward change successfully and with confidence.

Although MI therapists help clients envisage a better future and become increasingly motivated to achieve it, using coaching-like skills, the differentiator is the existence of pathology that behavioral change is targeted to treat. Addictions are, in fact, a contraindication to coaching.

MI *techniques* are sometimes used in a corporate environment as part of the human relations process or by corporations during sales and marketing presentations. But these applications are not called MI because MI is a therapeutic method that always looks out for the best interests of clients, not a set of techniques used to influence behavior that serves one's or a corporate entity's self-interest.

The one area in which MI has been used in coaching is health coaching, a relatively new behavioral intervention gaining popularity due to the need to control health care costs and its potential to address adverse behaviors, health risks, and illness self-management in the workplace (Butterworth, Linden, McClay, & Leo, 2006).

Coachability

On the basis of the distinctions between coaching and therapy, there are two issues. First, the client's motivation must be strong and the client must be self-directed. When a client is referred by a parent or a manager, she or he must independently recognize the value of coaching. Second, coaching must be appropriate to the client's circumstances.

These include life issues, work or business issues, and specialized areas such as ADHD or Asperger's syndrome when coaching is part of a comprehensive plan or is an adjunct to medical treatment for chronic diseases that require high levels of self-management (for example, diabetes, cardiac conditions, weight management).

Coaching is <u>not</u> appropriate

- as a "treatment of last resort";
- as a substitute for any kind of treatment when there are ongoing, long-term, or underlying mental and emotional issues preventing an individual from functioning optimally; or
- for individuals with a known history of psychosis, BPD, or addictions unless those problems are under good control.

Coaches who are not trained therapists can simply ask, "Have you ever been hospitalized or worked with a therapist in the past?" This will bring out the needed information. If a client responds by saying "that's personal," a coach can add that coaching can get very personal, and, although coaching is not therapy, it is helpful to know whether a client has ever experienced therapy and what the benefit was.

As you can see from my interaction with Julie, I will be very quick to pick up if an individual is not appropriate or ready for coaching. As a coach, I can pick and choose

---

Julie

Julie was a therapist who came to me to build a practice. She had recently been through some traumatic personal events, told me she had ADHD, and that she already had a therapist. When I tried to focus on her most pressing goal (stated several times on her intake questionnaire) of getting organized and creating an income quickly (she had just left a job), she became upset and told me she wasn't ready for that. She said I needed to "begin where she was at." I told her that perhaps in light of the trauma, she might not be ready for coaching just yet, but I would spend the rest of the session helping her think about how to get better organized, and she could think about whether coaching was right for her at this time.

I didn't expect to see or hear from her again and, in fact, felt badly about getting her so upset. I could see her perspective and agreed I had pursued an agenda with her without full permission. To my surprise, she e-mailed me a few days later and said she wanted to work together. When I asked her how she reconciled our bad start, she told me that when she had spoken to her young adult son about our session and told him how angry she was, he said, "Ma, you went to her for coaching, not for therapy!" His words helped her refocus on her original intentions. She also had found the structure we outlined immediately helpful and had done all of her homework and more, so she felt "more optimistic than I have in years."

with whom I want to work. This idea may seem heretical to human service and health care professionals, but many people in the field who have paid their dues can identify with the idea of working with the "ideal" client. Concierge physicians have embraced this idea as well. Coaching affords this opportunity and encourages practitioners to build their business on the basis of who they *want* to work with, not just whoever comes to them. Coaches are not bound by the same ethics around abandonment as therapists and, therefore, can at any time let a client know whether coaching is not working or appropriate; although it happens rarely, I am always careful to make an appropriate referral when it does.

Therapists' Ambivalence About Coaching

Although many therapists will say that they have been doing coaching for a long time, even though they have never labeled it as such, and that they enjoy the potential freedom from managed care that coaching can bring, a number of concerns become apparent when they are introduced more formally to the practice. I would be dishonest if I said that I have not experienced feeling many of them myself. They include the following:

- the idea that coaching is expensive and therefore reserved for the "well-off," which may run counter to the human service values of a helping professional;
- the concern that the idea that "anything is possible" is a seductive, "now-generation" marketing ploy that is hard to accept when recalling those clients one has worked with who are some of the most marginalized individuals in society (this concern may be particularly strong in an economic recession, although that is just the time when therapists themselves are looking for alternative sources of income and may be more drawn to coaching);
- the fact that nonclinically trained individuals can be coaches—what can they know? (trained helping professionals might see their oversights: failure to diagnose problems that need mental health intervention or people in over their heads with difficult clients);
- difficulty giving up the "expert" role—especially for those who have worked in hierarchical settings such as hospitals, mental health centers, and schools;
- guilt over charging and being paid what may feel like very high fees, even from those who can afford to pay;
- difficulty shedding a problem focus;
- the sense that coaching might seem shallow or simplistic, not intellectually challenging;
- lack of research or evidence-based data to support coaching results (although this is rapidly changing);
- the paucity of academic programs providing coaching education; and
- resistance to marketing and self-promotion (it can be hard to enter a new field that first needs to be explained before clients will become engaged).

Self-Exploration

- Do I feel the need for a more positive, upbeat way to make a difference in the lives of others?
- Do people tell me I am a natural coach or mentor?
- Am I ready to give up my identity as a therapist or other human service professional, or do I really just want coaching skills to add to my bag of tricks?
- Am I ready to put in the work involved in reinventing myself, including a reevaluation of some of my own core values and beliefs?
- Am I willing to give up my propensity to focus on or my attachment to suffering?
- Am I willing to give up the expert role?
- Am I ready to be a beginner again?
- Am I ready to "unlearn" some of the valuable things that I've learned as a therapist and trust myself to know what to retain and what to let go?
- Am I willing to be in a field with others who have no psychological training and still value their wisdom?

3

The Need and Opportunity for Coaching

My interest is in the future because I am going to spend the rest of my life there.
—Charles F. Kettering

In a 1997 marketing brochure for the Hudson Institute, founder and executive coach, Frederic Hudson listed the following eight reasons he believed we need coaches in our society:

- to help adults manage change,
- to model personal mastery,
- to elicit core values and concerns,
- to help stabilize and renew corporate and professional systems,
- to provide ongoing training in technical abilities,
- to sponsor "Generation X,"
- to teach collaboration and consensus building, and
- to tap the genius of older workers.

There is no doubt that coaching is even more relevant today. Since the recent economic downturn, companies are leaner, demanding more from fewer and more quickly. More people are being laid off, downsized, "right-sized," or just becoming frustrated with the lack of ethics and dehumanization in corporate life. Many want to flee and do something more meaningful with their lives. For those who are self-employed, the small business landscape is increasingly difficult to navigate due to rapid technological advances, and undoubtedly this trend will continue. We are also part of a global economy, with its unique challenges and opportunities.

In a white paper written just after September 11, 2001, and posted on the International Coach Federation (ICF) Web site ("How Will the Noise about the Economy Affect Coaching?"), ICF president Marcia Reynolds stated that

a downturn in economic times affects everyone in some way. A downturn in one nation's economy will affect many other nations' economies. Business is global now and there is acceleration in the impact of any world market news thanks to immediate communication and commerce via the web. So, what helps one country helps many, and what hurts one hurts many. *Coaching is the perfect solution* for so many people now.

Reynolds went on to describe how coaching is all the more relevant in an economic downturn:

- Coaching is perfect for larger corporations because development plans can be customized for individuals without requiring large company initiatives.
- Downsizing causes emotional issues that can be addressed through coaching.
- Coaching can help people focus in the midst of turmoil.
- The biggest impact in a downturn is *fear*, which can paralyze creative beings, and coaching can unlock the creativity and help people stay centered.
- Small business owners and entrepreneurs can benefit from the support of a qualified coach to navigate a tight economy.
- People will want to reduce the risks of their most important decisions—coaching helps people become smart about their choices, whether related to career, significant relationship, financial well-being, or company direction.
- Personal coaches are catalysts for big successes as people achieve their dreams. With each success story, another ambassador for coaching is born.
- Coaches actually love the creativity of helping people manage through the messes of living and working in a high-speed society.
- Coaches see the world as a possibility. They know that people can intend and manifest the changes they desire without buying into the fears of politicians, the media, and other sources.

There is a general lack of mentors and sense of community to support all of the changes around us. Coaching has filled the gap in many instances, helping people get what they want more quickly and more effectively without having to reinvent the wheel with each new transition. Some individuals feel they have maximized the impact of psychotherapy and just need something "different" or "more action oriented." Others would never dream of seeking help from a therapist anyway; they are well functioning but perhaps "lonely at the top" or in need of a "sounding board" when making difficult decisions, particularly in a fast-paced environment.

In a *Harvard Business Review* article, Steven Berglas (2002) asserted that therapists are best equipped to provide coaching because of their background and understanding of psychology and human vulnerability. One only has to think about recent corporate excesses and wonder whether there were nonpsychologically trained coaches in the boardroom missing or overlooking the levels of narcissism of the CEOs who brought down Merrill Lynch, AIG, and the auto industry, for example.

In the personal realm, we are a rapidly aging population of individuals who are committed to lifetime vitality. The term "Third Age" denotes a movement dedicated to passion and purpose beyond career, or at least beyond one's lifelong career.

The Hudson Institute (n.d.-b) has noted that the term "retirement" seems to be ill-suited for today's older population. Although the sort of retirement our parents planned for and dreamed about is more atypical, few of us have maps for how we want to proceed through these years. In addition, we are living longer, healthier lives with more options than ever before. In describing their program, ThirdLaunch: Passion and Purpose Beyond Career for individuals in their 50s, 60s, 70s, and beyond, the Hudson Institute (n.d.-b) observed the following:

- We are living longer than ever with mostly good health.
- We have saved less than past generations at a time when it takes more money to sustain our preferred lifestyles, and this means many of us will continue some form of work well beyond traditional retirement.
- Those of us turning sixty today are, by nature, more optimistic and we expect more.
- Workforce dynamics create some interesting convergences for us with shrinking numbers spelling new possibilities for all sorts of part-time work options that haven't existed in the past.
- People entering their sixties are the largest group within the total US population.
- Look around at the ads, the magazines, and you'll notice whole industries serving the "graying of America."
- We are looking for renewed passion and purpose that includes making a difference in our later years.
- Quite simply put, we are pioneering a new stage of life filled with ample challenges and opportunities for a rich new chapter.

Other current trends that I see affecting the future of coaching are

- a growing number of displaced workers who will need to reinvent themselves to remain economically viable in coming years;
- a new generation of "millennials" raised with high expectations but with more limited options and limited skills for entering the workforce;
- integration of coaching into health care as evidence-based research begins to emerge;
- the move toward increased professionalism of coaching, including greater emphasis on psychological knowledge;
- the growth of internal coaching programs, which are considered more cost-effective, may be limited in a down economy, but training of internal coaches and coach/managers and peer coaching may increase;
- nonprofit organizations will continue to multiply and, with reduced membership and charitable giving, will increasingly integrate a coaching approach in their leadership philosophy both within the organizations and the communities they serve; and
- health coaching, although slow to evolve, will likely be integrated into mainstream medicine.

The simple fact is that coaching has many useful applications, and it is here to stay.

4

Coaching as an Alternative or Complement to Existing Practice

Unless we change directions, we are likely to end up where we are going . . .
—Chinese Proverb

Therapist Dissatisfaction

In Norcross and Guy's (2007) book on therapist self-care, they indicated that "most therapists" are satisfied with their practices and would choose their profession again. Such an assertion makes it difficult to understand why 450 practitioners—social workers, physicians, nurses, psychologists, mental health counselors, and educators—attended a Harvard Medical School Conference on coaching in the fall of 2008, and 100 (I was told when I called to register) were still on the waiting list ("McLean Hospital/Harvard Medical School," 2009).

Among the satisfactions cited were the following:

At the office:

- the satisfaction of alleviating emotional distress and promoting personality growth in the lives of others;
- freedom and independence;
- variety of experiences;
- "permanent" membership in the client's world;
- intellectual stimulation;
- emotional growth of one's own; and
- reinforcement of personality qualities—relating to others, conversation, intimacy.

Outside the office:

- improved interpersonal relationships from learning from one's clients;
- improved personal effectiveness;
- life meaning;
- public recognition, including for one's education and degrees; and
- employment opportunities—teaching, writing, speaking, consulting.

37

Despite these sources of satisfaction, managed care has decreased the income potential of therapists and of all healthcare providers; interfered with the freedom to practice independently and the ability to be a "permanent" member of the client's world (all they need to do is change insurance); and, most important, led to frustration, anger about working conditions, and more burnout and dissatisfaction—beyond normal "service weariness."

Ask yourself whether any of the following common issues of therapist *dissatisfaction* are true for you. If so, then coaching may have an appeal:

- holding on to unreasonable expectations for your career (stable employment, a successful private practice with enough clients to go around);
- reaching an uncomfortable phase of career development (feeling that there is no room for advancement in the field, feeling stuck, having a flourishing practice disappear and feeling powerless to reverse this downward trend);
- feeling unable to support yourself or your family or feeling insecure about the future (not having enough income to live on, needing to work multiple jobs to make ends meet, no cost-of-living increases, declining fees, loss of benefits, feeling no better off than some of one's clients and feeling guilty about it);
- failing to set appropriate limits with clients and colleagues (continually agreeing to meet unreasonable demands, becoming emotionally involved in clients' problems, feeling limited in your ability to navigate effectively certain administrative demands or to make inroads with certain populations);
- feeling drained and burned out (related to the above but also a by-product of feeling insecure about oneself and one's future; cumulative anger about managed care, fee-for-service, declining fees, increased hours, falling into victimhood);
- toiling in an unpleasant work environment (accepting abuse or unreasonable demands, particularly around statistics and productivity; remaining in an environment in which coworkers exhibit frustration or low morale);
- wanting to work with a healthier and more motivated client population (frustration in working with difficult, resistant clients; feeling depressed and demoralized about the slow pace of change); and
- wanting and needing to make a bigger difference (frustration with limited resources, work loads that allow only patchwork interventions, the limited visions of agencies and institutions).

Therapist, Healthcare, and Human Service Professional Skills and Competencies

Now look at the array of skills of therapists and other helping professionals:

Client Work/Case Management
- Active listening
- Anticipating problems or needs
- Asking the right questions

- Assessing
- Clarifying values and goals of others
- Coaching
- Collaborating with those in other disciplines
- Conceptualizing
- Confronting others with difficult personal issues (such as denial of substance abuse)
- Conflict resolution
- Consulting
- Counseling
- Crisis intervention/management
- Developing rapport and trust
- Diagnosing
- Empathizing
- Exercising intuition
- Facilitating communication
- Grief work
- Identifying problems
- Innovating
- Intervening
- Maintaining confidentiality
- Managing
- Mediating differences
- Multitasking
- Ombudsmanship
- Performing needs assessment
- Problem solving
- Providing spiritual guidance
- Teaching, training, educating
- Troubleshooting
- Understanding complex human emotions and behavior
- Working as part of a team

Office/Practice Management

- Being computer literate/maintaining computer literacy
- Billing insurance
- Developing self-direction
- Following through
- Keeping accurate records
- Managing a budget
- Managing a staff
- Running a business (private practice)
- Supervising

Work Products/Processes

- Advocating
- Communicating
- Consulting
- Creating alliances in the community
- Demonstrate effectiveness (for example, case conferences)
- Delivering clinical interventions
- Delivering public presentations and trainings
- Gathering resources
- Interpreting documents and case records
- Keeping others informed
- Keeping statistics
- Leading meetings
- Managing information
- Networking
- Practically applying theoretical learning
- Preparing budgets
- Promoting diversity—education, training, management
- Record keeping
- Teaching
- Writing proposals and grants

Data-Related Skills

- Analyzing
- Establishing priorities
- Organizing
- Planning
- Seeing the "big picture"
- Working within models of varying systems (for example, medical, school, agency, government)

Below are some career alternatives I have come up with. Coaching comes up a few times. Other alternative careers for healthcare providers and human service professionals can easily be tied in with coaching.

Resistance Factors

Many of us who work in human service and health care are stuck ourselves. Below are common rationalizations that might prevent us from making changes. Do any of them sound familiar?

- Overall, it's really not at all bad where I am.
- At least work is predictable: Over the course of a week or month, I know I'll be facing the same good or bad things.

Career Alternatives

- Alternative dispute resolution
- Alternative healing—Reiki, yoga
- Art or movement therapist
- Business
- Career counseling
- Child-related services
- Coaching—life, business, health and wellness
- Consulting
- Corporate trainer
- Corporate diversity trainer
- Employee assistance
- Entrepreneurial ventures, especially those sensitive to human needs and concerns (elder-care consulting, day care centers, consulting businesses)
- Executive coaching
- Franchise owner, especially of a service-related business like a career center
- Funds development for nonprofit organizations
- Grant writer
- Grief counselor in a funeral home
- Human interest writer
- Human resources
- Lobbyist
- Mediation
- Ombudsman for the elderly/disabled/children
- Organizational development
- Outplacement counselor
- Planned giving director for a nonprofit
- Professional organizer
- Public speaker
- Researcher
- Relocation counselor
- Stress-management trainer

- What if it's worse where I go or what I do next? What if I have to take a fee-for-service job and I lose my benefits?
- I can't let my clients, colleagues, or organization down. They need me.
- How will I support myself? Pay for training? Pay for things needed to start something new—business cards and so on?
- The economy is bad. This isn't a good time to make a change.
- I really don't have time to think about this now.

- I'm a "good person." How could I think of doing something that's about my own needs?
- What will people think?
- I hate to market.
- I worked hard to get where I am now; I don't have the energy to start all over.
- What if I'm not good at it?
- I'm burned out now, but if I could take a vacation, I'd recover.

Clearing Exercise

Before embarking on a new path or embracing a new set of skills specific to coaching, it is useful to "clear" old thoughts, feelings, and beliefs that might block your access to what you want. Setting goals does not work if there are old conflicts or contradictions that underlie your belief system. Some of the typical techniques for clearing include psychotherapy, bodywork, yoga or meditation, and journaling. A simple set of questions in the Personal and Professional Inventory that follows will help you clear your thoughts.

After you have answered the self-exploration questions, complete the following questionnaires:

Self-Exploration: Personal and Professional Inventory

- What are your goals? Now? Long term?
- What have you done to achieve your goals?
- What worked? What did not work?
- What are your best skills (see the skill lists presented earlier)? Are you using them? How often?
- What do you value (see the value clarification list presented later)? Is your work and quality of life compatible with your values?
- If you could change your life, how would you change it?
- What accomplishments are you most proud of?
- Who or what would you like to eliminate from your life?
- What is one thing you could do that would make the most profound difference in your life?
- If you did not have to worry about money or other people's opinion of you, what would you be doing with your life?
- If you only had one year to live, how would you live it?
- In what ways are you most responsible? Least responsible?
- What are people afraid to tell you about yourself?
- What is your most significant obstacle (a boss, money, distractions, bad habits, fatigue)?

List 10 Things You Love to Do:

1. _____

    _____

2. _____

    _____

3. _____

    _____

4. _____

    _____

5. _____

    _____

6. _____

    _____

7. _____

    _____

8. _____

    _____

9. _____

    _____

10. _____

    _____

What Special Skills Do You Have as a Therapist or Other Helping Professional?

See the Therapist, Healthcare, and Human Service Professional Skills and Competencies section for ideas.

1. _____

   _____

2. _____

   _____

3. _____

   _____

4. _____

   _____

5. _____

   _____

6. _____

   _____

7. _____

   _____

8. _____

   _____

9. _____

   _____

10. _____

    _____

Tolerations

Tolerations are events, people, and situations that you put up with in your life that can drain your energy and prevent you from being yourself and enjoying life to the fullest. Tolerations are like "holes in your personal cup"—no matter how much you put into the cup, it will all drain out. Tolerations range from small chores, such as a car that needs to be washed, to more significant personal challenges, such as someone who repeatedly ignores your requests or a partner who refuses to communicate with you.

To discover your tolerations, write down at least 10 things you can think of that you would no longer like to have to put up with in your life. If you keep going, you probably will find you have about 100 tolerations at the present time. Once you start counting, the list just seems to keep growing.

List 10 Areas You Are Tolerating in Your Personal and Business Life:

1. _____

   _____

2. _____

   _____

3. _____

   _____

4. _____

   _____

5. _____

   _____

6. _____

   _____

7. _____

   _____

8. _____

   _____

9. _____

   _____

10. _____

    _____

Values Clarification

Choose 10 of the following values (or add your own). Rank order 10 in terms of their importance to you (left column). Then rank order *the same 10* under "Behavior" in terms of how you actually live. Notice whether both are aligned. Does this suggest any changes you might make?

Value	Importance	Behavior
Accomplishment/results		
Achievement		
Adventure/excitement		
Aesthetics/beauty		
Athleticism		
Altruism		
Authenticity		
Autonomy		
Clarity		
Collaboration		
Commitment		
Community		
Compassion		

Value	Importance	Behavior
Connection/bonding		
Creativity		
Decisiveness		
Ease		
Emotional health		
Environment		
Family or family first		
Financial freedom		
Fitness		
Freedom		
Fun		
Health/well-being		
Honesty		
Humor		
Integrity		
Intimacy		
Joy		
Leadership		
Lifelong learning		
Love		
Loyalty		
Making a difference		
Mastery/excellence		
Mediating differences		
Moving things forward		

Value	Importance	Behavior
Openness		
Orderliness/accuracy		
Partnership		
Philanthropy		
Power		
Privacy/solitude		
Recognition/acknowledgment		
Religion		
Risk taking		
Romance		
Security		
Self-expression		
Sensuality		
Service/contribution (as in "servant leader")		
Spirituality		
Success		
Trust		
Vitality		
Wealth/Financial freedom		
Wisdom		
Other _____ _____ _____ _____ _____		

Career Satisfaction

What Would Make Me Feel Really Satisfied With My Career Is:

_____

_____

_____

_____

_____

_____

_____

_____

What Would It Be Like if I Could Have My Career Exactly the Way I Want?

_____

_____

_____

_____

_____

_____

_____

_____

_____

What Might I Be Afraid of or Hesitant to Change?

_____

_____

_____

_____

_____

_____

_____

_____

_____

_____

Self-Exploration

Looking at your answers to the questionnaires in this chapter—including your transferable skills, what you love to do, your values, what you are tolerating and no longer want to tolerate in your life—write a statement that expresses where you want to go. Look at the lists presented earlier to see whether you have considered all the possible directions? Is coaching a good fit?

5

The Theory and Substance of Coaching

We see things not as they are. We see things as we are.

—Anaïs Nin

Coaching draws on a number of theoretical strains, including the humanistic psychology of Rogers and Maslow, the work of Milton Erikson, Bandler and Grindler's Neuro-Linguistic Programming (NLP), the solution-focused approach of Steve de Shazer and colleagues, and existential psychology. From Carl Jung (1960), coaching draws on the concept of "synchronicity."

As Patrick Williams (Williams & Davis, 2002) has pointed out, in *Therapist as Life Coach*, coaching developed from three streams: psychotherapy and counseling; consulting and organizational development; and personal development training such as est, Lifespring, the Landmark Forum, and Tony Robbins's programs. Here, I have put together my ideas about the theory behind coaching.

Motivational Theory

Psychologists such as Seligman (1994), Prochaska (Prochaska, Norcross, & DiClemente, 1995), O'Hanlon (1999), and Burns (1999) have told us that we can change behavior by consciously shifting our attention to our desired state of being. The so-called "New Age" writers, such as Deepak Chopra, have provided an even broader view of this goal. In *Ageless Body, Timeless Mind*, Chopra (1993) said,

> Every intention is a trigger for transformation. As soon as you decide that you want something, your nervous system responds to reach your desired goal. This holds true for simple intentions such as the intention to get up and get a glass of water, as well as for complex intentions, such as winning a game of tennis. . . . When you have an intention, your brain can supply only the reactions it has learning; if you are a good tennis player . . . your trained response will produce very different results from those achieved by someone less skilled than you. *Yet the deepest skill resides in managing intention itself* [italics added]. The people who succeed best at any endeavor are generally following a pattern of handling their desires without undue struggle in the environment . . . they allow the solution to present itself, trusting their own abilities to cope with difficult challenges. By creating a minimum of anxiety, conflict, worry and false expectation, they promote highly efficient use of their mental and physical energies. (pp. 103–104)

NLP

NLP is a practical set of models, skills, and techniques for thinking and acting effectively in the world. Its purpose, according to Joseph O'Connor and John Seymour (1993), who refer to it as "the art and science of personal excellence" (p. 1), is "to be useful, to increase choice and to enhance the quality of life" (p. xiii); according to NLP's "father" and cocreator, Richard Bandler (2008), its purpose is to provide " a way of organizing your internal world so you have more control over what the brain does. . . . If you change the way you think, it changes the way you feel, which changes the way you act" (p. 207). Today, NLP is used in psychotherapy, education, business, and sales.

NLP started in the early 1970s through the collaboration of linguistics professor John Grindler and Bandler, then a graduate student of psychology. They studied three top therapists: Fritz Perls, the originator of Gestalt therapy; Virginia Satir, the famous family therapist; and Milton Erikson, the world-renowned hypnotherapist. They found that these three therapists, although very different as personalities and in their therapeutic modalities, used surprisingly similar underlying patterns in their work. The "neuro" part of Bandler and Grindler's (1979) theory of NLP acknowledges that all behavior stems from our senses; the "linguistic" part indicates the importance of language in ordering our thoughts and behavior to communicate with others; and "programming" refers to ways we can choose to organize our ideas and actions to produce results.

One of the most revolutionary techniques introduced by Bandler and Grindler was to "change personal history." They found that although one could not change the past, *one could increase emotional freedom from the past by changing its meaning in the present.* Through "future pacing," one could also step into the future in imagination with the new resources developed through NLP and experience in advance how one would wish the future to be. Although it is not clear that coaching consciously borrowed these ideas from NLP, many coaches have had NLP training, and there is clearly a natural fit between the two approaches.

Language Theory

> *Basic words do not state something that might exist outside them; by being spoken, they establish a mode of existence.*
>
> —Martin Buber

As mentioned in chapter 2, coaching is, in part, grounded in a branch of philosophy that emerged in the second half of the 20th century called the *philosophy of language* (see Edelson, 2002b, on which much of the discussion in this chapter is based). The new claim of the philosophy of language was that when we speak, not only do we describe existing reality, but we also act. Language, in fact, is action. This definition contrasted the previous view of language as a way of accounting for what already existed.

Distinctions

Distinctions are concepts that separate what we previously might have "known" as the same. For example, Eskimos have numerous distinctions for snow and the color white. Distinctions are words that, when understood, cause a shift in one's understanding. They often affect one's beliefs, behaviors, values, or attitudes.

New distinctions are ways of reorganizing what we see, both with our eyes and with our minds. Someone with a rich body of distinctions in a particular area has power with respect to that area. So, the more distinctions you can draw, the more "power" you can have. Doctors can "see" things about the body and disease that the rest of us cannot because we do not have the distinctions. The same is true for other types of workers—from auto mechanics, who can hear a sound in a car and know what it is, to marketers, who can "see" what can be done to generate visibility or sales for a product. Artists see images differently than the average person. They may see nuances of color and perspective that a person without the distinctions of an artist does not have. They also have language to speak about the distinctions they see. Similarly, in human relations, the ability to draw distinctions gives us openings for new actions in effecting change. Distinctions in the way we speak can uplift or depress our clients. Asking what clients intend to "do" with information that they have distinguishes something different than asking them how they "feel." Articulated, the intended action can, and frequently does, change how a client feels.

⟡ The Biology of Language

Drawing on the work of his Chilean countryman Humberto Maturana, from whose work family systems therapists derived key concepts around entropy and change, and that of Searle (1970) on "speech acts," Fernando Flores has provided a "biology of language" and "conversations for action" (Winograd & Flores, 1986). Flores, who was Chile's Minister of Finance and, later, a political prisoner, is a key figure in the origination of the ontological approach to coaching. He saw that communication, truth, and trust are at the heart of power (Rubin, 2007). He said,

> "I made my own assessment of my life, and I began to live it. That was freedom." Fernando began his lectures saying, "In language, we build our own identities, our relationships with others, the countries we live in, the companies we have, and the values we hold dear. With language, we generate life. Without language, we are mostly chimpanzees." (Budd & Rothstein, 2000, p. 125)

The Linguistic Acts

This biology of language is based on five component parts that help us to produce effective communication (Winograd & Flores, 1986, p. 58). The first four are referred to as *action* acts. The fifth component is "assessments," which are nonvisible and can be described as acts of mental activity—they may or may not involve direct action, yet they can and frequently do provide the backdrop for the other linguistic acts. These five actions in language, according to Flores, encompass all human behavior. They are as follows:

Assertions. Assertions are statements about one's observations. They will differ according to one's biological makeup (as in color-blindness), tradition, and cultural differences. Eskimos, as mentioned, have many more distinctions for describing snow and the color white than do non-Eskimos. Assertions are also statements for which *one is willing* to provide evidence. They can be true assertions or false assertions, depending on whether they are verifiable. Changing one's assertions can alter existence by creating new paradigms. When it was asserted that the world was round, and this assertion was found to be true, life as it was experienced then changed dramatically.

Declarations. When we make a declaration, we can instantly alter a reality. We, in fact, generate a whole new world for ourselves. Some real-world examples of such declarations include *The Declaration of Independence* or saying "I do" to solidify wedding vows. Thus, declarations can also be historical or personal. A crucial declaration is forgiveness, which represents the declaration not to carry past resentment into the present and the future. When we make a declaration, we commit ourselves to behave consistently with the new reality we have declared. When we fail to honor this commitment, breakdowns occur.

Promises. Promises are linguistic acts that allow us to coordinate action with others. They involve a manifest commitment to another. Promises also live in time, distance, and form. Two actions are involved in the fulfillment of a promise: the making of the promise and the fulfillment of the promise. The completion of the action of making a promise occurs when both parties agree on the promise. When a promise goes unfulfilled, one is entitled to voice dissatisfaction. "A promise is like a buckle—it needs two sides to close" (Echeverria, 1990). We can, of course, make promises to ourselves, which might be more like a hook—namely, a point from which to suspend one's belt. Because there is less accountability involved when promises are made to oneself they might not be as readily kept, and this is a major motivation to work with a coach.

Promises are easy to make—possibly too easy ("I'll call you"; "I'll do that by Friday"; "I'll never leave you")—but often not easy to fulfill. Sometimes the inability to keep a promise is unanticipated ("I got sick"; "I didn't know my feelings would change"). At other times, the one making the promise knows in advance whether he or she can keep it and instead chooses to treat the promise cavalierly. Failure to fulfill a promise leads to a breakdown of trust, and the cumulative impact can alter the course of one's personal history. On a small scale, just notice how frequently plans are made and cancelled at the last moment. "Something came up" might be true, or it might mean that something was more important. In any event, no one can control the interpretation of the other, so each time a commitment is broken, it is important to remember the potential impact of that broken promise. Although it can be challenging to keep each and every commitment, the genuine intention to do so will increase one's record of success, which will, in turn, contribute to one's success.

- *Requests.* Requests are linguistic moves to elicit a promise from the listener. Although made in the present, they invite future action. There are four possible responses: to accept, to decline, to counteroffer, or to defer.

- *Assessments.* Assessments are the ungrounded truths that dominate and influence one's life. They frequently consist of beliefs based on early interpretations of one's environment without evidence to prove their truthfulness. This involves how we feel about our parents, ourselves and what we hold to be true about life generally. Positive assessments lead to better moods and more effective action. Negative assessments, such as "I'll never be number one" and "that's just the way life is," lead to negative moods and less effective action.

The Premises of Coaching versus Psychotherapy in Language Theory

The basic premises of psychotherapy can be said to be the following:

- Development is a life process, driven by biology.
- There are biological influences and deviations.
- History, of both the individual and the family, is important.
- Trauma and abuse alter the life course.
- The self is formed from the confluence of the above influences and factors.

The basic premises of coaching are the following:

- When we speak, we act.
- Language is generative.
- Listening does not necessarily result in receiving an accurate transmission of what is spoken but, rather, always involves an act of interpretation.
- If we change the language we use to describe our experience, we can change our interpretation and alter our experience—even regarding traumatic events.
- Language spoken into a future that is open creates the possibility of something new; language that is driven by the past will give us "more of the same"—what we have already had.
- In language, we have *choice*; our choices determine our actions; therefore, the language we choose to use can alter history—personally, socially, and globally.

In coaching, the emphasis is placed on the future and on creating results. Clients are encouraged through the nature of the coaching "inquiry" to generate new ways of viewing their lives and to consider what is possible as they move forward. In the process, a client may realize that what he or she previously viewed as shortcomings or personal failures can be reframed as lessons to be learned and clues about where he or she may need to develop new skills. The personal and professional coach, like a good athletic coach, is always raising the bar (appropriate to the clients' needs) and providing positive reinforcement (for example, "You can do it!"). Although coaching is similar to solution-focused psychotherapy in framing the direction of the work toward results, the absence of diagnoses supports the coach's ability to create a context that reinforces the client as "whole, complete, and resourceful."

Inquiry

The coach's inquiry is rooted in curiosity and based on collaboration rather than the aims of knowing and expertise that characterize psychotherapy. My coaching clients rarely turn to me as the expert, as therapy clients (who, no matter what, will see me as the "expert") do. Coaching clients do not seem to need to be judged and assessed as "healthy," because they were never ill or lacking to begin with. The inquiry is an adventure on which coach and client embark together, with the exception that one is holding the others' intentions for a better future. This very subtle linguistic difference gives coaching a very different feel for both coach and client.

Paradigm Shift

Listening always involves interpretation, and, therefore, interpretations can be reframed to be more empowering. The language used by a coach or therapist can have a profound impact on a client's readiness for change. It is the coach's or clinicians' job to use language to "cause" the client the greatest opportunity for movement—ideally, a paradigm shift.

A classic example of a paradigm shift is the shift that occurred when it was accepted that the world is round. Prior to that time, in a "flat" world, one did not venture far from home, and far less was possible in the world. A client had a paradigm shift when, after hearing her therapist (who was in coach training with me and open to using new language in her therapy sessions) use the term *contribution*, she realized she had made a significant contribution to her family. She was then able to spend time with them without the guilt and anger she had known most of her life. This left her feeling more "powerful" (that is, less helpless, less victimized, more whole) than she had ever felt before.

Although a variety of skills and techniques—such as value clarification, goal setting, and strategic planning—may be used in coaching, process is an integral part of the coaching relationship, and suffering is actively addressed when it arises. Coaching is particularly useful for individuals and systems in transition because it creates the context for asking what is wanted and what steps are necessary to attain it. Individuals and organizations can develop themselves in new areas that might not otherwise be available for "transformation."

Language and "Reality"

Without access to language, we have no reality. Language gives us existence, and existence gives us the desire to understand and make meaning of everything in our experience. Try as we may, we are unable to stop making meaning. We can, however, make meaning that is empowering versus disempowering and that connects us to our core essence.

Winograd and Flores (1986) used the analogy of a raindrop that falls on a mountainside and, as it courses downward, both affects and is affected by the slope down which it rolls. That raindrop's experience is its incontrovertible truth, though rain falling on an opposite slope finds quite a different path.

The Past and Emotions

The past is of interest in coaching as information but not as the focus of intense exploration, as it is in many forms of therapy. Language is critical and is seen as the key element in shaping the worldview of the client. As such, individuals have the opportunity to describe themselves and their circumstances in new language, develop competency, and *generate* certain emotions—trust, love, faith, and passion—that support their authentic life. When the client experiences his or her own authenticity, healing of the past can occur spontaneously.

A therapy client, for example, had felt stuck for years after being laid off from a job she loved. She worked only part time and lived paycheck to paycheck while, at 38, she completed her undergraduate degree at a state university. She double majored in English literature and psychology, professing a love for both, but I had trouble seeing her as capable of working in any human service capacity. It was painful listening to her at times; she was so filled with anger at her parents and previous employer. Despite myself, I still held her as whole, complete, and resourceful and tried to steer clear of my own judgments and assessments.

Following an eight-week exchange program working with developmentally challenged adults, the client experienced a profound emotional shift that allowed her to acknowledge the dissatisfaction she felt about her previous employer and to begin developing a path toward healing her relationship with her family. The client's "compelling way" of moving forward was through writing, which allowed her to redirect attention from her perceived deprivation to the gifts she brings to the world. She discovered her capacity to make things happen in her life *because she said she would!*

The Client's Story

The client's story is a powerful aspect of his or her life. It is formed in language (for example, "I'm not smart enough"; "I'm not lovable"; "I'm a loser"; "I'll always be second best") and perpetuated in language. The client described in the previous section had a very believable story about being a victim and about how hard life is. A new story is now available to her: "I don't have to be a victim. If I set my mind on what I want and have faith that good things can come to me, they will." She now has an opening for possibilities in her life. This opening immediately connects her with a larger purpose—her need to make a difference in the world.

People do not change their story because you ask them to. Our stories feel quite real; they are, in fact, our reality. In working with a client on perspective, a coach can open the door for him or her to a new alternate story.

Power

> *I feel it now: there's a power in me to grasp and give shape to my world. I know that nothing has ever been real without my beholding it.*
>
> — Rainer Maria Rilke

Coaching enables people, teams, and communities to find their "power." By *power*, I mean the ability to take action and effect positive change.

We gain power through the way we use language. Therefore, as coaches, we can *em*power others through the way we use language. Fernando Flores, like Nelson Mandela, felt his power in prison, an unlikely place, when he found a new language for his experience and could describe it as "freedom."

Choice and Declaration

We also have the power to chose our words—and, ultimately, our actions—carefully and, by doing so, to be fully responsible for their impact on others and on the world around us. Careless, toss-away comments can wound others and damage relationships. Thoughtless, hasty replies can commit us to undesired courses of action. Casual or flip responses, such as the "whatever" currently so common among teenagers, can render us victims. If we are willing to accept "whatever," then that may be exactly what we get.

Motivational writer and speaker Wayne Dyer has gone to the opposite extreme. In his keynote address at the International Coach Federation conference in 1996, Dyer admonished his listeners to "ask for what you really, really, really, *really* want!" He quipped that it is important to say it four times so it will be clear to the universe that you mean business.

A professional social worker I coach who had undergone nine difficult surgeries for a congenital condition declared his intention to speak to medical students and doctors about patient empathy. He recently received his first invitation to talk to a group of medical students and faculty at a major university medical school! He was pleased but immediately began to focus on how he could secure more speaking invitations so as to be considered successful. I told him that he already *is* successful, but if he did not make such a declaration, he might miss new opportunities that emerge.

In my early days of coaching, I declared the intention of working with women in corporations. I had no plan or track record, only goodwill and confidence in my ability to make a difference. So, I thought my idea could work. The universe delivered on my declaration. I met the vice president of a specialty bank in New York state, who, based on our conversation, wrote an impassioned letter to the CEO of the bank about the need to transform the way female employees were treated and praising my skills. Once it was clear that success in my endeavor was possible, my internal dialogue triggered doubts. The CEO actually contacted me by e-mail. Following that, my computer crashed, I lost the contact information and went into a tailspin, and I never actually succeeding in responding to the CEO. In my mind, like that of my client, I was not ready for such success. I was a "newbie" and an "imposter," and, in my internal framework, I felt the need to "work hard" before success was deserved. My internal dialogue shot me in the foot. How often do we see the same thing happening with our clients?

Taking deliberate care with the language we use with clients and instructing them on how to use language more powerfully in their own lives is crucial to our truly making a difference. Whether for the purposes of healing or empowerment, neither will be maintained if we continue to speak the past—that is, the way we always have. Change without a change in the language with which we describe ourselves and our circumstances will only be superficial, because we will not have truly chosen a new path until we speak it consistently.

"Problem" versus "Possibility"

Once the structure of language is understood, you and those you treat, coach, supervise, manage, or lead will be able to produce a more coherent approach to taking action. The word *possibility*, however, is perhaps the most crucial word we can use in helping create discontinuous change (such as water turning to ice or to vapor at certain temperatures) —what helping professionals refer to as *transformation*.

Although the word *possibility* has been used for many years by solution-focused therapists such as Bill O'Hanlon (1999), coaching goes a step farther to suggest that anyone can potentially have what they want in life *by design*. We are all "resourceful, whole, and complete" (Whitworth, Kimsey-House, & Sandahl, 1998). The coach's focus of attention is not on "pathology" or "problems" but, rather, on solutions and "possibilities."

The very language we use creates a different context. Language, as Fernando Flores and others have told us, is not just a description of our reality, it actually created our reality. "Possibility" (2004), according to *Merriam-Webster's Collegiate Dictionary*, is "the condition or fact of being possible"; "one's utmost power, capacity, or ability"; "something that is possible"; and "potential or prospective value" (p. 968). The coach's task, as I see it, is to uncover, in large part through the use of supportive language, "possibility," or even multiple possibilities for clients. Often such possibilities involve taking a client into the unknown or to a place they would never go alone.

The "possibility paradigm" is discussed by Steven Friedman and Margot Fanger (1991). No doubt, they were influenced by Matthew Budd and their experience of developing a brief treatment paradigm at Harvard Community Health Plan, where they all worked together. Friedman and Fanger (1991) saw that "nothing succeeds like success" and asserted that "the proper focus of treatment is not feeling but action in the world" (p. 17). Using metaphor, playfulness, and humor to "manipulate the frames" of the client's experience, Friedman and Fanger (1991) looked to transform the client's orientation to the future:

> An orientation to the future avoids, both for the client and the therapist, a position of absorption in the self-pitying morass of client guilt, shame and failure. The therapist, while acknowledging the past hurts of the client, empowers him or her to gain a renewed sense of competence, control and mastery. (p. 17)

This shift from problem to possibility describes the essence of coaching. "Possibility is not the opposite of problem; the possibility paradigm is rather *an entirely different frame of reference*" (Friedman & Fanger, 1991, p. 25).

In the problem paradigm, in which the focus is on what is wrong, solutions are sought through the application of "more of the same." In the possibility paradigm, discontinuity and a leap to "second-order change" (for example, from water to ice) is created through the inquiry of the client's desires, which suggests the possible existence of something different. Instead of getting away from the problem, the client is moved toward a new possibility.

What Makes Coaching Effective?

What actually makes coaching work? The most compelling aspect of coaching is that it is future oriented, which allows language to be used as a powerful vehicle for change. The simplest example is the words *I do* in the wedding ceremony. Two simple words (and a license) change everything from that moment forward. Words do truly give us our reality, explaining why affirmations can be an extremely powerful tool for change. Equally as powerful is having clients declare or commit to what they want to generate in their lives, their businesses, and their relationships (for example, "I'm successful"; "I'm an entrepreneur"; "I'm a coach"; "I'm a leader"; "I'm a survivor").

Writing down goals, making declarations, saying affirmations, and being accountable to another all work because our speaking sends a "no kidding" message to the unconscious. It allegedly takes 21 days to create a new synapse and repetition truly may lock positive thoughts in the brain. Negative thoughts, by contrast, seem to lock themselves into our minds on their own. We're simply unaware that in reality, we have repeated those negative thoughts to ourselves—"I can't do it," "I'm stupid"—so many times that they become like the air we breathe. By asking a client "When did you decide that you [were second best, not good enough, not smart enough, a loser, and so forth]?" the coach can find out the age of an internal dialogue. It may not be necessary that the client remembers the actual event from which the dialogue originated. Sometimes, the event is one that a helping professional might consider a "nonevent," such as the client's father not getting him or her a new baseball glove and the client equating that with "I'm not loved." Our brains remember. Such labeling, which often occurs at key times in one's development, steers one's direction in life. Because possibility is created through language, such internal dialogue also creates *negative possibility*. Thoughts also tend to come and go, and we easily lose some of our best intentions. "I am" compared with "I'm going to be" says we are already that to which we aspire. All we need to do is take the appropriate actions to solidify our intention. For example, the first-time bride and groom do not know how to be married yet; nonetheless, they have committed to living a new reality.

Holding the Client's Agenda

Saying that "sometimes it has to get worse before it gets better," a common platitude used by many therapists (including, at one time, me), has a far different effect on a client than saying "I am holding you to be big [strong, powerful, effective, competent] in your life." *Holding the agenda* could be seen as analogous to "support" in the classic definition of supportive therapy. Unfortunately, support too often has been interpreted as allowing the client to rely on the therapist inappropriately, sending an unconscious message that the client might not be competent to handle certain emotions or actions her- or himself. When we "hold" the client's agenda, we are simply saying we believe that what he or she wants is possible and that he or she will achieve it. I am often asked this question: What if you do not believe the client can achieve what he or she wants? My experience is that people are generally realistic about what they can and cannot do. The obstacle is more likely to be a negative internal or external dialogue (the latter taking place with the doubters in their lives). My opinion hardly matters, however, because I will always ask "What then?" or "What will it be like if you . . .?" or "Have you considered how you will manage if this doesn't go the way you want?" Through such a line of inquiry, the client will frequently come to his or her own decision and make different choices. My line of inquiry is always from the vantage point of what might be possible.

The "Gremlin"

Some possibilities create conflict, even wreaking havoc on our psyches. We want to go left, but we seem to always turn right. We think we will be happy when we get what we want, but, instead, we become depressed, overeat, or drink too much. We want to believe something is possible, but that nagging voice in our brain—referred to by some coaches as the "gremlin" (Carson, 1983)—has a different opinion: "You're stupid," "You're just a girl," "You'll never . . ." This is an area in which coaches really earn their keep. Knowing how to listen for and guide clients to combat their gremlin (also known as the "self-saboteur" or "negative self-talk") is often critical to the fulfillment of a client's dreams. Once the gremlin can be "tamed," a matter of guiding the client to greater self-awareness that involves considerable inventiveness on the part of the coach (because gremlins can be very stubborn), the path to possibility is cleared.

Accountability

The final ingredient in actualizing possibility is the coach holding the client accountable for producing intended results. Some coaches' favorite questions are "By when?" and "How will you let me know [that is, that you have done it]?" If the results are not achieved, then something can still be learned from the process, if only "what would be possible if . . . next time?"

Breakdowns and Breakthroughs

Matthew Budd has studied and eloquently outlined how we generate the life we live through our own language use. He also catalogued "the ten linguistic viruses"—10 common habits of speech that disempower, destroy relationships, and (ultimately) contribute to physical illness (Budd & Rothstein, 2000, pp. 141–155):

1. Not making requests—keeping one's needs and wants to oneself.
2. Living with uncommunicated expectations—often in the form of private conversations with oneself about what others "should" or "should not" do.
3. Making unclear requests—lack of sufficient clarity or detail to let the other person know what is wanted, communicating that one wants something but leaving the specifics to the listener to figure out.

4. Not observing the mood of requesting—making requests in the form of demands leaves others feeling resentful if they feel they have no choice; sounding like a beggar makes others feel manipulated.

5 Promising even when you are not clear what was requested—"committed confusion." Budd uses the example of giving his accountant a list of expenses he thought the accountant wanted (I laughed when I read that, having recently done the very same thing).

6. Being unable to say no—leads people to do things they do not want to do in life. On the receiving side of "yes"es, it is hard to differentiate authentic responses from inauthentic ones.

7. Breaking promises without taking care—leads to broken commitments to coordinate action and the undermining of trust. Current events are ripe with examples, notably the Middle East conflict.

8. Treating assessments as the truth or as assertions (facts)—because the coach's assessments are individual judgments, which are a function of individual and cultural histories, his or her personal truths may not be shared with everyone. To assume they are can lead to deep and irreconcilable conflict.

9. Making assessments without rigorous grounding (that is, without sufficient evidence to "ground" assertions)—the lack of grounding can lead to unfair treatment and prejudiced perceptions.

10. Making fantasy affirmations and declarations—assuming something you declare will happen all by itself. When President John F. Kennedy declared America would put a man on the moon by the end of the 1960s, what seemed like a fantasy was actually grounded in the appraisal of the country's scientific and technological capability, which led to the intended result.

Conversations for Possibilities And Action

Conversations that create new possibilities are the most common type of coaching conversation. Without the deliberate intent to heal past wounds and create positive outcomes through such conversations, negative possibilities (because they arise from past-based conversations) can inadvertently be created: "Another bad day," "I don't have any money," "I can't do it." To create new possibilities, we must *invent* them. Roz and Ben Zander (2000) have described the need to move out of the box and out of "scarcity" or "survival" thinking:

> Let us suppose, now, that a universe of possibility stretches . . . to include all worlds: infinite, generative and abundant. Unimpeded on a daily basis by the concern for survival, free from generalized assumptions of scarcity, a person stands in the great space of possibility in a posture of openness, with an unfettered imagination for what can be. . . . In the realm of possibility we gain our knowledge by invention. We decide that the essence of a child is joy, and joy she is. Our small business attracts the label, "The Can-Do Company," and that is exactly who we are. *We speak with the awareness that language*

creates categories of meaning that open up new worlds to explore [italics added]. Life appears as variety, pattern, and shimmering movement, inviting us in every moment to engage. The pie is enormous, and if you take a slice, the pie is whole again. (pp. 19–20)

The creation of new conversations for possibilities can be broken down into steps. The first and most important step is to declare a break with what happened previously. This is often the most difficult because as creatures of habit, we tend to resist change. It may be, however, that this very resistance to change is language based. Without anything more compelling, why change anything? *The Declaration of Independence* and wedding vows exemplify this. Both represent leaving behind something no longer wanted (being a colony, being single) for something more compelling. In co-active coaching, this is known as finding the "compelling way" (Whitworth et al., 1998).

Declaring Possibility

The next step is to declare a new possibility. One might begin with musings or considerations. Once "this is possible" is articulated, one can move to a declaration. This declaration ideally should contain these four elements:

- explicit *conditions of satisfaction* of the possibility,
- reaffirmation of the possibility by the speaker,
- specific actions that are now possible in the declared domain of possibility, and
- acknowledgment of the new possibilities opened by the conversation.

Using marriage vows as an example, the basic conditions of satisfaction are blood tests, a license, and a ceremony performed by an official with proper credentials, but the long-term conditions are creating partnership, intimacy in all areas of life, and fidelity. Failure to redeclare the vows can lead to a breakdown when one or both parties choose to have an affair rather than declare a breakdown in the partnership. Specification of the actions possible in the domain of marriage might be living together and sharing joint interests. New possibilities might include buying a house or having children. Although marriage is not a prerequisite for any of these possibilities, its continuing popularity suggests that declaration is a critical factor in strengthening commitments. The absence of declaration can cause serious social issues, such as those surrounding gay marriage, for example. Without the legalization of gay marriage, which makes it possible to have not only a public declaration of the relationship but also legal acknowledgment of the reality of the commitments, it is often difficult (and in some cases impossible) for a life partner to collect insurance and other benefits.

Integrity and the Power of One's Word

Given that what we say shapes our reality, it is important to know that the "integrity" of our words matters greatly. Few of us realize this. We fail to realize that when we say "I'll call you," the other will expect a call. In the movie *Harvey* (Beck & Koster, 1950),

Elwood P. Dowd (Jimmy Stewart) is always being politely brushed off by people who extend insincere invitations such as "You must come for dinner sometime," because he professes to be accompanied by his imaginary companion, Harvey, a large rabbit. Most of us would realize we are being brushed off, but Dowd does not see this and tries to pin down the invitation by asking "When?" which leads to more discomfort on the part of the other party. "Integrity" (2004) is defined not only as honesty, but also (in *Merriam-Webster's Collegiate Dictionary*), as "the quality or state of being complete and undivided: completeness." (p. 650). When we have integrity—being true to our values and to our word—life flows more smoothly because we are more whole. Literally, we are "undivided." Ruiz (1997) has given the following guidelines:

> Be impeccable with your word. Say only what you mean. Your agreement with yourself to keep your word is paramount. Avoid using your word to speak against yourself or to gossip about others. Use the power of your word "in the direction of truth and love for yourself." (p. 25)

Integrity is at the foundation of coaching. When we ask clients to be accountable for their commitments, we are asking them to have integrity with us as well as with themselves, which contributes to an increased experience of wholeness.

Synchronicity

Synchronicity was first described by Carl Jung (1960) and has more recently been written about by Julia Cameron (1992) and Joseph Jaworski (1996). Jaworski maintained that true leadership creates a domain in which people become ever more capable and "predictable miracles" can happen. Leadership is about the release of human possibilities, about learning how to shape the future. In his groundbreaking book, Jaworski used his own story to create an entirely new view of what leadership can be. When leaders are in a state of commitment and surrender, he said, they begin to experience what is called synchronicity, or predictable miracles. By shifting from seeing a world made up of things to seeing a world primarily composed of relationships, leaders can enter a realm of endless possibilities.

For everyone at any level in any organization—public or private, large or small—synchronicity provides a roadmap for achieving maximum leadership potential through nothing less than a fundamental change of mind and spirit.

Synchronicity occurs at the individual level as well. A client of mine who was following a particular pursuit that is best studied in a particular foreign country had not just one, but two opportunities presented to her to travel to that country within a year. She had never even been outside of New England.

Another client declared her wish to move from Boston to San Francisco to be near her only grandchild. Within seven weeks, the job of her dreams was offered to her. She was thrilled but not quite prepared, because her husband, who cavalierly agreed to move if she got a really good job, had yet to deal with his work situation. They agreed that she would go first, and he would follow a few months later. On our last meeting, she said, "Tell your other clients to watch what they ask for. Don't let them forget details like right timing!"

Summary

Coaching is a powerful technique that is based on a linguistic paradigm shift. The basic premises of coaching are simple and can be embraced by therapists in a variety of settings with a variety of populations, including those "resistant" to other interventions. Although conceived as an intervention to be used with executives and high-level clients, personal coaching has become democratized in recent years. It has become an attractive alternative to therapy for those who have had therapy but have not made the gains they desired and for those who would never seek therapy because they feel it is a sign of "weakness." It is also desirable for individuals who have been or are engaged in intense therapy but want to move forward toward specific goals. Because coaching is strengths based, coaches can converse with clients in a new language that is less threatening. By viewing clients as whole, complete, and resourceful, coaches draw from the well of human potential as opposed to underscoring weaknesses, deficits, and trauma. Coaches can still offer a healing environment, but it is one in which we say,

> Your pain is real; however, pain is part of life. I believe in the basic strength and resiliency of human nature and that you will find your strength and right path. I will hold your life's agenda, and pull for you to find higher ground.

Although speaking is of great importance, the most important skill is listening. What we listen to and listen for is also grounded in language. If I listen for the "gold" in my clients, they feel respected and pulled to a higher place within themselves and, ultimately, in the world. Using the "biology of language" as the basis for constructing the dialogue, it is possible to create clear, concise communication that moves people forward powerfully. When we look at distinctions in attitudes and behavior, it becomes possible to discuss virtually anything with a client without judgment or criticism and without causing defensiveness. In the space of the committed listening of the coach, the individual has tremendous freedom to "be." When we are called into "being," we can see our right path more clearly. Being attuned to the linguistic viruses described by Matthew Budd (Budd & Rothstein, 2000) can help us focus on the precise self-limiting mechanisms causing dysfunction in communication (for example, not making requests).

Finally, we come to the terminology unique to coaching. Appendix D contains a glossary of coaching terms found in both the ontological model represented by Winograd and Flores (1986) and the co-active model of Whitworth et al. (1998). Some of the terms will be familiar, others are new, and others are redefined. The vocabulary of coaching allows us to expand and deepen our conversations and to engage in an exploration of what is possible for clients, leading them into new and unforeseen futures.

Included in Tables 1 and 2 are examples of powerful words and phrases as well as weak or ineffective words and phrases used in everyday conversation. What we say can depress

Table 1: Powerful/Ineffective Words

Powerful Words/Phrases	Ineffective Words/Phrases
Yes/no	I think/don't think so
Will/won't	Would/should/have to
Do/don't	Could
By when	Some day
Promise	Try
Don't know	Maybe/probably
Choose	Made me
Create	Wish/hope
Cause	Couldn't help it
Intend/plan to	Can/can't
When . . . happens	If. . . happens
Possibility/invention	How it is/predictable
Assert	Right/wrong
Occurs/seems	Sort of/kind of
Declare	Don't care
Request	Need/want

Table 2: Conversations for Action

Requests	Promises	Declarations	Assertions
Ask	Accept	*Effectives:*	Testify
Beg	Pledge	Claim	Reveal
Beseech	Endorse	Hire	Pronounce
Instruct	Agree	Fire	Guarantee
Warn	Threaten	Resign	Negate
Advise	Warrant	Disclaim	Observe
Prohibit	Concede	Promulgate	Vow
Challenge	Swear	Nominate	State
Bid	Refuse	Denounce	Hypothesize
Charge	Contract	*Expressives:*	Predict
Urge	Consent	Congratulations	Recognize
Grant	Vow	Bless you	Conclude
Order	Commit	Thank you	Bet
Forbid	Guarantee	Forgive	Swear
Summon		*Verdicts:*	
		You are guilty	
		Is true/fair	

Source: Winograd and Flores (1986).

or uplift, disempower or empower, keep a client stuck and mired in the past or enable him or her to move forward into a new and different future. Just as therapy has much to offer coaching, coaching has much to offer therapy in understanding how the subtleties of language can alter futures. The unique use of language in coaching is universal. It crosses cultures and can unite in the same way as sports or music, through reaching people's inner purpose and passions.

> *Whatever you can do, or dream you can, begin it. Boldness has genius, power and magic in it. Begin it now.*
>
> —Johann Wolfgang von Goethe

6

Schools of Coaching

If you have built castles in the air, your work need not be lost; that is where they should be. Now put foundations under them.

—Henry David Thoreau

Although it is possible to coach with little or no formal training or with only "on the job" experience, most coaches are either formally trained or subscribe to a school of beliefs about coaching. I have selected six schools of coaching, each of which has a complete training program and each of which, I believe, have made the most significant and distinct impacts on the field.

Co-active Coaching

The Co-active Coaching Model

The co-active model of the Coaches Training Institute (CTI) is a simple but elegant design that embraces quality of life, the ability to choose freely, and the ability to "be" in the present and focus on moving toward an exciting new future. In co-active coaching, the answers come from the client. Co-active coaching also must address the client's whole life, and the agenda must come from the client. Finally, the relationship between coach and client should be an alliance of two equals.

Four Cornerstones of Co-active Coaching

The basic premises of the co-active model are the following beliefs and values:

- The client is naturally creative, resourceful, and whole.
- Coaching addresses the client's whole life.
- The agenda comes from the client.
- The relationship is a "designed alliance."

The five necessary coaching skills are these:

- listening,
- intuition,
- curiosity,
- deepening the learning/forwarding the action, and
- self-management.

69

There are three aspects to coaching: fulfillment, balance, and process. Co-active coaches ask their clients what it would take for them to be fulfilled and then help them discover how to get there. Balance is achieved by identifying new perspectives, choosing the appropriate perspective, and committing to a plan of action. *Process* refers to helping clients ask themselves where they are now and where they wish to be in the future:

1. *Fulfillment* coaching—focuses on the quality of life and being true to oneself; helps clients design their lives from the perspective of fulfillment, discovering the values that fulfill and nourish them. Values clarification is the primary tool.
2. *Balance* coaching—focuses on the client "being at choice" in life rather than reactive to what is and is not included in his or her life. The balance wheel is the primary tool. Balance is dynamic and therefore always changing. To operate effectively in life, one needs to have the facility to shift balance as life requires.
3. *Process* coaching—focuses on the state of *being* versus having or doing; most similar in flow to therapy, often involving intense emotions and ontological exploration, although the focus is on moving into the future (becoming) rather than on the past; frequently involves work with the "gremlin," the internal self-saboteur that tends to block forward movement.

Co-active Certification

Co-active certification is fairly rigorous and requires passing a written and an oral exam that includes interviewing a client after completing hours of teleclass, review in supervision of training tapes, and written homework.

Coach U and Corporate Coach U

Thomas Leonard, known as the "father of modern coaching," started training coaches in 1988 and founded Coach University (Coach U) in 1992. Coach U is recognized as the training school that establishing the coaching profession; to date, it is probably still the largest. Corporate Coach University (Corporate Coach U), a branch of Coach U, is recognized as the world's first corporate coach training school for managers, consultants, and business coaches. Classes in both programs are delivered as teleclassed with online support. The basic philosophy of Coach U is similar to that of CTI, but the training is completely through teleclass, and there is more emphasis on business coaching, forms, and structures.

Ontological Coaching

Ontological coaching, created by Newfield founder Julio Olalla, is a multidisciplinary approach that is immediately practical and grounded in contemporary principles and proven practices: the philosophy of language, phenomenology, the biology of cognition, the work of Clare Graves and contemporary philosopher Ken Wilber, recent advances in body/movement studies, emotional intelligence, and the latest in personal and organizational development theory and practice. This approach to coaching attempts to "transform" one's worldview and capacity for action while teaching one to coach others for sustainable change.

Olalla (2004) has defined ontological coaching as

> a practice that facilitates the emergence of new possibilities in the personal and/or professional life of an individual (or group) by making him [or her] aware of his [or her] participation in the construction and co-creation of the reality he [or she] perceives.

He went on to say that "ontological coaching addresses the concern for more effective action while also addressing the concerns of the human soul that are mostly left out of our learning practices today."

A primary goal of ontological coaching is to facilitate

> a shift in our coherence our habits of language, emotions, and physical presence—which then allows for the emergence of a new observer. This new observer becomes aware of the power and limits of [his or her] habitual ways of thinking and acting and becomes capable of foreseeing and taking new actions and producing unprecedented results, while caring equally for personal and collective concerns. (Olalla, 2004)

Brain-Based Coaching

Based on the work of David Rock, who partnered with neuroscientist Jeffrey Schwartz to formulate a way to help leaders be more effective, brain-based coaching is predicated on the notion articulated in Rock's (2006) book *Quiet Leadership*—coaches must "help people think better, not tell them what to do."

The ARIA model describes awareness, reflection, insight, and action as the common ways in which brain change occurs in coaching. This approach is the first to address the elusive question of why coaching works at all, particularly in contrast to other, more familiar approaches. Rock has claimed that whatever coaching model is used, change occurs when we stop and focus on a particular circuit (awareness), shift our perspective (reflection), see the situation in another way (insight), and then take action to embed the new connections. Some things that improve our efficiency through coaching, based on this new understanding, are the following:

• *Awareness:* The brain has limitations when processing new ideas. Our "working memory" overloads easily, so it is useful to simplify complex challenges to central issues by "chunking down" big issues into smaller ones and to tap into visuals representations by creating a collage or drawing of the "gremlin."

• *Reflection:* Research on the nature of insight indicates that prior to an insight, the brain is in an alpha state. Alpha states are quiet, representing minimal effortful activity or electrical noise. Alpha states are easily overwhelmed by anxiety, uncertainty, or even ambiguity. To help clients make new connections, we need to ask questions that help them quietly reflect on the solution to the challenge they face, not give more attention to the problem.

Thus, the phrasing of inquiries is critical. Asking "What's stopping you?" may not be the most useful way to facilitate insight. Instead, asking "What solutions can you sense might work?" is less likely to arouse defensiveness. When coaching conversations do not work, it is often because the client feels defensive. Recent studies have shown that the part of the brain needed for clear thinking becomes less active when a person feels threatened ("Brain Training Exercises and Coaching," n.d.; Vergano, 2006). Brain research points to the importance of rapport, trust, and clarity as essential components of good coaching, though these elements on their own are not enough to drive change.

  • *Insight:* The coach's job is to strengthen the client's insight by reinforcing his or her mental image when he or she has made a new connection.

  • *Action:* People are significantly more willing to commit to an action one minute after an insight compared with five minutes after. The energy released by an insight is short lived. The artistry of coaching is in knowing when and how to reinforce insights with calls to action.

   Although brain-based coaching focuses on making permanent workplace performance change, developing higher productivity, increasing workplace morale, and nurturing greater job satisfaction, this approach, which emphasizes thinking about how one is thinking, can be used effectively in any coaching model.

Coaching and Positive Psychology: Happiness Coaching and Appreciative Inquiry

Happiness Coaching

Happiness coaching represents the intersection of psychology and coaching. Stemming from the work of former American Psychological Association president, Martin Seligman, well-known for his work on "learned optimism," coaching is now being brought into academic settings such as the University of Pennsylvania and clinical settings such as McLean Hospital, a Harvard Medical School teaching hospital. Positive psychology represents a paradigm shift from the focus on studying and understanding psychopathology to a focus on what enables individuals and communities to thrive—what makes life more fulfilling. Happiness coaching represents the practical application of this new learning. How can people be counseled and coached to achieve and maintain happiness?

   Seligman (2002) has stated that "authentic happiness" comes from "identifying and cultivating your most fundamental strengths and using them every day in work, love, play, and parenting"(p. xiii). He refers to three elements that constitute happiness: positive emotion; positive traits (strengths, virtues, and abilities), and positive institutions (for example, strong families, democracy supporting free inquiry). One's "happiness formula" looks like this:

   H (Happiness) = S (Set or basic disposition) + C (Circumstances) + V (Voluntary control).
   (Seligman, 2002, p. 45)

Through a set of scales (http://www.authentichappiness.sas.upenn.edu/Default.aspx), Seligman measures individuals' self-rating in the areas relevant to their happiness, providing a basis for coaching individuals to improve their combined formula.

In partnership with Mentor Coach, a coach training program designed for therapists, Seligman and Mentor Coach founder Ben Dean trained over 1,000 professionals in the theory, assessments, interventions, and exercises of positive psychology between 1993 and 1995. Positive psychology is now fully integrated into Mentor Coach programs.

In 1994, Seligman, along with Mentor Coach instructor Christopher Peterson, introduced the *Character Strengths and Virtues Handbook* (CSV), representing the first attempt on the part of the research community to identify and classify the positive psychological traits of human beings, a companion to the *Diagnostic and Statistical Manual of Mental Disorders* (4th ed.) (American Psychiatric Association, 1994) of general psychology. The CSV provides a theoretical framework to assist in developing practical applications for positive psychology. It identifies six classes of "core virtues," made up of 24 measurable character strengths. These six virtues have considered "good" by the vast majority of cultures and throughout history and are organized as follows:

1. Wisdom and Knowledge: creativity, curiosity, open-mindedness, love of learning, perspective
2. Courage: bravery, persistence, integrity, vitality
3. Humanity: love, kindness, social intelligence
4. Justice: citizenship, fairness, leadership
5. Temperance: forgiveness and mercy, humility, prudence, self-control
6. Transcendence: appreciation of beauty and excellence, gratitude, hope, humor, spirituality

Several humanistic psychologists in the past—such as Abraham Maslow, Carl Rogers, and Erich Fromm—developed successful theories and practices that involved human happiness. Other proponents of positive psychological approaches, such as Jay Haley and Milton Erikson, have developed techniques that are more complex and difficult to practice successfully. Seligman's work is found at the intersection between psychology and coaching and gives clinicians a comfortable place to reside.

According to the Coaching and Positive Psychology Initiative, based at McLean Hospital in Belmont, Massachusetts, the philosophy of coaching is closely aligned with positive psychology. Both focus on building on what is right with an individual, executive, or organization, rather than fixing what is wrong (for example, weakness, pathology), making coaching a natural vehicle for the delivery of positive psychology interventions.

Although there are many articles and books on life and executive coaching, the Coaching and Positive Psychology Initiative believes that few are based on the kind of research studies that meet healthcare and general medical standards—a gap they believe needs to be filled to lend empirical support for the profession of coaching.

Appreciative Inquiry (AI)

According to the Center for Appreciative Inquiry (http://www.centerforappreciativeinquiry.
org), AI is "a way of being and seeing." It is both a worldview and a process for facilitating
positive change in human systems, (for example, organizations, groups, communities). The
fundamental assumption of AI is simple: Every human system has something that works
right—things that "give life to an organization or community when it is most effective
and most capable in economic, ecological and human terms" (Cooperrider, 2005, p. 8).

The AI approach to personal change and organizational change is based on the assumption that questions and dialogue about strengths, successes, values, hopes, and dreams are
themselves transformational. Developed by David Cooperrider of Case Western Reserve
University, and building on work by earlier theorists, AI is now a commonly accepted
practice in the evaluation of organizational development strategy and implementation of
organizational effectiveness tactics.

AI is a specific practice utilizing a particular way of asking questions and envisioning
the future that fosters positive relationships and builds on the basic goodness in a person, a
situation, or an organization. In doing so, it enhances a system's capacity for collaboration
and change, effectively coaching the organization or person to change itself or him- or
herself. A four-stage process is used in AI that focuses on the following:

1. *Discover:* The identification of organizational processes that work well.
2. *Dream:* The envisioning of processes that would work well in the future.
3. *Design:* Planning and prioritizing processes that would work well.
4. *Destiny* (or *deliver*): The implementation (execution) of the proposed design (the
   changes the organization will make).

The Organization and Relationship Systems Coaching (ORSC) Model

The ORSC model is based on the notion that

> relationship is the fundamental bond that defines living things. Within each relationship
> is the power to heal and the potential to harm. The impact of relationship is at once inti-
> mate and global in scale. Given current world events there is no time to waste. (Center
> for Right Relationship, n.d.)

ORSC shifts the focus from the individuals in the system to the relationship itself: an
important player called the Third Entity. It provides relationship systems practitioners
with a model to work directly with the system rather than doing individual work within
the group. The practitioners maintain that this subtle shift has a profound impact on the
results that are possible in systems coaching; it requires a very different skill set from that
of facilitating individual work within a group setting.

Nonetheless, there are many similarities between relationship coaching and relationship therapy (particularly family systems therapy), as shown in Table 3 (derived from an
unpublished white paper by Marita Frijohnn [used with permission]):

Table 3: Relationship Coaching versus Relationship Therapy

Relationship Coaching	Relationship Therapy
Uses a "discovery session"	Uses a diagnostic interview/history
Uses many skills similar to therapy	Uses many techniques similar to coaching skills
Works with the client's whole life	Works with the client's whole life
May work with emotional material	Often works with emotional material

Key to looking at system dysfunctions and dealing with them is understanding the role of John Gottman's (1994) "Four Horsemen," so named for the Four Horsemen of the Apocalypse, and their intense and lethal impact on relationships:

1. *Criticism:* attacking your partner's personality or character, usually with the intent of making someone right and someone wrong. Criticism includes generalizations such as "you always . . . ," "you never . . . ," "you're the type of person who . . . ," and "why are you so . . . ?"

2. *Contempt:* attacking your partner's sense of self with the intention to insult or psychologically abuse him or her. Contempt poisons a relationship because it conveys disgust; it includes
   - insults and name-calling ("bitch," "bastard," "wimp," "fat," "stupid," "ugly," "slob," "lazy," and so on);
   - hostile humor, sarcasm, or mockery; and
   - derisive body language and tone of voice (sneering, rolling your eyes, curling your upper lip).

3. *Defensiveness:* seeing oneself as the victim, warding off a perceived attack. The defending party usually reverses the blame for a situation, creating a no-win scenario by
   - making excuses (for example, external circumstances beyond your control forced you to act in a certain way: "It's not my fault . . . ," "I didn't . . . ");
   - cross-complaining: meeting your partner's complaint, criticizing with a complaint of your own, or ignoring what your partner said;
   - disagreeing and then cross-complaining: "That's not true, you're the one who . . . ");
   - yes–butting: start off agreeing but end up disagreeing;
   - repeating yourself without paying attention to what the other person is saying; or
   - whining: "It's not fair."

4. *Stonewalling:* Withdrawing from the relationship as a way to avoid conflict. An emotionally overwhelmed partner (usually the husband) tunes out and sits passively without saying a word or acknowledging his spouse. A partner may think he or she is trying to be "neutral," but stonewalling conveys disapproval, icy distance, separation, disconnection, and smugness through
   - stony silence,
   - monosyllabic mutterings,
   - changes of subject, and
   - physical removal of self from the situation.

The Four Horsemen show up in all relationships—in teams, where they show up as "team toxins"; corporations; and even between nations. One has only to look at the current world scene to see their devastating impact on humanity.

The relationship coaching approach can best be seen in the ORSC beliefs and values (Center for Right Relationship, 2009):

- Human relationships are inherently resourceful and wired for growth. If we reveal the system to itself, it is naturally self-correcting.
- All relationship systems have certain characteristics in common, whether they are our personal inner voices, a pair, groups, teams, communities, organizations, or nations. Training in the systems approach provides baseline cross-competencies in many areas of relationship systems work.
- Relationships, both primary and secondary, have a life cycle. The life cycle of relationship can be as long as a lifetime or as short as a day. The ending of a marriage or the dissolution of a team or an organization is a natural part of the system cycle. Relationship systems coaching can assist in the birth, creative expression, and constructive completion of relationship systems.
- Conflict is useful. It is the midwife to constructive change. It is the means by which relationships change. Relationship systems coaching demands moving from "Who is doing what to whom?" to "What is trying to happen?"
- Awareness is a critical but insufficient condition for growth. Awareness must be paired with behavioral change to be effective.
- Theory is useful but must be paired with research and outcome studies to determine efficacy. Good theoretical models are only as effective as the coach's ability to operationalize them.
- Everyone is right, but only partially! Only by listening to all the voices in the system can reality be accurately represented, and every voice is a voice of the system.
- We are at a critical juncture in human development. Individual interventions are important but no longer enough. To address such pressing issues as terrorism, global climate change, disease, and poverty, we must harness the power of communities and organizations—essentially, human systems built on relationships—to leverage change. Relationship systems work assists communities and organizations to "wake up" to both their creative power and their responsibility to make a difference.
- Every graduate of our program is a world worker. It does not matter whether graduates do their work on the personal, local, or global level. The inherent nature of our interdependence means all change ripples outward, touching everything. Our job is to provide our graduates with world-class tools and support to do their critical job.

Other Coaching Schools

Institute for Professional Empowerment Coaching (iPEC)

iPEC was founded by New Jersey–based psychologist Bruce Schneider; it offers instruction in the Core Energy Coaching process and provides certification as a certified empowerment coach. To date, approximately 4,000 to 5,000 individuals have been trained in this method, which emphasizes classroom training and mentor coaching and includes a strong business development component, mandatory reading, and a practicum.

Institute for Life Coach Training

The Institute for Life Coach Training (formerly Therapist University) was the first training institute specializing in training psychotherapists, psychologists, counselors, and helping professionals. Founded in late 1998 by psychologist Patrick Williams, its training is primarily conducted by teleclass.

SUN

The SUN program derives its techniques from sports psychology and management training, which can be applied to all life areas and brings a strong spiritual foundation to the business of coaching. The program was founded in 1981 by British company Results Unlimited; it was brought to the United States by master certified coach Teri E. Belf in 1987.

ActionCoach

ActionCoach was founded by Brad Sugars in 1993 and currently has more than 1,000 offices in 26 countries. It is identified with starting the business coaching industry, providing business coaching, executive coaching, and business mentoring to clients.

Wellcoaches

Margaret (Meg) Moore is the founder of Wellcoaches and cofounder of the Harvard Medical School Coaching and Positive Psychology Initiative. Moore left the biotech industry after realizing that her life's purpose was to help people master well-being and avoid disease, on a large scale, rather than to develop or market new medicines. Using positive psychology and a coaching approach, she organized five science-based areas of health and well-being—meaning, strength, energy, emotions, and relationship—into the DNA metaphor and wove them together to show that they are all vital and depend on each other (Moore, n.d.). Wellcoaches teach and coach on mastery of well-being, and Wellcoaches partner with employee assistance programs (EAPs) to offer coaching services as an adjunct to traditional EAP services.

More Information

See the Resources section for a list of approved coaching programs and credits. For a complete list of coaching programs, go to http://www.coachfederation.org/research-education/coach-training-programs/.

7

The Coaching Process

I think of myself as a "possibility therapist," that is, one who approaches a client with a naïve, curious, an open, and inquisitive mind; keeps assumptions simple; avoids elaborate explanatory thinking; takes seriously the client's request; respects the client's resources and creativity; thinks in terms of solutions rather than problems; takes a hopeful, future-oriented stance; looks for opportunities to introduce novel ideas or perspectives.

—Steven Friedman

The Client Inquiry and Sample Session

The coaching process begins with the client's first call or e-mail. Unlike therapy referrals, which usually result in an appointment after a brief phone call, "closing" a coaching client often takes more effort. Coaching is new to many; clients frequently call because a friend told them to, with little or no other explanation. For instance, I recently received an e-mail inquiry from a gentleman who had no knowledge of sending the e-mail. It turned out to be his zealous secretary who heard him make a positive comment about my Web site and knew he was interested in learning more. Potential clients often must first be educated. Given that coaching is hard to describe, experiencing it is the best way for the potential client to make an informed choice.

The coach with a background in the helping professions may have a keener ability to screen potential conflicts. The client population of coaches is, remember, healthy, already successful, and highly motivated to produce results. Therefore, some obvious red flags are an acknowledged mental health problem, confusion about whether therapy or coaching is more appropriate, and statements like "I've tried everything. I'm desperate!" Many might still be well served by coaching while they are seeing a therapist (if they are not already) or, sometimes, consulting a therapist for some sessions first.

The sample session or complementary call, therefore, is important to the coach as well as the client. When I began coaching, I found myself resenting the time spent in these sessions (after all, I would never consider offering free intakes to therapy clients!). Over time, however, I have learned how equally important it is for the coach to choose the client.

Informed Consent

The sample session is also the time to discuss informed consent. I inform my clients that I am a therapist but that I keep my coaching and therapy practices separate.

Many will ask whether they can use their insurance. I let them know that unless their reason for seeking coaching is deemed "medically necessary," it is unethical to use insurance for coaching and would be considered abuse of the healthcare system. It is important to remember that coaching is most effective with people who are healthy but want more out of life and/or their career or business and that it is not a healthcare service. (That said, we are beginning to see acknowledgment of the benefit of coaching as an ancillary approach in the treatment of medical disease and, as shown later, as invaluable in "making a difference" in the provision of social services.) A client who is unable to accept this is not a good candidate for coaching—he or she may have mental health issues that need to be dealt with first or be too attached to a victim stance to benefit from coaching.

Confidentiality

All information that a client shares with a coach is confidential; however, privileged communication is not granted to coaches. Any licensed professional with a dual practice needs to investigate their liability with the appropriate licensing boards and insurance carriers. A sample coaching agreement drafted by attorney/psychologist/coach Eric Harris can be found in Appendix G. In this agreement, Harris discusses confidentiality and distinguishes psychotherapy and coaching for clients.

Assessment/Intake Design

The typical coaching intake takes 1.5 to three hours, usually involving a variety of assessment tools as well as an in-depth interview. Unlike a psychosocial interview, the coaching intake interview is not historically based but, rather, has future-directed orientation. You will notice that questions designed to elicit information from the past are related to what has worked and what has not worked. The focus of coaching is on producing *results*, not insights.

A complete intake might include the following (see Appendix G for specific examples):

1. Questionnaire,
2. Coaching Agreement,
3. Wheel of Life,
4. Primary Focus *or* Top 10 Desires for the next 90 days,
5. Top 10 "Tolerations" to eliminate,
6. Values Clarification, and
7. Strengths/Weaknesses Inventory.

Other items that might be included are attention-deficit hyperactivity disorder (ADHD) assessments and the Work Performance Rating Scale. Many coaches encourage their clients to use tools; self-assessments; and surveys such as the Clean Sweep, which consists of 100 items representing all areas of life, from which clients can choose desirable options for self-improvement. Clean Sweep, which requires one to literally improve each and every identified area to self-satisfaction, can take as long as two years to complete. It can be found on the CoachVille Web site (http://www.coachville.com [a small fee may be required to obtain access]).

The longer I have coached, the shorter my intakes have become. Were I to use only a few tools, I would pick the Wheel of Life, Top 10 Desires, Top 10 Tolerations, and Values Clarification as the most useful. If I were limited to one, I would choose the Wheel of Life. Most human service professionals have superior interviewing skills and can address the kinds of questions in the questionnaire just as easily in a face-to-face conversation. Many coaches who work on the phone have, in fact, a list of powerful questions in front of them at all times when they coach.

The Personal Client Questionnaire

This measure includes powerful questions designed to encourage the client to think "outside the box." The following are some core questions for an intake questionnaire:

- What is your goal for coaching?
- What have you done up to now to achieve your goals?
- What worked?
- What didn't work?
- If you could have it any way you wanted, how would it be?
- What are the accomplishments you are proudest of?
- Who or what would you like to eliminate from your life?
- What one thing would make the most profound difference in your life?

Some addition powerful questions for an intake questionnaire are the following:

- If you didn't have to worry about money or people's opinions of you, what would you be doing with your life?
- If you only had one year to live, how would you live it?
- In what area of life are you most responsible/least responsible?
- What are people afraid to tell you about yourself?
- How should your coach relate to you?

Cheryl Gilman has suggested the following questions for career coaching (reproduced here with her permission):

- What is easy and effortless for you to do? Where and when are you doing it now?
- What was the first thing you ever did that you thought was fun? That you really enjoyed? That you felt special at? Or that really "turned you on"? What did you like about it? How are you doing that now?

- What was the first job you ever had (paid or unpaid) that you enjoyed? What did you love about it, and what gives you that same feeling now?

About one's current work, Gilman has added the following:

- When is work fun? When do you enjoy your work? What do you like about it? (Include such things as location, people, manager, hours, flexibility, structure, non-structure, benefits, culture, paycheck, and so on.)
- What do you hate about your job (You can use the previous list here, too.)

The intake process should always be geared toward the kind of coaching being requested. For individuals dealing with ADHD, for instance, I incorporate Hallowell and Ratey's (1994, p. 195) self-assessment.

The Business Intake

A corporate client profile might include questions like the following:

- What do you want from your job?
- What do you have to contribute that is unique?
- Are you in a position to contribute that now?

Other tools might include

- a business or leadership wheel;
- a job performance appraisal; or
- any of the more formal tools, such as the following:
  - *Not requiring certification: DiSC Universal Assessment, Skill Scope (360/multirater feedback tool), Skill Scan, Values Driven Work and Life Purpose Cards (Frederick Hudson), Leadership Practices Inventory, Stress Map, Kiersey–Bates Temperament Sorter (similar to the Myers–Briggs Type Indicator).*
  - *Requiring certification: Myers–Briggs, Firo-B.*

Designing the Working Alliance

Once a client and I agree to proceed with an intake, the client is a client, and we can "cocreate" the relationship. Does the client want a growth experience (what is the learning?), or does he or she want accountability so he or she can, for example, finally get that book written? Or am I needed as a sounding board as the client files and sorts ideas to clarify a new direction? Each coaching relationship is different and unfolds in its own way. I generally send the client a set of intake materials in advance, often by e-mail. (A complete set of these materials is provided in Appendix G.)

Intake materials are merely a jumping-off place. As I said earlier, if I were to use just one (as I often do now), the Wheel of Life is the one I feel has the most value, followed by the

Values Clarification. I now have a sense of the client's overall life balance, his or her satisfaction with all major areas of life, and the values that guide him or her in making choices.

Early in the process, I might also use one of the various assessments currently available, such as the Universal DiSC for an executive coaching client or team or the Myers–Briggs and Strong Interest Test for a career coaching client.

It is important to know the client's goals and vision—to determine that they are realistic—so that we can create an action plan. Often, however, the client does not even know or might have a vague idea of what he or she needs (for example, "need a change"; "feel more connected to what I am doing"; "manage better"). The assessment is designed to focus more clearly: "Get up each day and really look forward to going to work"; "write for myself, not just for my job"; "manage people without having to strong-arm them into doing what I need them to do." I know the focus is in the right place, however, when there is a natural "click" or an *aha* moment in our interaction. This cocreation of the alliance also involves asking the client how he or she wants to use me. Some primarily want accountability. Others want to process and "clear" their emotions so they can stay on their path. Others want to keep deepening their self-inquiry and expanding their list of goals. This aspect of the relationship can shift many times during the course of coaching. The client who hits his or her stride and is in "flow" will relinquish the need for deepening their learning unless they hit an obstacle. The client looking primarily for accountability will want to deepen his or her learning when they find themselves not doing their "fieldwork."

Here are some powerful questions to ask in the service of cocreating the alliance:

- What is a big enough "game" for you to play to warrant having a coach?
- What does fulfillment look like to you?
- What would you have to focus on to achieve fulfillment?
- What is your life's purpose?
- What else could you pay attention to in order to move forward with what you really want?
- How can you sabotage yourself? What would stop you from doing it?
- Take a step back and view your life as it is unfolding. What do you notice?
- How have you been "being" (versus what have you been doing)? Do you like it that way? If not, what would you change?
- What would your life be like without that story?

Coach Joshua Bloom has created the following list of powerful questions specifically pertaining to designing the alliance (http://www.quantumhealingcenter.com/):

- How can I be the best coach for you?
- What inspires you the most?
- What do you want in your life?
- What fun and exciting goals would you like to achieve?
- What obstacles do you foresee standing in your way that you would like to overcome?
- What situations facilitate your learning?
- What situations are obstacles?

- How can you use this coaching relationship in your life?
- If you had everything exactly as you wanted it, how would that look for you?
- What have you done so far that has either worked for you (so that I can support you in that) or has not worked (so that we can look for other ways for you to meet with success)?
- What would the ideal coach for you look/sound/feel/act like?
- What kind of person are you most comfortable with when talking about yourself and your feelings?
- How does a person have to be for you, in order for you to feel real relaxed with and happy to open up to?

Homework

"Homework," "fieldwork," "or "lifework," as it has been called, is often used in coaching. Unlike the homework used in strategic family therapy, coaching homework is straightforward and does not rely on paradox. If the client does not do their homework, the inquiries are simple: "What got in the way?" "Is this the right homework for you at this time?" "Will you recommit?" Homework may involve doing stretch goals, such as making 10 cold calls, or doing little or nothing for one week and observing the resulting reactions. It may also involve thinking about an inquiries such as "What are you tolerating that you really no longer are willing to?" and "What will happen if you actually succeed at this?"

Resistance

"Resistance" does occur in coaching, just as it does in therapy, but it usually presents itself in the form of failing to do homework or a feeling of not wanting to move. I first want to know whether there is a "gremlin" (discussed in chapter 5) or self-saboteur involved. Usually, understanding attachment to the status quo can be found in understanding the gremlin. Although somewhat psychological, the gremlin concept is playful and can get the client to view his or her resistance with humor. Occasionally, however, a client will resist—or as I put it, decline to "play with"—the gremlin concept. This occurred once when a client who wrote for a prominent business magazine came to me. I was enamored of the idea that he might write about the experience, but when I raised the idea of looking at his gremlin a second time, he quit coaching, teaching me a valuable lesson: Always, always, always listen carefully to your client!

The other major way in which resistance appears in unwillingness to do needed emotional healing, such as dealing with an addiction before availing oneself of coaching.

Logistics: Fees and Billing

Establishing a fee is a challenge for the experienced therapist. Many are very attracted to the coaching field because they expect a greater income from coaching and believe that their starting rate for coaching should be higher than their going therapy rate. Although a higher rate is a reasonable goal, the novice therapist/coach is competing with other new coaches, many of whom are willing to work for a significantly reduced fee or even on a pro bono basis until they build up a clientele. Because, however, the coaching client is always self-pay (unless payment is made by a third party such as his or her employer), billing is simple and straightforward.

Coaching can be billed hourly but is typically billed on a monthly retainer basis. The client pays a fixed amount per month, usually at the beginning of the month, for the service. Typical fees for personal or "life" coaching range from $250 to $1,200 per month for the equivalent of two to four hours, consisting of three or four 30- to 40-minute calls or two to four one-hour calls. There is no set or required format. Business clients sometimes prefer longer working meetings of several hours, often over lunch or dinner. Executive and corporate coaching fees are frequently higher and are often billed on a project basis.

I generally ask for a three- to six-month commitment, depending on the client's agenda. Thirty days' notice is asked of both parties to terminate the relationship, although I also inform clients that this is a guideline and that I am flexible if coaching is not meeting their needs or they achieve their desired goals sooner. Clients will drop out on occasion, as they do in therapy, but never leaving a large unpaid bill. Some coaches accept credit card payment that is set up to automatically bill on a monthly basis. Others accept checks but take a credit card number to use it if a client's check does not arrive on time or a check bounces. Those who have looked at issues of money in psychotherapy understand the power of the face-to-face interaction in motivating clients to pay. Because many coaches never see their clients, taking extra measures to insure payment is sensible.

The essential point is that as a coach, there are more flexible payment options available beyond fee-for-service or hourly wages.

Spiritual Aspects of the Coaching Relationship

Although coaches take good care of themselves in important areas that allow for financial as well as personal rewards, the most rewarding aspect of coaching might be the spiritual connection one makes with clients and finds in refocusing their work on what is most important to them. Phrases such as "making corporate America more human," "making a real difference" and "helping others find their life purpose" are common among coaches. Patrick Williams has pointed to several reasons therapists can "reclaim their soul" through coaching:

- the ability to design one's own work schedule and create the desired balance in one's own life;
- the ability to live and work where you desire because coaching is "portable";
- the egalitarian nature of the coaching relationship is liberating;
- financial rewards; and
- enjoying the transformation of one's own life as one takes pleasure in joining clients in their journeys of transformation.

The following description of spirituality I found in a Hebrew school guide written by Rabbi Harold Kushner , bestselling author of *When Bad Things Happen to Good People*, nicely sums up what the coaching relationship ideally provides the client and coach. Notice the contrast to feelings of burnout and alienation frequently experienced by human service professionals:

DO Feel	*DON'T Feel*
very close to and totally involved with other people; in harmony with nature	vindictive, manipulative, alienated
relaxed, yet energized	pressured, hassled, out-of-sync
very organized; things "click"	frustrated, unable to focus or concentrate
"whole"	"divided," distracted— different priorities compete for attention
important—your actions make a difference and you can change the world	apathetic, indifferent, complacent
open, ready to receive life	skeptical, cynical, critical

Self-Exploration

What is your personal growth edge? What are you striving for? What practices are you willing to incorporate into your life to support your growth? Some examples:

1. Develop a mindfulness practice;
2. practice yoga;
3. recite affirmations; or
4. do journal or "morning" pages (idea from Julia Cameron's, 1992, book *The Artist's Way;* these are three handwritten pages each morning on awakening to "clear" your mind for the day).

8

Skills

---

*Become a possibilitarian. No matter how dark things seem to be or actually are,
raise your sights and see possibilities—always see them, for they're always there.*
—Norman Vincent Peale

Six Skill Areas Adapted From CO-ACTIVE Coaching

Most coaching models embrace a similar core set of skills. I have adapted the five basic
skills outlined in the co-active model but separated action and learning, which I believe
are two separate skills. Skilled therapists, for example, may be very good at helping clients
learn about themselves but not at helping them accelerate action in their lives.

Listening

In the co-active model, listening is viewed as taking place on three levels:

- level I—focus on the self and the meanings we attach to others' words;
- level II—focused listening (the attention is on the other person); and
- level III—global listening, taking in mood, energy, nuance, and environment.

Figure 1: The Co-active Model

The most effective coaches operate consistently at levels II and III, regardless of whether coaching in person or on the phone, one-on-one or in groups. Coaches who practice telephone coaching develop an amazingly keen ability to read nuances of mood, emotion, and energy in their phone clients.

Intuition

The coach uses intuition to determine what path to follow in a given session and in the coaching relationship. Although therapists clearly do this as well, using intuition is not a skill that has been researched or discussed in the psychological literature. Coaches focus on having highly developed intuitive skills. Although, like therapy, coaching is an unfolding process, the pace of coaching can accelerate (especially if using half-hour phone sessions), often requiring the coach to respond more quickly. The analogy that comes to mind is the athletic coach who knows exactly what player to send into the game. Most often, however, the coach is following an instinct or "intuitive hit" not knowing where it will lead. Phrases like "I have a sense," "Can I check something out with you?" or simply "My intuition tells me" are examples of how the coach expresses his or her intuition. Unlike interpretations, which are pronounced with authority, intuitive responses of the coach are shared as curiosities, leaving room to acknowledge any misalignment of the coach's intuition and lessening the need for client defensiveness.

Occasionally, the coach "intrudes" with their intuition, interrupting the client. For those reluctant to interrupt a client, the co-active coaches remind us that one is not interrupting the client as much as their story. Because coaching calls can be brief, redirecting the client's storytelling may simply be necessary to stay focused on the client's core agenda.

Curiosity

Curiosity guides the coach's listening. The coach's job is to ask good questions and invite the client to respond. Curiosity is open, inviting, and completely nonjudgmental and allows the coach the opportunity to be curious alongside the client about what they will find together. The coach uses powerful questions, also referred to by Laura Berman Fortgang (1998) as "wisdom access questions," and occasional "dumb" or very simple questions such as "What do you want?" "What's next?" or "Where do we go from here?"

Action and Learning

Two main purposes of coaching are to "forward the action" and "deepen the learning." The clients' learning can vary widely, from specific skills such as how to be a coaching manager to intensive learning about oneself, such as how to limit oneself and what to do about it.

Action and Accountability

The power of coaching is in its emphasis on action and structures for accountability. Some of the tools used are brainstorming, planning and goal-setting, powerful requests, challenging, and creating accountability. The latter is, perhaps, the coach's most powerful tool and can be structured in three key questions:

1. What are you going to do?
2. By when will you do it?
3. How will you let me know?

The best accountability agreements should be *SMART*—**s**pecific, **m**easurable, **a**ttainable, **r**ealistic, and **t**ime-bound. The coach, although holding the client 100 percent responsible for his or her actions, also needs to take care to be accountable so that the client knows the coach is adhering to the coaching agenda.

Self-Management

Self-management can be likened to transference. It is the ability of the coach to get out of the way, put aside his or her own opinions and ego, and trust that the client, who is resourceful, whole, and complete, will indeed find his or her own answers.

Self-management also involves not only how the coach manages him or herself in the coaching relationship but also the coach's self-care. A good coach "walks the talk" and has achieved balance and fulfillment in his or her own life. Of course, because it is understood that balance is dynamic and ever changing, this is a coach's life work. This does not mean the coach must be perfect or have a perfect life but, rather, that he or she be honest about who they are and what they do.

Self-care is a critical aspect of self-management because burnout is an occupational hazard of coaching—not because of clients' neediness, but because there is a much greater learning curve than most imagine. Dealing with the challenges of a more technologically wired profession, clients in different time zones, and learning to pick and choose from the virtual department store of choices in direction, continued education, and networking opportunities can lead to burnout in coaches.

Other key skills of successful self-management include those that form the coaching contract (designing the alliance, holding the client agenda, holding the focus), that inspire the client's success (celebrating, challenging, championing), that create structures for the client (chunking, life design, mind-mapping), and that manage the client–coach relationship (asking permission, bottom-lining, clearing, getting unhooked). (Descriptions of these skills can be found in the glossary of coaching terms in Appendix D.)

Coaching on the Phone and by E-mail

Working on the phone and, on occasion, by e-mail is a skill in itself. Without visual cues to reference, the coach needs to rely even more on listening and intuition. The importance of powerful questions also becomes clear. Powerful questions reduce any ambiguity that might exist in the world of limited nonverbal communication. I personally still prefer face-to-face coaching if the client is local and it is convenient for him or her to arrange, but many coaches prefer phone coaching for some of the following reasons:

- It is possible for a client to find a coach who meets his or her ideal requirements without geographical limitations.
- Neither client nor coach will be distracted by physical actions or appearances of each other or the surroundings where they meet.
- Telephone coaching is much more efficient. It requires much less preparation time because neither client nor coach has to spend time traveling, and meetings can proceed without the social niceties usually exchanged when people meet in person.
- Telephone coaching is much less costly than face-to-face coaching. There is no cost for travel expenses or lost time due to traveling. Telephone coaching also requires less time than face-to-face coaching.
- Telephone coaching can be conducted from any location one wishes. It is easier to select a quiet, private, and relaxed place for coaching sessions.

Despite the above reasons, there might be times when face-to-face coaching would be best for clients. If either you or your client is easily distracted, phone coaching may not be the best choice. If you are a coach and are easily distracted, as I am, try closing your eyes and walking around (make sure you have a good headset). You will stay completely focused on the client. When I do this, I am always amazed at the depth of those sessions.

Face-to-face coaching might be better when there are physical considerations that are relevant to the client achieving her or his goals. Face-to-face coaching also might be more appropriate for coaching groups of people simultaneously, although many coaches are now coaching groups successfully.

9

Getting Started

Act as if it were impossible to fail.

—Dorothea Brande

Choosing a Niche

Choosing a coaching niche is the first challenge once you decide to be a coach. For some, it is easy—corporate executives will likely coach other corporate executives—but for the therapist or healthcare or human service provider who has functioned as a generalist, it can be difficult to narrow the field.

A niche is a very specific and small area of specialization. In fact, the more narrowly defined the better. This does not mean one need *only* to coach in that area or that it must remain one's niche forever. One's niche may evolve in time through experience. With experience, one also becomes clearer about what he or she wants and does not want to do.

Therapists need to be aware that they might naturally attract more needy clients and that they might not want to fall into a niche that will be too similar to their clinical practice. However, a clinical specialty such as attention-deficit hyperactivity disorder or breast cancer support might be a perfect niche choice as long as the emphasis is clearly distinct from therapy.

Creating Your Vision

If you have familiarized yourself with the process and still want to dive in, you need to take the next step and declare yourself and your intentions. This is best done by thinking about the nature of your ideal work situation using a vision statement.

Your future vision is where you get to design your life according to your desires. Many of us are good at visualizing; others are not. Do your best. Using a three-year horizon, describe your life as you ideally would want it. Imagine it *really* being that way. Be precise and use clear detail, stating it in the present tense (see Example of Future Vision box on p. 92).

Once you have a future vision, you can then create a tangible mission statement. The example below is based on a prototype once used by Ben and Jerry's. It is broken down into product mission, business mission, and social mission. If you prefer, then you can use just one mission, but this format

---

Example of Future Vision

I have a successful coaching business and work three days a week from 8 or 8:30 a.m. to 4 p.m. with clients who are highly motivated and can afford to pay. This allows me to see some low-fee or pro bono clients and do some work for some nonprofit organizations. I have one day for personal activities, including writing, and one day for education. My schedule allows me time with friends and family as well as time for myself for exercise, painting, and personal growth. My clients include 10 to 12 coaching clients, some of whom I work with on the phone, and two to three business or nonprofit clients. I continue to work with some therapy clients, as I enjoy the work. Coaching provides the perfect balance.

I do organizational coaching and consulting, which creates a few travel opportunities a year. By 2010, I will be working internationally. I am completing my second book and developing online courses so I have more passive income.

People who are highly supportive of my choices surround me. My living space is well organized and uncluttered. I have 4 to 5 weeks of vacation per year, much of which I spend at the beach where I can coach on the phone if I wish.

---

often helps human service professionals see clearly that they can have a business mission while retaining core values.

Defining Your Mission

Mission Statement

Draft a mission statement about your ideal work situation. In *The Seven Habits of Highly Successful People,* Stephen Covey (1989) says "begin with the end in mind." You can break your statement down to include the following examples of three aspects and relate them to tangible goals and action steps.

* *Product Mission:* To use my clinical knowledge to practice in a highly ethical and client-focused manner.

   Related goal: To make my business accessible to individuals regardless of income level.

   Related action steps: Decide on my desired income. Set markers for increments that will increase from my current income to that level. Create a spreadsheet that will track my income. Include the minimum number of pro bono/reduced-fee spaces I feel I can afford. As I reach each desired increment, add an additional pro bono or reduced-fee client space.

* *Business Mission:*

   1. To run a business that allows me to work with my preferred clientele and live comfortably.
   2. To have the capability of responding to clients' needs efficiently and effectively.

Related goals:

1. Have a *minimum* of half of my practice in personal and professional coaching.
2. Be able to respond effectively to client requests within 24 hours.

Related action steps:

1. Explore marketing strategies for reaching my desired population. What other professionals have contact with those desired clients (for example, therapists, employee assistance professionals, human resource personnel)? How can I best reach them (for example, newsletter, mailing, writing pertinent article for local newspaper or trade paper, an effective educational brochure)? Create a list of projects with due dates and treat those projects like client commitments so they get done. (Chunking can be used for this goal in order to make it more manageable.) Track monthly the percentage of the desired specialty in my practice. (You may also want to track the monthly percentage increase.)
2. Review all office procedures every three to six months and institute any needed changes immediately. Update computer and software. Hire a virtual assistant to support my vision and represent my office well to the public.

• *Social Mission:* To raise awareness of the contribution coaching has made to the health care and human service community.

Related goals:

1. To teach coaching to other human service and healthcare providers.

Related action steps:

1. Submit course proposal(s) for academic courses at a local college or university.
2. Publish articles.
3. Send out quarterly newsletter and biweekly calendar.
4. Create a pilot project to present to local health care organizations.

Once you have clarified your vision for coaching, you can begin to experiment with an "elevator talk" (which is detailed further in the next section). Feel free to change and update it as your circumstances change. Your elevator talk should flow easily once you have practiced it for a while. If it does not, then look for areas in which you are not bringing complete integrity. Try to be more authentic. Have someone else listen. Once you have it, memorize it, be prepared to use it at all times, but also be prepared to extemporize.

The "Elevator Talk": Creating Your First and Lasting Impression

• State outcome in simple, plain, clear language,
  – keep it active versus conceptual
  – keep it specific versus general

- design a repeatable phrase with a "memory hook,"
  - keep it positive as you can for your particular group
  - paint their dreams, not their pain
- include your target audience, and
  - use two groups
  - match your audience
- state the group's most common or pressing need.
  - use two group-identified frustrations, plateaus, challenges

Example: I am a personal and professional "Results" coach and clinical social worker. I coach human service professionals who want to renew their careers and experience both job satisfaction and financial reward.

Try yours:

I, _____work with _____

and _____who _____ and

_____.

End with an open-ended question, something that either piques the audience's curiosity to learn more or inspires a call to action. ("When would you like to talk further? I would be happy to offer you a complementary session. I think you would really understand the benefits.")

Some extra tips on your elevator talk:

- Make it sound effortless, conversational, and natural.
- Focus on how you can benefit the listener and help him or her solve his or her problems.
- Make it memorable and sincere.
- Show your personality.
- Write and rewrite it so you really sharpen your focus.
- Make sure it would interest you to hear it from someone else!
- Practice saying it.
- Consider including a compelling "hook," an intriguing aspect that engages the listener, prompts her or him to ask questions, and keeps the conversation going.
- Project a passion for what you do.
- Do not hesitate to develop different versions of your elevator talk for different situations and audiences.
- Include your unique selling proposition or competitive advantage—in other words, how you can perform better than anyone else.
- End with an action request such as asking for a business card or interview appointment.
- Do not forget to update your speech as your situation changes.

Consider joining a group such as Toastmasters International to boost your confidence if you are uncomfortable with the kind of speaking that elevator talk entails. Through such an exercise, you will access a noncritical audience that will give you good, honest feedback.

Once you have defined your niche, have a vision of where you want to go, clarify why it is important to you (your mission), and have even a rudimentary way to communicate it to others. With that, you are ready to begin marketing your practice.

Self-Exploration

1. Is my vision clear? Does it excite me?
2. Am I willing to own the vision and do what I need to in order to actualize it?
3. Am I ready and able to tell others about my vision, mission, and coaching niche? (If you cannot tell those closest to you, then think again about whether this is something you really want to do!)
4. Have I tested the need for my niche? Have I asked friends and colleagues whether they would use or need this service? Would they refer? What would they be willing to pay?
5. What other ways can I be paid (for example, grants, workshops, consulting)?

10

Marketing and Practice Building

If you want to build a great enterprise, you have to have the courage to dream great dreams. If you dream small dreams, you may succeed in building something small. For many people, that is enough. But if you want to achieve widespread impact and lasting value, be bold.

—Howard Shultz, President and CEO, Starbucks

According to Patsi Krakoff, being a successful coach means the coach is involved in two businesses—coaching and marketing.

If you are reluctant to market yourself, you are at a disadvantage in growing a coaching practice or business. Don't be discouraged. You can still, however, use the coaching skills discussed in this book. But before you abandon the idea of marketing yourself, consider that marketing doesn't mean using "sleazy" practices or having an "over the top" personality. It does mean understanding what marketing is, how to use your own personal style and niche, and what you are committed to doing in order to attract clients.

What Is Marketing?

Marketing is not selling. It refers to everything that goes into the process of getting to the point of sale. Branding, advertising, direct mail, and cold calling are some of the marketing techniques with which people are familiar. Marketing is also multidimensional. At the highest level, it is referred to as "new business development" and tied to corporate strategy.

Marketing a product is quite different from marketing a service. When we speak about marketing coaching, we need to think specifically about how one markets services. Services vary widely according to the individuals who deliver them. Many of us only want specific people to provide the service we need or want because they have a good reputation or have been referred by someone we know. Marketing of a service can be said to consist of the following:

- an *attitude*—it is about *who* you are . . . and are not (Avis was not afraid to be number 2!);
- distinguishing *yourself as the product*;
- having a *vision* of where you want to go, a clear *mission* statement, and a detailed *plan*; and
- the *willingness to self-promote* and overcome any negative ideas about marketing.

97

The Unique Aspects of Marketing Coaching

Coaching is not only a service and a very personal one in most cases but also new and not well understood; many coaches even have difficulty explaining what coaching is. Although many report great results from coaching, research on coaching is only in its infancy. Some of the issues of marketing coaching are general to personalized services and some are specific:

- Services are intangible and can be very difficult to describe.
- Service businesses have a variable quality among providers.
- The perception of risk by the consumer is greater than with a known product. You may or may not produce for them. Just because you helped one person or one business does not mean an exact replication of this success will be appropriate for other people or other businesses.
- The explosion of coaching in recent years has increased competition. You will now frequently hear, "Everyone seems to be a coach now."
- The variety of coaching options available may be confusing.
- People may be confused about the difference between therapy or "positive psychology" and coaching as well as between coaching and mentoring.
- During an economic downturn, although the need for what coaching offers is greater, it is harder to sell services not considered to be "necessities." Marketing efforts need to be better than ever, but budget constraints that clients experience may compel the coach to reduce some marketing efforts. (I like the approach of a personal trainer I know: Although personal training is not a necessity, the benefits of training are long-term benefits.)

Reach, Repetition, and Relevance

Judy Feld, past president of the International Coach Federation and cofounder of Smart-Match Alliances, aptly described three core functions of successful marketing in a teleclass she delivered a number of years ago:

- *Reach* refers to how many potential buyers know about your product/services—how many people are reached by your newsletter, access your Web site, see your article in print, or attend your workshops.
- *Repetition* refers to how often people see your name. What is your plan for mailings, articles, speaking engagements, and other channels for repeat access to your niche population? You are unlikely to produce results if you have no plan and no consistency. If you have a print or an electronic newsletter, for instance, send it out at regular intervals. People will expect it and may even look forward to it. Random access to your target audience yields random results. Once your business is established, the impact of your marketing can and should be measured. If you make one small change and have measured your baseline results, you then have a comparison.

Are your results better or worse than before? Such a determination can help you shape your efforts in the right direction. Too many people give up on a good business idea when they do not succeed at first, never testing the effects of tweaking their efforts.

- *Relevance* refers to your message. Avoid making the message problem oriented. Instead, make it expansive, stressing success and goal achievement. In the teleclass, Judy stated, "People who come with problems leave after they solve their problems." An example is as follows: "I work with successful business owners to achieve a joyful balance" versus "Are you drowning in your work and needing help?" In a challenging economic environment, one needs to strike the balance, "I help people in job transition get ahead of the pack so they actually get interviews."

Authentic Marketing

"Authenticity," according to the Microsoft Encarta College Dictionary, is "the genuineness or truth about something." "*Authentic* marketing," therefore, is marketing genuinely. Because many human service professionals have negative thoughts about sales and marketing, finding one's authentic voice can be a challenge. Do you like to speak, write, and/or teach? What are your natural strengths and abilities for putting yourself and your thoughts forward? What do you want to say to others? Most important, what is the difference you make and how can you let others know? Your method can be simple and straightforward, but if you do not let others know what you do and that you are available, the likelihood of attracting clients is greatly diminished. *In*authentic marketing is not about lying or overinflating one's skills but rather refers to people looking inauthentic or who are ill at ease about marketing in ways that are not a good fit for them.

Specialty and Niche

A *specialty* describes what you are good at (for example, helping others create a vision for their life or business, fostering creativity, and the like). A *niche* is actually a market segment—for instance, "entrepreneurs." A niche describes your target population and is very concrete and specific. The more narrowly you define it, the better off you will be. Many coaches try to be all things to all people and fail to distinguish their uniqueness. It is better to say "I coach 40- to 50-year-old female entrepreneurs with ADHD" than to say "I coach midlife women." You may not have thousands of potential clients who fit the description, but you will in all likelihood attract virtually all of the potential clients in that group (as long as you make it possible for them to find you).

You can, in fact, actually "own" a niche. I am a trained family therapist and pretty much "own" "family-business coaching," appearing among the first five Web sites from a Google search without ever having paid for positioning. I do coach family businesses, but it is a relatively small percentage of what I do. I had, however, brought me a high ranking on the Web, some newspaper articles, and periodically an inquiry from a potential client.

Find a niche or two that represent *your* authenticity—what you love to do and are already skilled and/or trained at doing. Your niche need not be all that you do. Even if it is a relatively small percentage, it should be what you become known for. Below are lists of coaching issues and niches. Many of the potential issues in coaching can be expanded into niches. For example, the issue: finding the right relationship; the niche: relationship coaching or life partner quest.

A niche will also provide areas in which to market (for example, a relocation coach might contact relocation companies or human resources departments).

Issues for Coaching

- Productivity and effectiveness
- Motivation
- Focus
- Leadership/vision
- Career change
- Starting a business
- Facing a big challenge/supporting a project
- Financial problems—personal
- Financial problems—business
- Solving a big problem/making a big decision
- Balance/integration
- Improved self-care
- Clarify values/align life purpose
- Integrity
- Strengthen character
- Management skills
- People skills
- Marketing assistance/selling skills
- Self-confidence
- Relationships
- Marital issues
- Personal Development
- Lifestyle design/retirement coaching
- Divorce/starting over
- Goal-setting management
- Team building
- Time Management

Coaching Niches

- Career coach
- Executive coach
- Life coach

- Transition coach
- Entrepreneurs
- Female entrepreneurs
- Attention-deficit hyperactivity disorder coach
- Whole health/wellness coaching
- Financial wellness coach
- Life purpose
- Management/team leadership
- Leadership skills
- Sales coaching
- Relationships/life partner quest coach
- Retirement/lifestyle design coach
- Divorce/starting over
- Presurgery coach
- Relocation coaching
- Writing coach
- Creativity coach
- Parents of college-bound students
- Time-challenged entrepreneurs

Creating a Business Plan

Writing a business plan is highly recommended. It need not be elaborate, but be sure to include a simple spreadsheet. A coach and colleague who left a lucrative career in another field saw that she was losing money in her coaching practice. Within a month of writing a business plan, she created a lovely new brochure targeting her desired population and had gotten seven new clients.

A template for a simple business plan is included in Appendix J (and the Small Business Administration provides a number of useful resources at http://www.sba.gov/smallbusiness-planner/index.html). Be sure to include a complete assessment of internal (personal) and external factors such as collateral and money to invest. If you have a web-savvy teenager who can design and maintain a Web site for you, then you are already ahead of the game. Market research on coaching is hard to come by; you will have to be creative in measuring the need in areas in which you wish to work.

Here are some questions, provided by a professional marketing executive, that can also guide you:

1. What is the current business challenge?
2. Why is this challenging?
3. What objectives are suggested for a successful solution?
4. Which of these are the most important?
5. What are the ways that these challenges can be overcome?
6. How would these be achieved?

Strategic Plan

Your strategic plan is a plan of how you can apply your vision or mission statement to the real world. This should include the decision regarding becoming involved with partners or working for others as well as the degree to which you might continue to work in your existing field either part time or full time.

Establishing a Referral Network

Networking is an essential aspect of coaching. Your existing network of human service professionals may or may not refer to you, depending on how well you educate them. You will need to help them realize you complement rather than a threat to their practice. It is also helpful to develop new networks of professionals who work with your target population and, if you are interested in business coaching, people in the business community. There are numerous networking groups in existence, including local chambers of commerce; referral groups such as Business Networking International; various women's groups; and, more recently, an explosion of meet-up groups you can find online for just about every interest, primarily in metropolitan areas. If you cannot access in-person meetings, there are also many online networking venues. I discuss these venues in the pages that follow.

Your Image and Presentation

Everything about your presentation is part of your marketing. It is said people decide about physical appearance within seven seconds and draw conclusions about written materials probably in an equally short period of time as well. Make sure your appearance and your materials express your authenticity in a professional way. Think about yourself as always being ready for a job interview. You might meet your next potential client on line at the supermarket or on a plane (I have!).

Make sure you make it easy for clients to reach you. When people call and get a busy signal or do not get a timely return call, they get frustrated and look for someone else. Make your message friendly and upbeat. When you record a voicemail, make yourself sound ten times more excited than you might normally because the phone flattens out one's tone. Have others listen to it and make sure it is professional but friendly and upbeat. First impressions count! If possible, get a separate line for your coaching calls (for incoming calls only it is pretty inexpensive) so you do not pick up other calls when your client is scheduled to call in.

Responding in a timely way is essential, as any therapist who did not return a call to a new referral within hours has learned. Never make excuses such as "my voicemail wasn't working," even if it is true; it simply is not professional. Always take responsibility: "My apologies. I am aware I should have gotten back to you sooner." If you cannot respond right away, then send an e-mail and explain when you will and then follow up when you say. As a coach, you want to project the image of success and good self-management.

Creating Your Marketing Plan

General Tips on Authentic Marketing

Below are some tips for developing a successful practice. Following them will be easier if you have your own coach. Having a coach will give you a role model and help you overcome your gremlins about marketing and find your authentic expression. Choose someone who is successful and for whom marketing is easy. Those who have overcome challenges in building a successful practice can probably help you avoid costly pitfalls. Once you internalize the principles, it will become easier for you as well. The key is to find your own unique marketing voice.

- *Become very comfortable at describing exactly what you do:* Coaching, as mentioned previously, can be very difficult to describe. Make it clear how the results of coaching, specifically of *your* coaching, can be measured—the bottom line in business coaching is generally more profit, less loss, improved morale; in personal coaching, the goals include life satisfaction and living authentically; in career coaching, obtaining the advantage in getting and keeping a job. Make sure you communicate in terms of creating possibilities rather than solving problems and in terms of what coaching is and not what it is not.

- *Write a marketing plan that includes* specific, measurable *goals:* These should outline finances, number of clients, and a timeline of actionable steps to market your services (for example, have an article published by October, call 10 potential clients by Friday). The more specific you are, the more likely you are to be drawn to that future.

- *Be accountable to another*—a coach, a partner, and a friend—for the results you intend to produce.

- *Market "shamelessly" in a way that fits your own style and personality:* Do not try to market the way others do if their techniques make you feel uncomfortable. If you are reluctant to "self-promote," for instance, write articles or produce a free pamphlet about a subject that you believe is important and will make a difference to others. Use writing as a way to spread your name around. However, do not hesitate to challenge yourself to learn new skills if you wish to incorporate them into your skill set. I once had a fear of presenting in front of groups but really wanted to be able to, so I completed a rigorous leadership-training program. I am now able to give workshops and even have a lot of fun doing it!

- *Share your successes!* Do not be afraid to brag or to post a new business client on your Web site or write a press release, making sure to honor client confidentiality.

- *Do a thorough self-assessment and set out to develop the areas that you need to develop in yourself as soon as possible:* This might involve learning or becoming certified in a new skill (such as using assessment tools such as the Myers–Briggs or Universal DISC) or honing skills in public speaking or writing. It might also involve mastering a way of being (for example, learning to approach others at a networking function rather than waiting to be approached or overcoming procrastination).

- *Try to create a referral pipeline* so that you always have people in various stages of the selling cycle. Unlike therapy, there is a sales cycle to coaching—initial phone call or e-mail, first personal contact, complimentary session, setting up the contract. The cycle will be longer often for corporate coaching, especially in an uncertain economy where funding may be scarce or even disappear overnight. It is always good to have a few things in the pipeline to cover those contingencies.

- *Always be helpful—even when you are not the designated person for the job:* Help the prospective client find the right coach or resource. Make suggestions, provide tips, and send an article. You will be surprised how often people remember small gestures over time. Whenever we give something away, it will come back to us—not necessarily from the same source, but it will come back.

- *Be appreciative of others:* Send handwritten (more personal) notes and appreciation gifts.

- *Keep in touch with your past clients:* They might be your most valuable resource. Keep in touch with them, show interest in their ongoing progress, and keep your name on the client's radar.

- *Be aware of clients you do not want:* They may be too time-consuming, emotionally draining, or just not the right fit for your skills. Refer them to others, and you will likely receive the kindness back.

- *Be impeccable in how you run your business:* Satisfied clients may not always boast about their success (although many do), but unhappy ones will broadcast their dissatisfaction loudly.

- *Offer clients free coaching time in return for referrals:* Such an offer would be unethical for a therapist but is accepted practice in coaching.

- *Be prepared to invest a little cash in your business:* You really cannot get something for nothing! Also be prepared to put solid blocks of time into the marketing effort. Take the time to think about your actions. Invest in having nicely prepared materials developed. Hire a professional. If you cannot afford to do so, use a simple "white paper" format that describes what you do. It can be equally effective as a nice brochure if it gives real, tangible information about coaching and specifically about *your* coaching.

- *Consider bartering services:* Web design, graphic design, or editing, for example. One coach I know barters coaching for massage. Although not part of her intended plan, the massage therapist client also now sends her referrals!

- *If you "cannot" do certain things, get others to do it for you:* Find a coaching partner with a different specialty whose business you complement and cross-promote each other's work. It is often much easier to promote someone else.

- *Don't be a perfectionist:* You will never succeed if you wait to get it "perfect." I spent too much time when I started coaching on perfecting my marketing message and materials and creating my Web site. You are in a relationship business, and your "brand" is you and the results you help others achieve. If you are not doing the work, you have little to market. A very successful executive coach, for instance, recently told me he had a new business name after 17 years of coaching, "I finally got it [my brand] right!" That never derailed his success.

- *Don't be afraid to "fail"*: Take some risk. Be prepared to give time to see your efforts work. Do not be discouraged, for instance, if an ad fails to get a response initially. Keep it in place for at least six months. People may keep your name for a long time before calling. It never hurts to have your name in front of people. Professional marketers believe one needs to see a product name at least seven times before buying. Marketing, even according to professionals, is trial and error. Even when market research is used, conditions change and results are not always predictable. Eventually, you will hear, "I've heard [or seen] your name before ."
- *Practice "extreme self-care"*: Apart from "walking your talk" so you can be a good role model for clients, your self-care will give you the best foundation of all for a successful business.

Marketing Skills and Tools

I once heard someone say marketing involves only two things: speaking and writing and writing and speaking. I would add "networking" as a third element. You need to network to have people to speak with and send your written materials or give your card to. A good network can get you speaking opportunities, an article in your newspaper or alumni magazine, an opportunity to offer a workshop or speak at a conference, or, better yet, a champion who will sell your services to others for you for no charge.

Networking

According to Sandra Yancey (2006), CEO of eWomenNetwork, networking is "the art of creating connections and building relationships. You build a network through the reciprocal process of giving and sharing referrals, contacts, information, business, leads, idea resources, and advice" (p. 41).

Networking is part art and part science. With the advent of online networking opportunities, one no longer has to leave one's home or office to network with others worldwide. Someone with good writing and technical skills can excel in this process. In-person networking, nonetheless, still has its place. At a time when trust is more in question than ever in our culture, nothing replaces face-to-face interaction.

You are networking when you

- strike up a conversation with someone else waiting at the doctor's or dentist's office;
- talk to your doctor, lawyer, or accountant about being in law school;
- speak with your neighbors;
- visit with other members of social clubs or religious groups;
- connect with others through an alumni association;
- talk to someone at the health club;
- volunteer at your child's school or help out at a charity event;
- post messages on mailing lists or in a chat room; or
- participate in an interest group such as a book club or an investment club.

Diane's Very "Effective Networking"

Diane Darling is the founder of Effective Networking, Inc., author of two successful books, a professor, well-known speaker, and an expert resource on the subject of networking. She also won the prestigious 2009 Rising Star award from the Center for Women & Enterprise (CWE) for her entrepreneurial endeavors.

After surviving the loss of a previous business, Diane rebuilt her career literally from scratch (at one point, she ran her company while living out of the YWCA) using her natural networking skills. A naturally shy person, she was nonetheless successful at connecting with others. After being asked how she was able to easily get meetings with CEOs no one else could get access to, she knew she was on to something. Most recently, she began speaking to groups about using networking to find employment, sharing with them how she can really relate to their anxieties. Her experiences encouraged her give back to other women entrepreneurs as a volunteer and champion of women in business, resulting in her CWE award with the following description: "Diane's inspiring story of her journey towards success is emblematic of what CWE helps women to do every day—survive and thrive."

Possible contacts:

- Family
- Friends
- Employers—present and past
- Faculty and administrators
- Fellow students
- Undergraduate classmates and faculty
- Alumni associations
- Undergraduate clubs
- Professional associations
- Community and volunteer activities
- Religious groups
- Athletic teams
- Neighbors
- Meetings and conferences
- Networking organizations

Supporters, Shakers, and Mentors

- *Supporters* are the backbone of your network. They are the ones you go to for support and affirmation.
- *Shakers* are people who know and care about you but also have the guts and confidence to shake you up and give you honest feedback (Yancey, 2006).

- *Mentors* are people who have already paved the way and can provide knowledge, inspiration, and practical information.

Advantages of Online Networking

- There are thousands of discussion groups and community forums covering hundreds of subjects.
- You can "break the ice" before meeting someone in person.
- You can listen, engage, or be engaged as you wish. No one can see you sweat, and you do not have to feel like a wallflower because no one can see you standing by yourself.
- You can work on it during "no pay" or "no study" hours.
- You can make yourself visible to recruiters who routinely search online sites to find potential candidates.

Disadvantages of Online Networking

- Networking online is just as difficult as networking in person! In fact, it may be harder because you cannot really establish a true personal relationship online.
- First impressions count even more. Be very careful with your first public posting.
- Your online behavior matters more than you think. Be careful. Once online, you have an online persona and reputation.

Where to Network Online

Many professionals use chat rooms, Web forums, and social networking Web sites for networking, discussing recent developments in their occupation or industry, and asking questions of each other. Anyone seeking business or looking to sell their product or services can benefit from following these online public discussions, learning about current trends and developments and the interests and concerns of those involved.

Job seeking is a little more challenging, but it can be done online as well. Some of the most popular online resources today, referred to as "social networking" sites, are Facebook (http://www.facebook.com), Twitter (http://www.twitter.com), and LinkedIn (http://www.linkedin.com). People are increasingly using Facebook, the most popular social networking site, for business purposes, setting up separate pages on which they ask others to be their "fans." LinkedIn, however, is still considered by many to be the best purely professional networking site. LinkedIn allows members to show their resume and experience, request that others recommend them, join common interest groups, ask others for "e-introductions" to people they wish to meet, and broadcast activities such as talks and article and workshop offereings to their entire online network.

LinkedIn Tips

- Start slowly.
- Do not invite many people you do not know well.
- Do not try to connect with the whole world. It will defeat the purpose.

- If you receive an invitation from someone you do not know, then it is best (for their reputation) to say "don't know."
- Try out all the features.

An example of an appropriate online inquiry I received on LinkedIn follows below:

> Marilyn,
>
> You may be aware that I'm looking for new employment and professional development opportunities, as a result, I'd like to add you to my LinkedIn professional network. If you accept, please note that I'll only pass requests on to you from people I trust, and I hope you'll do the same for me.

Writing

There are two ways you can gain exposure through writing—*being written about* and *your own writing*—and two types of writing—*writing for a professional audience* and *writing for the general public.* When you write for a professional audience, you may be writing to your niche clients or to your referral sources. When you write for the general public, you may reach a wider audience, but because your audience is less specific, results may depend more on a compelling presentation.

Being Written About

Typical mediums include the following:

- Newspaper articles
- Magazines
- Trade journals
- Professional publications
- Newsletters
- Alumni publications
- Listings on referral sites (which occasionally provide an opportunity to be profiled)

All of the above will give you exposure, but the first three are the most challenging opportunities to find and often feature a very unusual story, require great luck, or a good publicist. Diane Darling is one person I know who not only is lucky enough to have a name that is compelling but also is most adept at networking. She managed not only to get a column of her own in the *Boston Business Journal*, but also, as millions were being laid off from their jobs in March 2009, to get a full spread on the first page of the *Boston Globe* Lifestyle section (complete with photos) about rebuilding her finances after the loss of her business, starting a new business, getting two books published, and building a national reputation for herself.

Writing and Relevancy

The most important thing to know when you are writing is that you need a *point of view*. If you are writing for an audience that knows little or nothing about coaching, then do not just say what coaching is, but tell them how it will help them. If your audience already knows about or has been exposed to coaching, then tell them something that is relevant to them. Use themes that are relevant to current events, such as "How to Succeed in Coaching in Challenging Times," or highlight new niches, such as "The Growth of Coaching in Healthcare." Just as it is helpful to have a ready list of topics to address, it is also helpful to have a ready list of topics you can write about. Most readers have a professional specialty already, so linking specialty to coaching should be relatively easy—for example, "What Every Social Worker [or Psychiatrist, Nurse, Mental Health Counselor, or Consultant] Needs to Know About Coaching" or, from a scholarly perspective, "From the Sidelines: Coaching as a Nurse Practitioner Strategy for Improving Health Outcomes" (Hayes & Kalmakis, 2007).

Some online writing mediums include the following:

- newsletters—print and online ("ezines");
- articles you submit to local newspapers and professional publications;
- papers for scholarly journals;
- white papers (which can be posted on your Web site);
- articles you write for colleagues' newsletters;
- online articles;
- Web site content (some of which can be turned into articles and newsletter content); and
- blogs and Twitter.

Speaking

There are many opportunities to speak and get yourself "out there." Speaking is regarded as one of the most anxiety-producing experiences for many, so finding opportunities to practice, such as attending (free) meetings of Toastmasters International or taking a class in public speaking, can be very helpful.

Leading workshops, seminars, and trainings is an art in and of itself, but it is not necessary to reinvent the wheel. What is most important is to know your potential audience, the level of their knowledge, and their expectations. The organizer of an event is usually knowledgable about audience members' profile and can provide you with this information to help you better tailor your presentation. If you are bold enough to promote a speaking engagement yourself, ask a few friends and colleagues who might represent your target population or who work with your target population to give you ideas.

Whether as an invited speaker or as the self-promoter of an event, it is helpful to begin your presentation by asking two simple questions: How many of you know something about [your specific niche if appropriate] coaching? and What would you like to learn today?

Here are a few types of speaking venues and opportunities:

- classes (including being a guest speaker at someone else's class),
- workshops and seminars,
- lectures and small or informal talks,

- keynote addresses,
- trainings,
- panel presentations, and
- leading or facilitating an organization's meetings.

A simple way to start is by giving small talks—to professional interest groups or committees, clubs, or community organizations. Deirdre Danahar, who specializes in working with "academics who are interested in exploring creative paths to further their pursuit of knowledge in all aspects of their life" and "mid-career professional women in social services/public health impassioned to follow their creative paths to exciting outcomes in their life and work," began her business by giving talks at a local bookstore in central Illinois where few people were acquainted with coaching but many were interested in the title of her talk, "Get on Balance."

I began by speaking to the private practice committee of my NASW chapter and, before long, had invitations to present at conferences regionally as well as locally. When I felt comfortable enough, I then branched out and submitted a workshop proposal to the Boston University School of Social Work (my alma mater) continuing education program. My programs were very well received so, loving travel and having committed to working abroad as part of my coaching vision, I reached out and submitted a proposal to the International Conference for the Advanced Professional Practice of Clinical Social Work in Lisbon, Portugal, in 2000. I also began offering my workshops in New York, New Jersey, and Massachusetts. I was in the process of signing a contract to take my workshop on the road to 30 U.S. cities when 9/11 occurred, and so I decided to rethink my plans and later formed a relationship with Commonwealth Educational Seminars, a Massachusetts learning company that continues to promote my work.

You can create and offer an interesting program on a popular subject that other speakers are not talking about. That is what Kathleen Burns Kingsbury, a psychologist/coach with an MBA, did by focusing on women and money. In addition to her Web site (http://kbkconnections.com/speaking_workshop.html) and blog, *Chicks Make "Cents"* (http://kbkconnections.blogspot.com/), she also speaks at women's groups on topics like "Finding Your Value: The Art of Self-Promotion," "Women and Money: Why Setting Fees is Emotional Business," and "Women and Money: The Next Steps for Financial Freedom." For instance, in her "Women and Money" talk, she raises important issues about setting fees: "Do you squirm when someone asks you for your fees? Do you undercut your price to be 'nice' or because 'you should'?" She then goes on to say, "This workshop will address how you can tap into what is driving your pricing strategy and how to make sure your self worth is not president of the company."

When you speak, you will be included in a printed program, in a catalogue, or on a flyer that provides potential clients with your name and qualifications. You can use the event to create postevent publicity by sending releases to your local newspapers and alumni publications. Call some journalists and tell them about the event. They may just attend your talk and write about you. Although your sponsor will not be your publicist, the sponsor can publicize you on their Web site and in their newsletter, which will aid you in reaching a new audience. Many organizations post their programs in the local business journal, which also usually has an online calendar, providing another link to you on the Web! You can coordinate starting a new program with your speaking engagement—for example, start a professional women's group two weeks after speaking to a women's networking organization.

Workshops are another great way to present to a target population, such as your own professional group or to local business people you have located through your chamber of commerce. Business presentations need not be focused on business topics such as finance; rather, they can tailored to relevant issues in the news, such as "How to Tell if Your Employee Is Depressed and What to do About It."

Leading workshops is great experience and opens up areas such as corporate training. Leading groups is good practice during a recession, as it makes coaching accessible to more individuals without you having to reduce your income. These skills can easily be transferred to teaching teleclasses and webinars, both of which allow you to post a permanent sample of your work on your Web site or snippets on a blog so people can "meet" you with low risk.

Steps to Developing Your Speaking Program

Your first step is committing to do it. Your next most important step is to determine your niche and target audience. The biggest mistake I have made is spreading myself too thin. Do not try to be all things to all people:

1. *Determine the result* people would receive and the niche you wish to target.
2. *Develop a list of topics* for workshops or groups you might be able to lead. If you have never led a workshop and have the desire to learn, take a course such as one offered at Kripalu (http://www.kripalu.com) to build your confidence.
3. *Plan carefully:* Set the date for your workshop or event and work backward to create a timeline to complete needed tasks.
4. *Create programs that can be modified to fit various formats:* Prepare an all-day workshop that can be abbreviated for a presentation to a networking group meeting.
5. *Practice your presentation in advance:* Tape it (video or audio), and, if possible, have others critique you.

Teleclasses

A teleclass or teleseminar is a live, interactive workshop that is conducted over the telephone like a conference call. Teleclasses have been an extremely popular way of introducing coaching to large groups and spreading the word around the world. (One or a series of free teleclasses are used in many training programs as an introduction to prospective students.)

Teleseminars are used to provide information, training, or promote or sell products to groups of people interested in a particular topic. They are similar to traditional seminars, in content and purpose, but they are conducted in a teleconference or over a bridge line rather than at a specific location. A teleclass/teleseminar audience can vary in size from a few callers to thousands of participants, depending on the size of the bridge lines used and the popularity of the topic being discussed.

Teleclasses are frequently recorded and available either as permanent downloads or for a period of one week or until the next class is recorded over the previous one, depending on the choice of technology used by the host. Many free conference lines exist, my favorite being http://www.freeconferencecall.com, which provides a detail report of the numbers of participants and times of the call.

Teleclasses are an opportunity to provide information to a large number of people at one time. It allows a trainer to train many participants at once and eliminates the need for travel, expensive preparation, and presentation material costs, making it a very cost-effective delivery method. Some are one-time classes, whereas others are a series of weekly classes over time. Some, particularly those geared toward other coaches, are skilled based, giving vital information on topics such as marketing, creating effective ezines or online newsletters, or publishing a book. There are also a number of motivational and supportive teleclasses, with names such as "Financial Success for the Overspender," "Finally, a Lifetime Solution to Procrastination!" and "Create Your Perfect Life for Suddenly Single Women Over 40," and health and wellness teleclasses such as "How you Can Improve Your Health Using Mind-Body Techniques 10 Minutes a Day."

Many teleclasses are offered for free. Others are for a fee, which ranges from $25 to $79 per hour of class time. Even when there is a fee for participation, students benefit by saving on the hassle and expense of traveling to a live seminar. They can join the teleconference from home or anywhere that they have a telephone connection.

Free teleclasses provide a low-risk opportunity to become familiar with a particular coach and his or her specialty. From a coach's perspective, teleclasses can expand your network dramatically and provide an opportunity to recruit one-on-one clients. The more specific the coach's niche, the more likely the right clients will sign up for teleclasses. If the classes are effective, then clients become engaged. Many potential clients try coaching on the basis of the coach's approach to practice.

Not all classes are equally popular; however, "fit" is the most important factor. People prefer to buy something that speaks to them. Therefore, teleclasses that are more situation specific will attract more subscribers. The "Eliminate Delay Program for Hard Core Procrastinators" had more appeal than the "Eliminate Delay Program," and "7 Steps to Crafting Your Personal Marketing Message" attracted more interest than "Marketing 101—Finding the Heart of your Personal Marketing Message."

Statistics show that the right title makes a significant difference in the "buyability" factor of products on the Internet, especially e-products such as teleclasses.

Delivery is important. Once you attract people to the class, you need to offer real value. People have come to see through teleclasses offered purely for marketing purposes.

Providing a white paper, tip list, self-assessment, or other tools participants can take away adds value. There is an art to teaching successful teleclasses, and many teleclass listing sites require presenters to take some form of "certification" before listing a class—free or paid—on their site. The skills for this type of distance learning are a good fit, however, for coaches who frequently work on the phone and involve identifying the mood and tone of the group (level III listening) as well as creating a structure that allows everyone to participate if they want to and to achieve specific learning goals for the session. The key success factors include the following:

- Be well prepared.
- Have more material than you might get a chance to use.
- Send out preclass and postclass notes.
- Be timely in your follow through.
- "Underpromise and overdeliver." Many of us make the mistake of doing the opposite.

What follows is a random selection of classes listed on various Web sites at the time of writing:

- Parents (Loved Ones) of Military Personnel Discussion Group
- Finding a Career that Fits Your Life
- 7 Biggest Mistakes Solopreneurs Make and How to Avoid Them
- Healing High Anxiety: Moving Into Alignment with your Highest Self
- Is Your Body a Burden? Find a More Vibrant Life through Body Knowledge
- Marketing a Meaningful Career as an ADD Coach
- How to Forgive Yourself So You Can Have More Joy in Your Life
- Website Development on a Shoestring
- 10 Hidden Keys to Effective Forgiveness: Move Past Fear and Anger to Reconnect With Your Dreams
- High Energy, Healthy Weight and Anti-Aging
- Bio-Identical Hormones—The Wave of the Future
- Understanding Adrenal Stress

As you can see, there is room for almost any topic, although topics appear to be clustered along the lines of personal development, health and well-being, and business (sales, marketing, business building, and Web skills).

Webinars

Webinars are online seminars delivered through Web conferencing via the Internet. In a Web conference, each participant sits at his or her own computer and is connected to other participants on the Internet through either a downloaded application or a Web-based application where the attendees will simply enter a Web site address to enter the conference.

Webinars are usually one way—from the speaker to the audience—and entail limited audience interaction. There are instances, however, when a webinar can be collaborative and include, for example, polling and question-and-answer sessions. In some cases, the presenter may speak over a standard telephone line, pointing out information being presented on screen, and the audience can respond over their own telephones.

Webinars are increasingly replacing teleclasses as a means of both marketing and providing information. Generally, marketing webinars are free. The exchange of information provides the presenter with valuable e-mail addresses, and this can be the first step in creating a "sales funnel." Paid webinars can cost anywhere from $59 and up and are often resold to organizations for as much as $259 and up, with the idea that the organization will own that information and retain it in their library.

Webinars can be a challenge for relationship-oriented presenters. After getting over the feeling of no one being "out there," however, I have come to appreciate webinars. They force you to organize your thoughts carefully and rehearse your presentation so it flows smoothly. A well-advertised webinar can reach several hundred people, and at the conclusion of the session, you retain ownership of the participant list—a major selling point for offering webinars. I have done them both through my own business and as a presenter for other organizations such as Business Expert Webinars (http://www.businessexpertwebinars. com), Computer Aid, Inc.; and the Performance Institute, Government Executives Network (http://www.performanceweb.org/events/e-learning/ [formerly http://www.Goven. org]). The top providers of webinar services are Go to Meeting (http://www.gotomeeting. com) and Webex (http://www.webex.com), but other companies are entering the field.

Internet Marketing

Internet marketing refers to the marketing of products or services over the Internet. It is also referred to as Web marketing, online marketing, or "eMarketing."

The Internet has brought many unique benefits to marketing, one of which are lower costs for the distribution of information to a global audience. The interactive nature of Internet marketing is a unique and, to the uninitiated, somewhat daunting quality of the medium. Internet marketing is more than marketing on the Web; it also comprises the management of visitors' (customers') data and relationship management systems. Internet marketing also pertains to the placement of media, because it is possible to buy online placement such as Google Ad words to advertise yourself online.

Internet marketing is associated with four different business models, which are frequently used together:

1. e-commerce: goods are sold directly to consumers or to businesses;
2. publishing: the sale of advertising;
3. lead-based Web sites: an organization generates value by acquiring sales leads from its Web site; and
4. affiliate marketing: a process in which a product or service developed by one person is sold by other active sellers for a share of the profits (the owner of the product normally provides some marketing material—for example, sales letter, affiliate link, tracking facility).

Affiliate marketing used for selling information products is the fastest growing and most profitable business on Internet, as it requires only a small financial investment. There are many coaching products one can sell along with one's own services. Affiliate marketing can be fairly time consuming and is not recommended if you are just entering the coaching field, unless you have someone to help you.

Web Sites

According to internet World Stats (http://www.internetworldstats.com), as of March 2009, the following numbers of people use the Internet:

- 248 million in North America (73.6 percent of the population and 17 percent of the world population);
- 390 million in Europe (48.5 percent of the population); and
- 650 million in Asia (17.2 percent of the population).

According to Nielsen online (http://en-us.nielsen.com/), the average number of Web pages viewed per month are 1,600 per person, with 36 sessions and 72 domains visited. The average time spent during a surfing session is a little more than one hour, and the average time spent viewing a Web page is 50 seconds.

In other words, it is very difficult to get noticed on the Internet. If you do, then you only have 50 seconds to capture someone's interest. Getting them to move to a new page once they reach your home page is another matter.

When the Web was in its infancy, it was easier to get noticed. Initially, many simply used their Web sites as an online brochure. As the Internet grew, search engine optimization became popular, but it too failed to cut through the masses of information, giving way to newer strategies such as blogging and tweeting.

If it so difficult to get noticed on the Web, then why is it so important to have a Web presence, and how can one use it to his or her advantage? The answer to the first question is simple: It has come to be expected. If nothing else, then one can gain credibility by having a professional looking site. I am consistently surprised by the positive response I receive about my site (http://www.ontrackcoaching.com), now in its third iteration: "very professional, easy to navigate, good information." On the basis of my site, I was selected as one of the top two coaching firms by *Boston Magazine* in 2005 and by major companies interested in coaching services. More recently, I have had an increasing number of contacts from local businesses, in contrast to only one all of last year resulting from my *Yellow Pages* listing. More than half of those have actually become clients!

Creating the Web site was a "labor of love," though like labor, often painful—simply because I did not know what I was doing initially. Coaching was so new, it was hard to know how to position it to distinguish myself from other coaches, who all seemed to be saying very similar things. I used many sources of input, but the best guidance I received from Lisa Rigsby of Big Pond (http://www.bigpond.net), who managed my Web site and development, was to make it interactive so people would keep returning.

The process of developing a Web site is much easier today. There are companies that will do it for you easily and cheaply, such as WebFlexor (http://www.webflexor-websites .com/), which specializes in coaching Web sites, and a blog site is a type of Web site one can set up completely on one's own. Before doing either, here are a few things to consider. Make it *easy* for people to do the following:

1. find your Web site,
2. connect to who you are and what you can do for them,
3. join your e-mail list,
4. navigate the site to know what you offer,
5. receive updates and new information,
6. interact with you and ask questions, and
7. buy your services and products when they are ready.

Make sure that you create a professional-looking Web site. You can do it yourself or hire an inexpensive web designer. If you have a little money or talent for doing it yourself, contact a local high school or college technology or art department, or put an ad in a local newspaper for a high school student with interest in Web site development. Having a logo and a snappy name is helpful, but do not get stuck there. A low-cost professional Web site building company can help you with your brand as well. If you go with a student or do it yourself, there are plenty of stock images at sites like (for example, http://www.iPhoto.com, http://www.vistaprint.com) that you can use on your site as well as on business cards. The key is consistency. Make sure your site reflects who you are. The colors I chose to use are a fire engine red and gray. Red is simply my favorite color—I often wear red, I am a Sagittarius (fire sign), and I even have red chairs in my office to "light a fire" under my clients. Gray, to me, represents being professional, but it also symbolizes seeing "shades of gray" and provides a sense of balance—something I talk about a lot with clients—by adding a cool element to balance the fiery red.

Although I started with my OnTrack brand before building the Web site, many coaches are now doing the opposite—creating the brand when they build their Web site. There are many interesting coaching Web sites of varying quality. Feel free to borrow ideas you see. Many coaches already do that. A few ideas for a site are the following:

- Keep it simple and direct.
- Do not get stuck in deciding on a good design. Get into action. The rest of the world is already on the Web!
- Decide whether you want your site to be a source of many direct referrals or more of an online brochure. (You can, in fact, put an actual brochure right on your site in PDF format.) When someone wants to know more about you or what you do, refer him or her to your site and suggest you speak after they have had a chance to look at it.
- Make sure potential clients find you. Include an e-mail link and a way to sign on to your Web site to receive your newsletter, your LinkedIn link, or other contact information.
- Update your site or blog frequently.
- Offer something to either get them to call, return, or refer—a complementary session, a free pamphlet or white paper, or back editions of an online newsletter.

- Make it easy and desirable to sign up for your list. This is usually tied in with one of the offers suggested in the previous bullet point.
- Include interactive materials such as recorded messages, recordings of trainings, or video clips if you have them. If you don't, consider making them.
- Include valuable reciprocal links to other sites. That will increase your traffic.
- Include a way to track the "hits" you get—for example, Google Analytics.
- Create a chat room if you have a topic that is unique.
- Create additional "passive" income by selling a product online—a book, coaching tool, software, or an assessment tool. You can also do workshop registration directly, saving hours of phone conversation and administrative time. You can even link to a direct payment system where the customer does all the work.
- Create affiliate relationships.

Blogs

A blog (which is the shortened version of the term *weblog*) is a type of Web site, usually directly maintained by the author with regular entries of commentary, descriptions of events, or other material such as graphics or video. The verb *blogging* refers to maintaining or adding content to a blog. Blogging is a great way to get your thoughts out there and to attract followers.

Many blogs provide commentary or news on a particular subject; others function as more personal online diaries. A lovely example, by life coach and therapist Karma Kitaj, owner of Life Spring Coaching and author of *Women Who Could . . . and Did* (2002), is *Retirement As You Want It* (http://www.retirementasyouwantit.com).

Blogs can do almost everything a Web site can do, are less costly, and do not even require a Web designer to maintain. There are many coaching blogs available, so check out what others are doing before you launch yours. A "blog catalog" can be found at http://www.blogcatalog.com/directory/coaching. A sample award-winning coaching blog is available at http://findyourcoach.blogharbor.com/blog.

Twitter

Twitter is a social networking and micro-blogging service that enables its users to send and read other users' updates, or "tweets," which are text-based posts of up to 140 characters in length. Updates are displayed on the user's profile page and delivered to other users who have signed up to receive them. Senders can restrict delivery to those in their circle of friends, but someone can "follow" you (you will receive a message if they do) unless you restrict them from your circle.

In November 2008, Forrester Research estimated that Twitter had four to five million users, making it the third largest social network after MySpace and Facebook (the largest in the world, with 55 million monthly visitors). Even Twitter's founders are amazed at its growth and are the first to admit they have yet to define their ultimate business model. It is clear, however, that in our fast-paced world, there is a need being filled by having a place for snippets of personal information.

From a marketing perspective, both blogs and Twitter took off in late 2008 to early 2009. One does not have to be a "techie" to use them, but there is a learning curve to make the *best* use of them.

Affiliate Marketing

Affiliate marketing is an Internet-based marketing practice in which a business rewards one or more affiliates for each visitor or customer brought about by the affiliate's marketing efforts. Affiliate marketing—using one Web site to drive traffic to another—is a form of online marketing that is thought of as one of the best online marketing programs available to small business. It involves usually hosting links, banners, and product information on a Web site or blog and then getting paid a flat fee or percentage of a sale when a visitor clicks through on these links and makes a purchase. There is no risk because you only pay after the results are delivered. By using an affiliate marketing program, you agree to pay your affiliate partners a referral fee for each lead or sale that is generated. Here are some tips on how you can make a coaching affiliate program stand out from the crowd:

1. Find a niche market.
2. Locate niche partners—Web sites that have viewers interested in your niche market or programs and products to which you can refer your audience. You will want to find partners who have already built traffic and would benefit from your affiliate offer. Your offer should be a win–win for both you and your affiliate partners.
3. Provide your affiliate partners with creative and promotional material. Make the job of marketing your products or services as easy as possible. If you are marketing partners' products, then make sure they provide everything you need.
4. Be on the lookout continually for new affiliate partners.
5. Take care of your partners. Communicate with them by welcoming them to your affiliate program, and send out updates on product additions or changes. Give them tips and advice on how to be successful in marketing your products. Always pay them on time, and make sure they do the same.

It takes time to build a successful affiliate marketing program, but the financial reward can be significant. Coaching can link to so many other products and services, such as books, training, and healthcare products, to name a few.

Crafting Your Plan

On the following pages are lists of possible direct and indirect actions that you can take in building a client base. Go through them all and mark them according to your level of effort:

- very willing,
- neutral (I will if I have to),
- a challenge (I would if I believed I could), or
- strongly opposed (against my values; I could never bring myself to do it).

Once you have established these rankings, group them accordingly. If you know yourself to be someone who does best with a big challenge, start with the "challenge" grouping first. If you are a pretty straightforward person, then start with the "very willing" group first. Only go to the "strongly opposed" list if you have had significant success and are willing to risk failure to learn something. That group probably represents your greatest growth edge as well as your best business potential. Over time, you want to confront it.

Once you have your list, you can organize it into a strategic marketing plan. There are many ways to do that, but most important are having a clear time schedule and budget. Start by figuring out how many hours per week you plan to devote to marketing. You might want to take your own inventory of values and do a personal mission statement first. That will ground you in how you want coaching to fit into your life. Appendix G includes some additional forms to help you get organized. You may see "comments" sections on some of them. This is where you can record your emotional responses to doing the specific tasks. Here, you can gain valuable insight that will reveal where you need to develop your marketing muscle and bring to your own coaching. Remember, many of your clients will be dealing with similar issues—especially if they are in business!

Highlight the techniques below that most attract you. Then, use the ranking system suggested previously. Notice which ones you find most challenging; those may be areas in which you need more training, such as taking a writer's workshop, going to a networking class, or joining Toastmasters International to get comfortable with public speaking. Do not assume you cannot do something just because you have not done it before. Your small business owner clients will face the same issue. What would you help them do?

I. General Marketing and Networking Ideas

- *Get on referral lists* with appropriate organizations.
- *Join your professional group's or training program's referral services.* All are online.
- *Contact other professionals in your area and let them know the benefits of coaching.* If you get lists and write letters, then make sure you follow-up with a phone call and regular mailings of brochures and updated materials. Do not deluge people, but keep your name on their radar.
- *Create an informal network of practitioners* with complementary skills and niches that do not compete with yours. Develop "strategic alliances" with other businesses.
- *Join one or more* professional, educational, recreational, social, religious, or spiritual groups. Let people know what you do.
- *Always carry business cards* with you. Keep brochures or flyers for date-sensitive programs with you as well.
- *Join your local Chamber of Commerce and/or Rotary club.*
- *Set up a booth* at conferences or job fairs.
- *Attend networking functions* with the goal of meeting a certain number of new people each time. Do not forget to follow up.
- *Write thank-you notes* each time you receive a referral. Many professionals do this routinely. Let people know: "Your faith and trust in referring to me meant a lot."

- *Send an appreciation gift* to those who refer more than once or who make a substantial referral. Christmas is a good time, but any time is good.
- *Join a leads group,* such as Business Networking International or a local business owners group.
- *Volunteer to be a speaker* at groups you belong to. Seek out groups in your area of expertise (for example, singles clubs if you are a relationship coach!).
- *Volunteer your services* for a nonprofit or a company you would like to work with. Or offer your services to a client for free. It will be easier to "claim" clients.
- *Use your own waiting room* to market. Create an informative brochure on coaching or a "tips" pamphlet on your niche topic (for example, "The Top 10 Tips for Planning a Successful Retirement").
- *Accept charge cards.* It makes it easy for clients to pay you.
- *Limit the amount you spend on advertising*—unless you have a clearly thought-out plan. Be willing to run the same ad in the same publication over a minimum of six months. Avoid jumping from one publication to the next.
- *Try to recession-proof your services.* Work stress and job loss coaching are good areas to incorporate in your personal coaching practice for down times; creative problem solving and making do with less are good themes for corporations and entrepreneurs.
- *Do not drop a good idea if it is not immediately successful.* A friend spent a number of years seeking the ideal spot for a day spa before he opened it. It was wildly successful when he finally did! He had also learned a lot during the period of time he looked for a location and probably avoided many costly mistakes. We can learn as much from what does not work sometimes than we do from what does. When things do not work, do market research (even if informally) and find out why. Call other people doing something similar and ask how it worked for them. For instance, did putting an ad in a particular publication bring them results?
- *Get and stay educated in your field.* Take classes, participate in meetings, keep increasing your learning and your expertise. You do not want to assume the expert stance with your clients, yet you do want to be an expert at coaching and in your niche area.
- *Look at your current referral sources if you are already in private practice and send notices to them detailing your transition into coaching* or the addition of coaching to your existing services. Distinguish the differences between coaching and therapy and offer a complementary session to acquaint them with coaching. If they are reluctant, then make sure they know you give complementary sessions to anyone new to coaching. That will lessen the risk to them in referring to you.
- *Give a free talk at your local library, school, or church.* Volunteer to speak at a nonprofit organization.
- *Do a press release and send it to your local paper.* Call to follow up. Press releases work best if associated with a community service–oriented or newsworthy event. You can also tie your coaching into issues in the news that might be relevant to your practice.

- *Improve your speaking and writing abilities.* Go to Toastmasters or take a train-the-trainer course, attend a writing class, or get a ghostwriter to write for you if writing is not something you like to do. Writing and speaking are your main marketing tools!
- *Get a list of local small and medium-sized businesses and offer special reduced-fee sessions or a complementary session to employees.* In an economic downturn, offer coaching to the corporate "survivors" (that is, those who survive layoffs). Employees in reduced workforces experience a range of emotions: They may be angry about their work loads and are under tremendous stress; they miss their coworkers who were terminated and may feel guilt about being able to keep their own jobs.
- *Read the newspaper and become educated* on current trends and local news in order to anticipate changing needs in the marketplace.

II. Specific Ways to Create a "Pipeline" and Generate Referrals

Writing and speaking are the primary ways in which to market yourself.

Writing

- *Write an article for a professional publication.* Try to submit it to time it with a workshop or presentation you may be giving.
- *Have an article written about you* in a local newspaper or professional publication.
- *Send a press release to local newspapers* about anything new or newsworthy you may be doing—for example, a talk for a local business or professional organization, a new publication, a new group, or running a 10K for charity.
- *Write an educational pamphlet* on a topic that may be of interest to a number of people. Make the giving of valuable information the goal of "10 Tips for Meeting Your Ideal Partner" or "How to Balance Your Business and Personal Life: A Short Guide for Entrepreneurs." Provide your contact information on the back of the pamphlet and ask professionals you know whether you can leave it in their waiting room.
- *Create a newsletter.* Keep it simple and informative. You can send out both online (e-zines) and print versions. Sending an online newsletter is inexpensive, but you need to make it worthy of people's time or they will resent it. Make sure you include helpful information, including dates of upcoming programs or events relevant to your niche that might be of interest to them.
- *Put a pamphlet or brochure on your Web site in PDF format.* It will open in full color, look and read just like an original, and appear very professional.
- *Prepare a press packet* that is always available to send immediately when you receive a call. Update it frequently. Make sure to include a bio and business card, brochures if you have one, separate sheets on special programs you may offer, and articles about coaching. It is okay to use general articles on coaching if you do not have any about you or written by you, but you may want to make every effort to get at least one article with your name (and photo). It definitely adds to your credibility.

Speaking

- *Develop a speaking program.*
- *Do a workshop with another professional* if you are anxious about presenting on your own. If you do, then plan to divide your topic to showcase each of you individually during the talk.
- *Have a more experienced colleague invite you to speak* for a short time during one of their presentations. Bring business cards with you.
- *Develop a free, one-time workshop and plan an ongoing paying group to follow.* Keep your fee relatively low to start. Build goodwill, and you will soon have a following on your topic.
- *Put individual clients who have similar issues together to form groups.* You will get more new referrals to a group that already exists than to one forming for the first time.
- *Learn to conduct teleclasses* and lead a phone group around your topic.
- *Start an online chat room* that meets weekly, and bring all your clients together around a common theme (for example, building a business, parenting issues).
- *Join Toastmasters International.* This is a free group that can help you develop skill in and comfort with public speaking. If you already are comfortable, then you can practice and improve your speaking abilities.
- *Take a "train-the-trainer" class* with the American Society for Training and Development or at Kripalu.

Print Materials

- *The "press kit" or information packet:* This packet contains a brochure (if you have one), biography or resume, business cards, articles written by or about you, and product information sheets (for example, "What is Personal Coaching?").
- *Brochures:* These materials receive mixed reviews. They can be expensive to produce (entailing printing and designing costs if you want them to look professional) and may not yield the reward commensurate with the expense. You also get locked in once you go to print, and often the nature of people's work changes over time. Let your practice evolve until you are confident it will not change much before you print a brochure. The exception might be producing one on your computer with minimum expense. A simple white page can be used instead.
- *Business cards:* It pays to spend money here. Try to be as specific as possible about what you really do, and place this information on the back of your card or use foldover cards. Do not hesitate to say all the things you do on one card to keep it simple—for example, coaching, counseling, and consulting. Some of you may prefer different cards. It does not matter as long as you keep both on hand at all times.
- Try to make your card interesting but not too unusual. If it is a unique size or shape, people will not know what to do with it. My card is red on the back with white lettering and always gets a positive comment from people, but it is very difficult to get

printed correctly. Make sure you have white space somewhere on the card so you or the person you give it to can write added information on it if necessary.

- *Biographies and resumes:* A resume is rarely needed. A white page biography, however, can be useful for including in (corporate) proposals.
- *Information sheets:* These materials describe coaching clearly, particularly the kind of coaching work you do. Use case examples of successful coaching or client testimonials. When using testimonials, try to get your clients' permission to use their name and position.
- *Newsletters and e-zines:* These sources are a great way to get your name in front of people. Include solid and useful information. People will take note! Although there are a few prepackaged coaching newsletters, most coaches prefer an e-zine (a periodic publication distributed by e-mail or posted on a Web site). The word *e-zine* is the abbreviated version *electronic magazine*. E-zines are typically focused on a specific subject area, and coaching lends itself well to this format.
- *Pamphlets and white papers:* Write a "tips" pamphlet or "top 10" list (for example, "10 Tips on Growing a Successful Business"). If your material is educational and informative, then it will not seem like marketing. You also help referral sources solve the problem of talking about you when they do not fully understand what you do.
- *Specialty items:* These items include bookmarks, buttons, bumper stickers, even T-shirts and offer a creative way to promote your services and your company.

Advertising

- *Periodicals* (newspapers, magazines, other companies' newsletters) give you repeat exposure but may be costly. You also usually lack control over where your ad is placed. Some are worth it usually when your niche specifically matches a publication, when cost for repeat placement is relatively cheap. The worst mistake is to place an expensive ad and then pull it after the first month because you have not garnered results. You really want to give advertising six months.
- *Yellow Pages:* Some cities such as Boston now have sections for coaching. Many coaches also list under "Career Counseling."
- *Professional conference program booklets,* including preconference publications, are overlooked sources of advertising.
- *Professional or trade papers and organization newsletters* (church, temple, condo) are good ways to reach a niche audience.
- *Learn to lead teleclasses and webinars:* These can be a valuable source of exposure and, eventually, income. There are several sites that will list your classes and even train you to lead them. This modality is great for anyone who loves to and is good at leading groups.
- *Open up to use technology to maximum advantage:* Coaching lends itself to a number of cutting-edge technologies that may not always be suitable for therapists. If you

are not computer savvy, *take lessons*, especially in using the Internet. Hire a computer consultant to work with you (or barter coaching with them).

- *Get yourself on or start a cable TV show or radio show in your area:* Invite other coaches. When I began coaching, I was on a cable show in a neighboring town where the coach host interviewed a different coach each month. The show appeared about 40 times during the month at various times of day. One of my clients' mothers happened to see the show on which I was the guest and told my client, "your coach is famous . . . I saw her on TV!" More recently, I appeared on cable TV in my own town with two of my clients, which was very inspiring. I had no idea of what a big impact coaching with me really had on them. The show also gave me a tape, and I can upload segments on my Web site. Another cable TV appearance in early 2009 was focused on the job market and gave me an opportunity to reach viewers struggling with their job searches.

- *Develop an "add-on" skill or a product:* Use of an assessment tool (see the Resources section for an extensive list). Pick one that does not require certification. This technique is particularly good for those interested in corporate work. Develop an expertise, for example, in stress reduction, emotional intelligence, or mediation/alternative dispute resolution training.

Referrals

- Happy coaching clients are your best resource. *Serve your clients (and their families, friends, colleagues) well*, and they will multiply.
- *Meet and surpass your clients' expectations:* Be effective. "Underpromise and overdeliver." Be impeccable in all of your client interactions.
- *Do not hesitate to tell your therapy or counseling clients you are developing a new service in your business or practice:* Be clear that it might be a conflict of interest (depending on the ethical code of your first profession, licensing issues, and so forth) for them to become a coaching client if they have been a therapy client. You can, however, bring coaching skills into an existing therapy relationship. You still want your clients to be aware of the services in the event that they know someone who might benefit. After all, they are the best judges of your work. (If your clients are interested in coaching while still in therapy with you, refer them to a trusted colleague. Most professional codes of ethics recommend that the primary relationship, in this case the therapy relationship, is honored and protected.)
- Always *be helpful:* If you cannot see someone, make sure they get to the right person. Leave a prospective client with a helpful tip. Champion the efforts of and acknowledge your clients sincerely but liberally. They may think of you and give your name to someone else even if they do not become a client themselves.
- *Measure customer satisfaction:* Use an exit interview similar to one you might use for weekly calls, but add a few ending questions.

- *Always follow up with clients who drop out unexpectedly* and make sure you understand the specific reason for their departure. Ask, "Is there anything I might have done differently for you to continue?"

Summary and General Pointers

1. *Create a tracking system* to assess the results of your marketing efforts.
2. *Create a timeline for what you wish to accomplish.* Reward yourself when you complete tasks and reach markers on your timeline.
3. *Develop a 30-second "elevator talk"* (see Appendix K) to tell people you meet what you are doing. Practice saying it easily and enthusiastically.
4. With each new contact you make, *ask for other names* to contact.
5. *Become an effective networker:* If you are shy, then be remembered by your graciousness and follow through.
6. *Always carry business cards* with you.
7. *Always have a professional appearance and demeanor:* Being seen at the supermarket yelling at your child may not be what you want to project!
8. *Read the business pages:* Watch for trends and opportunities.
9. *Have a good plan for self-care*, especially during times of intense marketing efforts. Do not burn yourself out!
10. *Think of your coaching practice as a business:* It may be easier to make business decisions when it feels less personal. Get a name and a "tagline." My business is called *On Track Coaching and Consulting:* "Grow. Develop. Evolve." Here are a few other examples:
    - **CoachLink:** "Your success matters." Coach referral Web site (Cenmar Fuertes, Loma Linda, CA; http://www.coachlink.net)
    - **In Motion Consulting and Coaching,** "Creative Paths to Logical Outcomes" (Deirdre Danahar, MSW, MPH, LICSW; http://www.inmotioncc.com)
    - **Think People,** "Playground for Creative Change" (Jean DiGiovanna, Chestnut Hill, MA; http://www.thinkpeople.com)
11. *Consider filing a doing business as documents or incorporating:* Becoming a legal entity is a serious step, so get good advice from your accountant and a good lawyer. There may be other advantages or disadvantage, depending on your specific situation. You will feel different when you are the president of your business, and such a designation creates a serious impression of the business. If you work in an agency, set up a separate division for "coaching and consulting."
12. *Plan to spend some money on developing your business:* Try not to get caught up in feelings of lack. You are investing in yourself! If you have difficulty seeing this, or feel unworthy of such as investment, take note and find a book or tape about creating abundance in your life. If you continue to have negative self-talk or experience a "gremlin" about this, get some help (see the Money and Prosperity section in the Resources for references on money and abundance).

Marketing to Businesses

Marketing to businesses is challenging. Success in this area generally depends on a unique offering, either a good personal connection to someone in the company or a good system (one that is well organized, systematic, and replicable) and a bit of luck. Services such as Salesforce (http://www.salesforce.com) are helpful in tracking leads, setting reminders, and researching news on the companies you are interested in.

Many companies have internal coaches or human resource departments that already have contracts with external coaches. Employee assistance programs (EAPs) might eventually become a good source of referrals, but to date, the majority of EAPs focus on services covered by health insurance. The exception may be health and wellness coaching, which is just beginning to be used by EAPs.

One EAP in Massachusetts—KGA, Inc. (http://www.kgreer.com)—has successfully incorporated coaching. KGA says, " Leaders are more responsive when they set their own goals" and offers to guide participants through "the process of defining the characteristics and qualities that are important for a leader as well as the importance of improving for oneself and for the company" providing assessment, development of a plan, and follow-up support to "a variety of organizational and leadership development initiatives including developing current and future leaders, building alignment and teamwork, improving communications and relationships, and sustaining the success of training programs." Upper-level executives that companies tend to invest in rarely go through their EAPs and, in many cases, are allowed the option of working with an external coach. Some executives will hire a coach for themselves and, if satisfied with the results, offer the service to other key members of their team. "Remedial" coaching is needed when one is called to work with a key employee who the company does not want to lose but who is creating problems (usually anger-related behavior) within an organization. In this instance, the coach needs to be careful about the contract. Is the client motivated? Will he or she value the coaching? Is the coach free to follow the client down a path that might, in fact, cause them to leave the company? All of these are issues to consider. As with therapy, the existence of a third-party payor can have an impact on the service provided.

Team coaching and coach training are two growth areas of corporate coaching. Increasingly, organizations are interested in bringing coaching into their corporate culture but are no longer willing to pay the high cost of individual coaching. Connecting with the right buyer is the major challenge. Large organizations are very difficult to navigate and, even when there is a need and interest among some, an initiative can get caught in indecision, red tape, or budget constraints. If you are marketing to corporations, make sure you are targeting real buyers—people who have a budget and can make decisions.

"Being" Issues

"Being" issues are the subtle, often intangible ways of being that are consistent with developing a thriving practice. Over and over, one hears that integrity and authenticity are two of the most important qualities of any successful business. No matter how well

---

"Being" a Corporate Coach

Although I traveled to another state, by coincidence the brother of one of my social work colleagues from Massachusetts just happened to be part of the team I was coaching. I saw the family resemblance immediately, and we realized the connection. During the lunch break, he told the group I was a social worker. Being "found out" was one of my worst fears at that point. (I had never even worked in a corporation . Who was *I* to be there coaching them?)

After lunch, the group joked that I was a "head doctor" and said they must really be in bad shape if I was called in to work with them. When the conversation became more serious, they wanted to know how I got into doing the work I was doing with them, which involved leading them through a strategic planning process and following them for an entire year. What happened in the months that followed was truly extraordinary.

Members of the team opened up and shared very personal things with me such as their dreams and plans for retirement and interest in doing more in their communities. One woman wrote a very poignant e-mail after her mother died, expressing what her mom had meant to her. Another wrote about his wish to retire and work in his church. The richness of these connections translated into the team accomplishing their goals, which was noticed by their leader, a vice president who had hired me and later, after he left the organization and bought his own consulting company, became a business partner!

---

you market your services, if your "way of being" does not match your offering, people will not trust you. I learned this lesson the hard way when I did one of my early corporate engagements (see "'Being'" a Corporate Coach" box).

The intangibles are every bit as important as any of the marketing techniques described. All of your efforts and "doing" will not be fully rewarded without "being" a coach from the inside out—being peaceful and stress free, making a difference in the world, being a champion for health around the world.

The following quote that a client shared with me speaks to the challenge and possibility:

Where Great Dreams Begin
Before a great dream can become a reality, there may be difficulty. Before a person begins a great endeavor, they may encounter chaos. As a new plant breaks the ground with great difficulty overshadowing the huge tree, so must we sometimes push against difficulty in bringing forth our dreams. Out of Chaos, Brilliant Stars are Born.

—Unknown

Summary

- Make a difference.
- Walk your talk—live your own life powerfully even in the face of feelings and circumstances that would dictate otherwise.

- Be generous and loving in what you do, even when being firm.
- Be highly professional, but give up the expert stance.
- Operate at the highest level of integrity.
- Become an educator. Coaching is a young field; spread the word even if you do not get clients. The more people become familiar with coaching, the more likely you will become known to potential clients in the long run.
- Promote others heartily, and they will, in turn, promote you. You can create a free salesforce for yourself by being generous with referrals. What goes around truly comes around.
- Follow your "bliss"—listen to your own quiet, still voice in making your choices.
- Be open to learning and to feedback from others.
- Always do your best.
- Take good care of yourself.
- Have fun.

Self-Exploration

1. Am I in touch with any gremlins I have about marketing?
2. Am I willing to do whatever I need to (including learn new skills) to market effectively?
3. Am I willing to put in the time or money I may need to spend?
4. Have I thought through my vision and mission and made an actual plan?
5. Does my plan express my authenticity?
6. Do I have a coach or coach colleagues with whom I can discuss my marketing strategies and from whom I can receive honest feedback and support?

11

Personal, Legal, and Ethical Issues

Some people regard discipline as a chore. For me, it is a kind of order that sets me free to be free.

—Julie Andrews

Certification Requirements

The International Coach Federation (ICF) is accepted as the certifying body for the coaching profession. There are currently three levels of certification, each of which can be obtained through completion of a coaching certification program (ACTP) or through assembling a "portfolio" of coach-specific approved coursework (ACSTP) in addition to documenting client contact hours, coaching or mentoring by a certified coach, and *adhering to the definition and ethics of the ICF*. Note: The ICF is reevaluating requirements for certification of new coaches and changes may be made in 2010.

Professional Certified Coach (PCC)

Portfolio

- One hundred and twenty-five hours of coach-specific training (not personal development, psychology, or counseling) taught from the "core competencies" of coaching;
- 750 client hours or 25 clients for 1.5 years actively engaged in the business of coaching (clients must have hired you for coaching and not in any other capacity);
- no more than 75 volunteer or pro bono client hours;
- three letters from ICF-credentialed coaches;
- three months of coaching or mentoring for a minimum of 10 hours by a certified coach;
- satisfaction of a written and an oral exam; and
- at least three documents demonstrating you have been, and are, actively engaged in coaching.

Accredited Coach Training Program

- Successful completion of a full coach training program through an ICF-certified ACTP.

Master Certified Coach–Portfolio and ACTP

- Two hundred hours of coach-specific training (graduating from an ACTP fulfills 125 hours);
- 2,500 client contact hours (five years of 20 clients at 0.5 hours per week or 10 years of 10 clients per week);
- no more than 250 hours of volunteer or pro bono client contact;
- 10 client references;
- three letters of recommendation;
- 10 hours of coaching or mentorship by a PCC or an MCC over a minimum of three months;
- a professional contribution to the coaching profession, including books, articles, speaking engagements, or volunteer coaching activity; and
- satisfaction of a written and an oral exam.

Associate Certified Coach (ACC)

- Sixty student contact learning hours of coach-specific training (for example, actual classroom work, direct observation, teleconferencing, cyber courses, and so forth [excluding lunch and breaks]). Training received from a nonaccredited coach training entity must align fully with the ICF Core Competencies (see the Core Coaching Competencies section). The coach-specific training must include 48 hours of *direct interaction* with the trainer(s) (defined as voice-to-voice or in-person training; it does not include cyber courses, mail-order courses, or self-study unless these are used to accommodate a documented disability).
- Two hundred and fifty client coaching hours (60 minutes of actual time spent coaching a client).
- No more than 25 client coaching hours may be pro bono or volunteer.
- Client references for at least five clients.
- Two letters from coaches who hold an ICF credential.
- Satisfactory completion of an oral examination.
- At least three documents demonstrating that the applicant is currently and actively engaged in the business of coaching.
- Agreement to attend ICF-sponsored educational teleforums that will be given especially for those who hold the ACC designation.

The ACC credential is good for three years and then expires. To maintain an ICF credential after an ACC designation expires, the applicant must apply for and receive a PCC or an MCC designation. A fourth certification—relationship or team coach—is pending approval.

Core Coaching Competencies

The following competencies are used as the foundation for the ICF credentialing process examination. The core competencies are grouped into four clusters according to those that fit together logically on the basis of common ways of looking at the competencies in each group. The groupings and individual competencies are not weighted; they do not represent any specific priority in that they are all core or critical for any competent coach to demonstrate. The details can be found in Appendix B.

Setting the Foundation

1. *Meeting ethical guidelines and professional standards:* understanding coaching ethics and standards and the ability to apply them appropriately in all coaching situations.
2. *Establishing the coaching agreement:* the ability to understand what is required in the specific coaching interaction and to come to agreement with the prospective and new client about the coaching process and relationship.

Co-creating the Relationship

1. *Establishing trust and intimacy with the client:* the ability to create a safe, supportive environment that produces ongoing mutual respect and trust.
2. *Coaching presence:* the ability to be fully conscious and create spontaneous relationship with the client, using a style that is open, flexible, and confident.

Communicating Effectively

1. *Active listening:* the ability to focus completely on what the client is saying and is not saying, to understand the meaning of what is said in the context of the client's desires, and to support client self-expression.
2. *Powerful questioning:* the ability to ask questions that reveal the information needed for maximum benefit to the coaching relationship and to the client.
3. *Direct communication:* the ability to communicate effectively during coaching sessions and to use language that has the greatest positive impact on the client.

Facilitating Learning and Results

1. *Creating awareness:* the ability to integrate and accurately evaluate multiple sources of information and to make interpretations that help the client gain awareness and thereby achieve agreed-upon results.
2. *Designing actions:* the ability to create with the client opportunities for ongoing learning, during coaching and in work–life situations, and for taking new actions that will most effectively lead to agreed-upon coaching results.
3. *Planning and goal setting:* the ability to develop and maintain an effective coaching plan with the client.
4. *Managing progress and accountability:* the ability to focus attention on what is important for the client and to leave responsibility with the client to take action.

Ethical Issues and Standards

Coaching is a self-governed profession similar to mediation. The ICF as it exists today was formed in 1996 when the two existing professional associations—the Professional Coaches and Mentors Association and the ICF—merged. Standards of practice, credentialing, and ethical guidelines were soon established. An older version of the ICF Code of Ethics stated that coaching

> adheres to a form of coaching that honors the client as the expert in his/her life and work, believes that every client is creative, resourceful, and whole. Standing on this foundation, the coach's responsibility is to:
>
> 1. Discover, clarify, and align with what the client wants to achieve
> 2. Encourage client self-discovery
> 3. Elicit client-generated solutions and strategies
> 4. Hold the client responsible and accountable

The 2009 standards (ICF, 2009, Part One, Section 1) have been revised to include the following definitions:

- "*Coaching:* Coaching is partnering with clients in a thought-provoking and creative process that inspires them to maximize their personal and professional potential."
- "*A professional coaching relationship:* A professional coaching relationship exists when coaching includes a business agreement or contract that defines the responsibilities of each party."
- "*An ICF Professional Coach:* An ICF Professional Coach also agrees to practice the ICF Professional Core Competencies and pledges accountability to the ICF Code of Ethics" (the complete Code of Ethics can be found in Appendix A).

To clarify roles in the coaching relationship, it is often necessary to distinguish between the client and the sponsor. In most cases, the client and sponsor are the same person and therefore jointly referred to as the *client*. For purposes of identification, however, the ICF (ICF, 2009, Part One, Section 1) defines these roles as follows:

- "*Client:* The 'client' is the person(s) being coached."
- "*Sponsor:* The 'sponsor' is the entity (including its representatives) paying for and/or arranging for coaching services to be provided."

"In all cases, coaching engagement contracts or agreements should clearly establish the rights, roles, and responsibilities for both the client and sponsor if they are not the same persons."

Some tension exists between coaches, who sometimes believe psychotherapists are trying to usurp the profession, and therapists, who may feel increasingly threatened by coaches moving into neighboring territory—especially during a recession. There have, however, been remarkably few legal cases involving coaching, while, at the same time, ethical standards and the call for research have intensified.

The most significant threat to coaching as a distinct profession was evident in a 2003 case in Colorado, in which an MCC, whose clients lived out of state, was charged with practicing without a license and asked to register as an unlicensed therapist. When she refused and decided she could not afford the legal costs involved in defending her practice, she was forced to close the practice. The case led to the ICF beginning a lobbying effort that led to an amendment of the *Colorado Mental Health Act* exempting coaches from oversight. In 2004, the Act was signed into law, with a statement that the "the provisions of this article shall not apply to professional coaches who have had coach-specific training and who serve clients exclusively in the capacity of coaches."

Subsequently, according to Pat Williams, founder of Therapist University, a concern arose in Ohio that was quickly resolved (see Williams & Anderson, 2006, p. 19). At the time of this writing, I am told there is a possible problem in Nevada concerning the legitimacy of Reiki practice; it is being called into question as an unlicensed form of massage therapy, which may affect coaches who are also Reiki practitioners. The Colorado Act is also "sunsetting" in 2010.

The ICF is committed to maintaining coaching as a distinct profession, and due to both the worldwide nature of the profession and the business applications of coaching, it is my belief that coaching, like mediation—which is conducted by both therapists and nontherapists (lawyers)—will remain unregulated.

When to Refer to a Therapist

The following 10 indicators that a client should be referred to a mental health professional, provided by clinical nurse specialist Lynn Meineke, appear on a part of the ICF Web site access to which is restricted to members only and in Appendix C along with suggested ways of recognizing and dealing with them:
Your client:

1. Is exhibiting a decline in his or her ability to experience pleasure and/or an increase in being sad, hopeless and helpless.
2. Has intrusive thoughts or is unable to concentrate or focus.
3. Is unable to get to sleep or awakens during the night and is unable to get back to sleep or sleeps excessively.
4. Has a change in appetite: decrease in appetite or increase in appetite.
5. Is feeling [excessively] guilty because others have suffered or died.
6. Has feelings of despair or hopelessness.
7. Is being hyper alert and/or excessively tired.
8. Has increased irritability or outbursts of anger.
9. Has impulsive and risk-taking behavior.
10. Has thoughts of death and/or suicide.

It is important to note that the appearance of any one of these indicators, except for indicator 10, which must be referred and followed up on immediately, does not indicate the immediate need for a referral to a psychotherapist or community mental health agency; everyone can experience a very brief episode of any of the indicators. However, if you see that several indicators are emerging and that the client is not presenting as whole, competent, and capable, then it is time for a referral to a mental health professional.

Conflicts of Interest

At the other end of the spectrum are questions regarding business ethics and professional conduct with clients. Like therapists, coaches are asked to avoid sexual intimacy with clients and sponsors and to avoid "knowingly taking any personal, professional or monetary advantage or benefit of the coach-client relationship, except by a form of compensation as agreed in the agreement or contract." This may explain why some well-known business coaches may receive fees in the thousands (Coutu & Kauffman, 2009, p. 91). Because business coaches can sometimes save companies millions of dollars, early practices, particularly prior to the dotcom bust in 2002, often involved taking a percentage of a company's profits as part of the fee.

Coaches, however, are not totally discouraged from being friendly with, socializing with, or even touching clients as long as they maintain a clear focus on the clients' needs. Professional guidelines state the following: "I will be responsible for setting clear, appropriate, and culturally sensitive boundaries that govern any physical contact I may have with my clients or sponsors" (ICF 2009, Code of Ethics, Section 3, 17).

Confidentiality and Privacy

Confidentiality is addressed in the ICF (2009) Code of Ethics (Part Two, Section 4) as follows: As a Coach,

- "I will maintain the strictest levels of confidentiality with all client and sponsor information. I will have a clear agreement or contract before releasing information to another person, unless required by law."
- "I will have a clear agreement upon how coaching information will be exchanged among coach, client, and sponsor."
- "When acting as a trainer of student coaches, I will clarify confidentiality policies with the students."
- "I will have associated coaches and other persons whom I manage in service of my clients and their sponsors in a paid or volunteer capacity make clear agreements or contracts to adhere to the ICF Code of Ethics, Part 2, Section 4: Confidentiality/Privacy standards and the entire ICF Code of Ethics to the extent applicable."

Duty to inform is not mandated, raising the question of whether a coach can be asked to testify against a client. However, there have been remarkably few, if any, known cases of coaches who have been implicated in legal situations.

Diversity

Although not specifically stated, the view of clients as "creative, resourceful, and whole" can be construed to address issues of culture, religion, gender, and race. Although some coaches and coaching practices specifically address these issues, it was only clearly stated in the Association for Coaching's Code of Ethics and Good Practice that "coaches must be sensitive to issues of culture, religion, gender and race."

Diversity is addressed in relation only to following ICF criterion for committee member participation (italics added):

- Visionary
- Strategic
- Passion for the profession
- Strong personal and professional foundation
- Desire to be collaborative, creative, and innovative
- *Open to different perspectives*
- *Represent the diversity of our field across geography, culture, and training*

Cultural diversity presents itself in a number of aspects of coaching. In private industry, organizations are flatter, less hierarchical, leaner, and more focused on the customer. As corporations seek to adjust to rapidly changing markets, with "just-in-time production," delivery, and marketing, community development professionals agree that no one-size-fits-all program can meet the diverse needs of communities and organizations. Every community has its own unique issues. Coaching offers an opportunity to use strategies flexible enough to work in diverse situations and effectively apply new tools and best practices currently available.

In communities, the issues that might be dealt with in this process are a declining economic base, a lack of skills and insights about how to work together to figure out how to move forward, the exodus of residents, and conflict and the need to work with diverse populations. Coaching helps in these situations by enabling people to find common ground and a common focus and, in so doing, building on the strengths and assets of the group to increase local capacity. In chapter 15, I provide a number of examples, both in the United States and abroad, in which these principles have been put into practice.

One-on-One Client Work

Many clients who seek coaching cannot afford to pay for it. An unwritten ethic among coaches is to work with a number of clients for a substantially reduced fee or pro bono. "Jane" was one such client.

During the time I was working with Jane, I also had a chance to lead a balance workshop for 20 staff members of a well-known Boston homeless shelter. Half the staff had been residents of the shelter themselves at one time, and although employed, many were living a marginal existence, commuting long distances and feeling stressed out. They wanted to "give back" but were struggling. Not only did their personal challenges allow them to connect with the workshop, particularly with the wheel of life exercise about life balance, but they also saw how they could be more effective in their interactions with the current residents by using the principles of coaching. It was an inspiring day.

There are many opportunities to coach individuals who otherwise would languish in the community. By treating them as "creative, resourceful and whole," and helping them make a plan, coaching can make a big difference with otherwise marginalized individuals.

Community Impact

Nowhere is coaching more suitable for affecting a culturally diverse population than in education. One of my early trainees, for example, instituted a coaching and mindfulness

Jane

Jane was in her late 50s and had experienced intermittent homelessness for many years. When I met her, however, she was living in a small rented room. She had seen my name in an article on coaching in the local newspaper and called stating, "I'm in my late 50s, and this is my last chance to 'get a life.' Will you help me? " She had given up on therapy many years earlier, saying that she knew why she was homeless (she had witnessed extreme violence in her home as a child, which made having a home feel dangerous to her) but that knowledge did not help her "get a life." She was extremely motivated, had some friends and acquaintances who appeared willing to support her effort, and so I took her on as a "pro bono" client.

We met monthly—sometimes more frequently than others—for several years. I helped her make a plan for her life—something no one had ever suggested to her. We mapped out what she wanted for herself and brainstormed how she would get there. She has two interests: yoga and photography. She had learned yoga in a homeless shelter and was practicing daily. I helped her get funding from the state to get her yoga certification, and she began trading yoga lessons for things she needed. She convinced a local merchant to accept a barter agreement for some presentable clothes, and she started walking into local businesses. Soon after, she was hired by a new hotel in her neighborhood to give yoga lessons at their spa. She also managed to find an old but workable camera and demonstrated a wonderful eye—particularly for unusual glimpses at human nature. A friend paid for her to enlarge some digital images that she donated to a charity auction, where it sold for $750. This boosted her confidence and encouraged her to do more.

She was estranged from her only sibling, a sister, but when she learned her sister was dying, she begged me to help her have a "family coaching" session by phone with her sister so she could say goodbye. Her sister died a few weeks later, and my client vowed to stop smoking. (Her sister died of lung disease.) She said she felt "in control" of her life for the first time and it would be easy. It seemed it was. A few months after that, she decided to move closer to her nieces and nephews with whom she reconciled. Her parting gift was a copy of the photo that had sold at the auction and a small check that she insisted on giving me. Periodically, I receive short notes of gratitude from her. "Thanks for believing in me," "I'm doing okay. Thanks for giving me back my life."

school-to-work program in the Boston public school system. The success of the program can be summed up by a remarkable achievement. An important student–faculty–parent meeting, held on a very icy December evening, had 100 percent participation. Individually, the students had greater success in their placements than previous cohorts.

Another training participant brought the Wheel of Life exercise to over 250 freshman high school students in a disadvantaged school system in northern Massachusetts. The principle and teaching staff were so impressed with the impact on the students, they asked the participant to return annually.

Administrators at North Carolina State University are using "Extension Educators." They not only have identified coaching as entirely new but also have isolated several key factors in motivating and empowering students:

- Coaching empowers people to control their destiny.
- Coaching involves a kind of facilitation that builds community capacity. Coaches are on the side, nudging, supporting, jumpstarting, encouraging inclusivity, helping people "name the elephant," and be more reflective.
- Coaching builds capacity for developing and implementing projects.

One participant trained by the program observed that, "If coaching is a new thing, then perhaps the program area best suited to coaching is civic participation."

Corporate Coaching of Diverse Employees and Teams

More leaders will be needed to coach those who have backgrounds and experiences drastically different from their own (Goldsmith & Lyons, 2006).

In a global economy, a manager in Massachusetts might be responsible for a team of software engineers in rural Lithuania. An executive might be working with a team distributed in both urban and rural areas of the United States, in London, the Philippines, India, and Mexico—each working for local organizations with different cultural norms and expectations. Not being able to recognize and deal with resulting biases can have huge negative consequences for organizations. Social workers are ideally trained to bridge these gaps and help leaders adjust their styles to work successfully with multicultural teams and to help individuals from other cultures adapt to U.S. norms.

A Newton, Massachusetts, coaching company, Diversity Coach (http://www.culture-coach.biz), has addressed just this issue. Although Diversity Coach has more consultants than coaches (they partner with an executive coaching organization for coaching services), they perform the role of coaching their clients in the importance of addressing diversity issues. Their vision is "to create an inclusive environment of mutual respect and trust across cultures and in diverse groups." Their mission is "to enhance people's understanding of how culture impacts their daily lives and to empower them to thrive in an ever-changing world."

The leader–coach can improve outcomes when dealing with diverse teams by questioning his or her own assumptions about the individual or the cultural group they represent. Rather than taking actions based on past beliefs and conclusions, which the leader–coach has made on the basis of on their own prior experiences, and cultural background, the coach should question those assumptions, gather input, and explore meanings with the client an understanding of differences are fully examined. This approach should lead to improved results when coaching those of diverse backgrounds.

12

Specialty Coaching

It is those who concentrate on but one thing at a time who advance in this world. The great man or woman is the one who never steps outside his or her specialty or foolishly dissipates his or her individuality.

—Og Mandino

Coaching Attention-Deficit Hyperactivity Disorder

According to the Attention Deficit Disorder Association (ADDA) (http://www.add.org), there has been an "explosion" of diagnosis, treatment, and research regarding attention-deficit hyperactivity disorder (ADHD), also referred to as attention deficit disorder. ADHD coaching is a perfect fit for therapists, educators, and learning specialists.

ADHD can profoundly compromise functioning in multiple areas of living. Research and clinical experience suggest that ADHD-related difficulties can lead to significant educational, occupational, and family dysfunction and contribute to a variety of health, social, and economic problems. For some individuals, traditional methods of treatment—such as medication, behavioral or psychological therapies, and education or workplace accommodations—are not sufficiently effective and different intervention approaches and services are needed.

Within the scope of new services and treatments, ADHD coaching has emerged as a distinct new field. ADHD coaching is practiced by coaches who work one-on-one with people with ADHD and occasionally with their families, including the spouses of adults. ADDA supports ADHD coaching as an "effective nonclinical intervention" and as an adjunct or additional intervention within the range of available methods of treatment. Coaches who specialize in ADHD coaching can be very creative, for instance providing daily 10-minute phone conversations to some clients to create daily accountabilities. Other clients benefit from support in the areas of choice and focus.

Like all coaching, ADHD coaching is an ongoing partnership that helps clients live more effective and satisfying lives by deepening their learning, improving their performance, and enhancing their quality of life. Clients with ADHD have the same human needs as any coaching clients, but in addition they face unique challenges related to ADHD, which can interfere with their quality of life. These challenges may include hyperactivity, impulsivity, or inattention as well as the belief that they cannot reach their goals because they have ADHD. Individuals with ADHD, in fact, are more likely to describe themselves as "lazy, stupid, or crazy" (Kelly & Ramundo, 1995).

ADHD coaches support their clients in developing a comprehensive understanding of both the nature of ADHD and the impact of ADHD on their quality of life. In addition, ADHD coaches work with clients to create structures, support, skills, and strategies. Coaching assists clients with ADHD to stay focused on their goals; face obstacles address core ADHD-related issues like time management, organization, and self-esteem; gain clarity; and function more effectively. ADHD coaches work with their clients to develop strategies to move forward toward their goals, to deepen their self-awareness, and to continue moving toward fuller and more satisfying lives. The client is seen by the ADHD coach as resourceful and, thus, with increasing self-awareness, as fully capable of discovering his or her own answers.

ADHD coaching also helps clients to

- understand that the sources of many of their challenges are the results of ADHD, not of personal shortcomings or character flaws;
- safely examine areas of failure and areas where they want to be held accountable;
- heighten self-awareness and self-observation skills and use those heightened skills to improve decision making and performance;
- change perspective when "stuck" (for example, by learning new ways to work with procrastination, perfectionism, staying on task, or being more consistent); and
- become aware of their own learning styles, processing styles, and learning preferences so they can enhance their ability to learn and comprehend information and situations.

ADHD coaching can be an important part of a comprehensive program for individuals with ADHD. The coaching process initiates and encourages taking ownership and self- responsibility. Coaching is individualized and action focused, so the client is working to build productive habits and systems that lead to a fulfilling life. ADHD coaching also provides support from an understanding coach who is knowledgeable about ADHD.

ADDA believes that one of the most critical steps in advancing ADHD coaching services is to establish a standard of care for people seeking coaching, and it has published a set of guiding principles. These guiding principles are not a coaching cookbook or intervention manual, but, rather, they seek to define the essential elements of ADHD coaching to help consumers increase their understanding of ADHD coaching and its benefits.

Several organizations now certify ADHD coaches, including

- ADHD Coaches Organization (http://www.adhdcoaches.org/education);
- ADD Coach Academy (http://www.addcoachacademy.com); and
- the Optimal Functioning Institute ADD coach training program (http://www.addcoach.com).

How ADHD Coaching Works

Nancy Ratey (2002) has emphasized the role of coaching in forging new neural pathways in the brain, allowing the brain to develop new competencies in areas that had been deficient. Coaching paves the way for such new learning to occur. Ratey further emphasized that a coaching intervention can make a real difference in how people with ADHD negotiate their particular deficits and cope with life on a daily basis, describing five major deficit areas that can be seen playing out in the lives of people with ADHD and for which coaching can offer successful compensatory strategies.

Coaching Maintains Mental Arousal and Focus on Completing Goals. Motivation frequently lags for individuals with ADHD, particularly around routine or uninteresting tasks, due to mental underarousal. For instance, people with ADHD often have a hard time pursuing abstract goals. Coaches seek to bring the more abstract goals to the forefront of their clients' minds, keeping attention aroused to work on a goal and stay focused until it is completed. The ADHD coach will work with a client to create deadlines and stay on top of schedules, conducting meetings and regular phone check-ins aimed at reaching goals, keeping the client's brain aroused, vigilant, and on track.

Coaching Helps Modulate Emotions. Shame, guilt, and fear plague many people with ADHD. Years of being labeled "lazy," "stupid," or "irresponsible" add an emotional burden that can derail their actions, throw them off course, or even paralyze them. The ADHD coach helps clients learn how to deal with disempowering feelings and their triggers and explore effective ways to modulate emotional responses and reduce self-blame.

Coaching Maintains Motivation and Sustains the Feeling of Reward. The ADHD coach helps clients maintain motivation by reminding them of their top priorities and of all the gains they have made, boosting self-confidence. By breaking large projects down (referring to as "chunking it down") into smaller, more manageable tasks, coaches keep clients more focused on their goals. Some clients might need help in discovering a system of tangential rewards to sustain motivation and progress forward.

Coaching Acts as the "Executive Secretary of Attention." Clients with ADHD are challenged in their ability to gather and focus ("gross prioritize") their attention in a more global way. By keeping the big picture in mind, the coach helps clients to sustain their attention on their primary goals, pointing out distractions and helping to create strategies when distractions do arise.

Coaching Supports the Client's Ability to Self-Direct Actions and to Change Behavior. The ADHD coach compensates for client deficits in the ability to self-direct by providing daily reminders and helping the client sequence out the details of needed actions. By asking clients to process and evaluate outcomes and consequences, the coach encourages clients to be more proactive in their choices and less reactive to the environment. Coaches also help clients develop the ability to estimate the time it takes to complete tasks by having ongoing discussions, reviewing plans for timelines, and processing out the details and sequences of tasks. The coach helps clients to, in effect, observe themselves in action, by processing out events, asking questions, and providing feedback. Clients with ADHD are also very adept at self-deception and forgetting the pain of past procrastination and other self-defeating behaviors. The ADHD coach can remind them of both the negative consequences of old behaviors and the positive rewards of change.

What to Look For in an ADHD Coach

The relationship between coach and client is one of partnership. As in all coaching, a good fit between coach and client is vital. Below are questions suggested by ADDA that can be asked of a prospective ADHD coach in determining the specifics of how the partnership will work:

1. What can I expect from a coach and from coaching?
2. Can the coach clearly explain what I will get from coaching?
3. What would this partnership look like?
4. How exactly would we work together to accomplish what I need to accomplish?
5. What would an individual session look like?
6. How, where and, when would we meet—face-to-face meetings, telephone, or electronic mail?
7. What happens if I miss a session?
8. How much will it cost?
9. What is the method of payment (check, credit card)?
10. Can I access my health insurance to pay for coaching?
11. Does the coach have a sliding fee scale?
12. Are my records and information kept confidential?
13. Are there ever times when information about me would be shared with other professionals?
14. Under what arrangement?
15. How long has the coach practiced?
16. What is his or her experience in the coaching profession?
17. By whom and when was he or she trained?
18. Is this coach certified?
19. Does he or she have a specialty: executive coaching, spiritual coaching, career coaching, lifestyle coaching, and so on?
20. Does he or she associate with other coaches belonging to coaching organizations?
21. Does this coach have specific ADHD coach training?
22. Does he or she have knowledge of medications, other professionals who diagnose and treat, and relevant resources?
23. Does the experience of this coach match my needs?
24. What else would I like to know about this coach and his or her work to discern whether we might work well together?
25. Does this coach's philosophy, style, or approach fit with how I believe I function best?

In addition, having some direct experience with ADHD—in oneself or one's family—is often a plus, particularly if you are a good model for overcoming ADHD issues.

As with the choice of any coach, in choosing an ADHD coach, the prospective client should be as clear as possible in stating specific needs, challenges, and desired goals. The coach's ability to listen, answer important questions, clarify, and be a total support and advocate are even more important. ADHD coaching is an area of coaching in which expert knowledge is invaluable.

ADHD Coaching Competencies

Even though there is currently no standard training, licensure, or certification of ADHD coaches, according to the ADDA, ADHD coaches should possess the following core set of standard competencies:

1. the ability to use a structured goal-setting and goal-achievement orientation as the primary method of working with clients;
2. training and facility in active listening, questioning, strategizing, planning and goal setting, designing actions, monitoring progress, and creating accountability;
3. knowledge about ADHD, including a thorough understanding of the neurobiological nature of ADHD, comorbid conditions, and the effect these conditions have on the client's quality of life;
4. familiarity with current literature and research about ADHD and ADHD coaching;
5. commitment to stay abreast of rapidly expanding information on ADHD and ADHD coaching, demonstrated by ongoing professional reading and regular attendance at professional conferences, workshops, and trainings;
6. a fund of ADHD coaching tools, strategies, and interventions and the skill to use them appropriately to assist clients in areas like daily living (that is, areas like sleep, eating, exercise, medication management, and social skills), time management, organizational skills, and work or school issues;
7. the ability to help clients move back and forth between the big picture and the details;
8. skill in helping clients self-advocate;
9. the ability to collaborate with psychiatrists, psychologists, psychotherapists, educators, employers, and others on the client's behalf;
10. consistently demonstrating professional ethics;
11. the knowledge needed to give appropriate professional referrals; and
12. the skill to explain coaching logistics—frequency of contact, fee structure, and coaching format.

Professional Guidelines and Standards for ADHD Coaching

The following standards represent a framework for ethical ADHD coaching practices:

1. ADHD coaches provide access to ADHD coaching for all appropriate clients regardless of age, gender, race, religion, or sexual orientation.

2. ADHD coaches respect and hold in confidence all client information, obtaining permission to discuss or disclose client information only when a formal release form, specifying the terms of release, has been signed.

3. ADHD coaches clearly and accurately represent their level of competency, expertise, training, and credentials.

4. ADHD coaches explain in detail the terms of the coaching contract, including administrative details and financial arrangements.

5. ADHD coaches define the coach–client relationship and under no circumstances take advantage of a client personally, socially, sexually, or financially.

6. ADHD coaches avoid all possible conflicts of interest by disclosing to the client any personal gain they might receive by referring the client to another professional or advising the client to take some specific action.

7. ADHD coaches continue learning about coaching and ADHD specifically, attending and participating in professional conferences and organizations.

8. ADHD coaches build strong and ethical professional relationships with colleagues to enhance and promote communication and collaboration for the benefit of the ADHD client.

9. ADHD coaches maintain full compliance with any institutional or governmental regulations and laws that may apply regarding research.

All ethical guidelines and standards for practice are directed toward maintaining and promoting quality assurance in the field of ADHD coaching. All ADHD coaches have a responsibility to uphold and advance the values, ethics, and knowledge of the profession.

Andy

Andy was a highly successful young man in the real estate business. Despite his history of long-term behavioral and learning issues related to ADHD, he had formed a positive relationship with his employer and demonstrated the capacity to handle complicated problems in managing commercial properties and making deals. He was so valuable to his employers that they agree to pay for coaching, which his mother requested for him when she noticed he was mismanaging his money, not caring for his nice condominium, and having problems with his girlfriend, whom mother liked and felt was a very positive influence. Andy had no intrinsic interest in being better organized but did realize he had narrowly escaped what could have become big problems for his employers, to whom he felt indebted, so he accepted coaching.

We worked first on eliminating "tolerations," which led him to take control of his schedule and finances. He realized he needed to devote time every day to staying on top of his life or it would deteriorate quickly into chaos. When he saw how much money he could save just by paying attention, he was further motivated. Despite the fact he saw having a plan and accountabilities as "insulting [his] intelligence," he followed the plan diligently and was promoted.

Professional Collaboration in ADHD Coaching

Professional collaboration is often essential with the ADHD client, making ADHD coaching particularly well suited for social workers, who are generally experienced in working with a network of professionals from various disciplines.

Increasingly, other professionals—including physicians, who frequently become frustrated with ADHD patients—welcome the input of a knowledgeable ADHD coach. In addition, a primary function of the ADHD coach is to empower clients to speak, negotiate, and better manage for themselves, so it is often important for interventions to be conveyed and strategies planned in cooperation with other individuals living and working with the client.

Professional collaborations occur with the express written permission of the client. These collaborations are for the purpose of providing first-hand communication of details, information, assessments, or observations, as well as for establishing or fine-tuning goals, strategies, and resources.

Coaching Asperger's Syndrome and Autism Spectrum Disorder

According to Wikipedia ("Asperger Syndrome," n.d.),

> Asperger syndrome [also called Asperger's syndrome, Asperger's disorder, Asperger's, or AS] is an autism spectrum disorder [ASD], and people with it therefore show significant difficulties in social interaction, along with restricted and repetitive patterns of behavior and interests. It differs from other autism spectrum disorders by its relative preservation of linguistic and cognitive development. Although not required for diagnosis, physical clumsiness and atypical use of language are frequently reported.

Experienced learning disabilities educator Ellen Korin (http://www.ellenhkorin.com/) has published the first books on coaching individuals with autism: *Asperger Syndrome: An Owner's Manual—What You, Your Parents and Your Teachers Need to Know* (2006) and *Asperger Syndrome: An Owner's Manual 2 For Older Adolescents and Adults—What You, Your Parents and Friends, and Your Employer Need to Know* (2007). The books are based on the premise that despite a common diagnosis, each individual with Asperger's syndrome is genuinely unique and that to create successful plans for living, learning, and loving with Asperger's, strategies must be derived from the individual's profile. The strategies Korin presents are generally recommended for people on the higher level, or "upper end," of the spectrum (Asperger's syndrome and high-functioning autism).

Coaching, Korin (2007) states, is "best seen as an adjunct or add-on service rather than a sole solution" (p. 42). The model relies on the ability of individuals to

- work on identifying behaviors they exhibit that may be hindering them in life and work;
- have the ability to identify neurotypical behavior ("neurotypical people have neurological development and states that are consistent with what most people would

perceive as normal, particularly in regards to their ability to process linguistic information and social cues" ["Neurotypical," n.d.]); and

- try out "unnatural" ways of behaving to improve in certain areas.

The manual suggests the availability of increased self-awareness, as in other forms of coaching, and the necessity of motivation and willingness to try new things. The coach, Korin tells readers, does not act as an "expert" who has all the answers but as a "partner in a collaborative effort for the purpose of solving problems" (Korin, 2007, p. 42)

The areas of life in which Korin suggests coaching can help Asperger's clients are

- job,
- school,
- social skills,
- organizational skills, and
- life skills.

In a way that reflects her years of experience in simplifying information for achieving clarity with her client population, Korin (2007) presents one of the clearest and best summaries of coaching that I have seen. Coaching, she states, is

- therapeutic but not psychotherapy;
- focused on the here and now and on the future;
- concrete and practical;
- directive;
- a pragmatic problem-solving approach;
- metacognitive—using knowledge about your own thoughts and the factors that influence your thinking; and
- collegial—a sharing of knowledge and insight between equals. (p. 43)

Coaching is not

- psychotherapy,
- focused on the past,
- concerned with others' roles in the cause or solution to problems, or
- a relationship between an "expert" who withholds insights and a "patient" who must discover what the expert already knows. (p. 43)

Like with other coaching clients, the process begins with self-assessment along the lines of a whole-life review, starting with where the individual is at that moment. In what areas might they have developmental delays? Typical areas are these:

- use of money,
- time management,
- organizational skills,
- tasks of daily living, and
- relationships and socialization.

As with other clients, the next step is helping clients create a vision for where they want to go, set goals, and make a plan to help them get there. In helping readers create their vision, Korin (2007) asks them to "think big but not off the planet" (p. 15). She likens the vision to a "fantasy with a reality base." Examples might be owning one's own home or being married and living in the country, but the recent appearance of an Asperger's finalist on *America's Top Model* and a cardiologist with Asperger's being portrayed on *Grey's Anatomy* suggest that big visions can become realities for individuals with Asperger's too.

Noting that individuals with Asperger's may lack skills in certain basic areas that many of us take for granted, Korin outlines ways to address issues such being invited to dinner or how to act in social situations, ranging from weddings to funerals. Specific skills and strategies include charting anticipated events by cataloging the situation in advance. Goals are looked at in relation to hindrances, and interventions are systematically targeted. Here are two examples (Korin, 2007, p. 42):

Goal:	Hindrance:	Intervention:
1. Obtain a job	Come to job interview in messy clothes and uncombed hair	Notice what others wear, ask for help to create a more traditional appearance
2. Make a friend	Avoid eye contact, not know name	Greet by name with eye contact

Korin (2007) also suggests use of the *PAPI* model, which she suggests can be used for preparing for new situations and comprises four steps:

- **P**redict
- **A**nticipate
- **P**repare
- **I**mplement

For example, in transitioning to independent living, an individual might need to

- predict:
  - shopping,
  - cooking,
  - bill paying, and
  - transportation.

He or she might need to

- anticipate:
  - needing to learn simple cooking,
  - making a schedule so as to remember to do chores,
  - needing to take a driving course;

- prepare:
  - break learning skills down into small steps (for example, getting a driver's permit); and
- implement:
  - follow the plan and review as needed to move onto the next skill.

Korin (2007) describes many more excellent examples of the application of coaching, but of particular importance is her guidance not to be stopped by the "fear that changes in behavior will compromise your identity" (p. 87). She points out that despite "loneliness and disappointment with everyday life," most people with Asperger's become accustomed to and, in many cases, even "proud of" their "quirky" image (Korin, 2007, p. 87). (We see this frequently in the high tech world.) She then goes on to help readers distinguish the core identity characteristics (the "essential you"), including intelligence and personality characteristics, such as honest and kindness, from "behaviors that can be changed," such as style of address, learning to make eye contact, looking for "shades of gray," and practicing flexibility.

Korin happens to be an old friend of mine, with whom I had the pleasure of reconnecting recently when I attended her first book signing. We have since marveled at how she arrived independently at a model that is so consistent with both basic coaching principles and reflects principles similar to those of ADHD coaching. She is an adjunct faculty member at Antioch University New England, where she has created and presented professional development workshops for educators, parents, and clinicians, and she also does presentations for the Asperger's Association of New England, universities, public and private schools, and school districts, and educational collaboratives. These workshops for professionals and parents focus on "Understanding and Working Effectively" with people on the autism spectrum and coaching with this population. Korin has also designed and conducted workshops for teens and adults on the autism spectrum, focusing on post-secondary planning, preparing for college and independent life, time management, and presentation of self.

Coach Kristina Elaine, a trained scientist, describes the advantages of Asperger's Syndrome as including focus, attention to detail, and logical decision making—traits that are invaluable leadership and entrepreneurial skills. She coaches Asperger's clients

> because I love the way your mind works. My son and many members of my family have Asperger Syndrome. I've lived with them. Worked with them. Listened to them. Coached them. Loved them. I enjoy the Asperger mind; the creative logic, the straightforward honesty and the ability to piece together intricate puzzles. It is a challenge and a delight to keep up with your mind. (Elaine, n.d.)

Coaching Health and Wellness

There are two benefit areas to health and wellness coaching—the indirect benefit of wellness coaching on disease prevention and the direct impact coaching can have on disease management.

Wellness and Positive Psychology

Positive emotions have been linked with better health, longer life, and greater well-being. Money, however, beyond having enough to get by, has little incremental effect on one's sense of well-being. On the other hand, chronic anger, worry, and hostility increase one's risk of developing heart disease and other chronic diseases. A 2005 Harvard School of Public Health study found that people who were generally hopeful were less likely to develop hypertension, diabetes, or respiratory tract infections than those who were less hopeful. Another, more recent Harvard Medical School (2009) study discussed techniques and approaches for enhancing well-being. Many of them are emphasized in coaching techniques:

- Mindfulness: being "present" to what is versus what is not (abundance versus scarcity) reduces frustration and anger.

- Use your personal strengths and values: people are likely to feel more energetic and to perform better when drawing on personal capacities than they are when they are trying to use a capacity that comes less naturally. Likewise, when you set out to do something in alignment with your highest values, those values you hold dear, you are likely to work harder and have more energy and persistence for the task at hand. The key is knowing what your strengths are, and coaching, as we have seen, focuses on just that. The strengths most closely linked to health and well-being are gratitude, hope, vitality, curiosity, and love.

- Develop gratitude and appreciation: Gratitude helps people feel more positive emotions, relish positive experiences, have better health, and deal better with adversity. A University of California study asked three groups to write down a few sentences each week, focusing on five things. One group wrote about things they were grateful for that had occurred during the week, the second group wrote about what had displeased them, and the third group wrote about events they had observed with no emphasis on positive or negative. The gratitude group, over 10 weeks, felt more positive and optimistic than the other two and also had fewer medical visits!

- Become more engaged through "flow": The more engaged one is in meaningful activities, the more satisfied and greater one's sense of well-being. As a landscape painter, when I am "in the groove," I am always amazed at how several hours can pass without my being aware of even one distressing thought. It may be a coincidence, but one well-known woman artist from New England lived to age 107!

- Celebrate: Do not keep the good moments of life to yourself. Let yourself be happy when you complete a project or when something goes well. Savor your accomplishments.

- Slow down: Having the time to enjoy your life and participate in the activities you want predicts happiness better than does monetary affluence. Try to eliminate some of the less enjoyable ways you spend your time (tolerations?) so that you can enjoy the more pleasurable experiences in your life.

Wellness Coaching

Wellcoaches, whose founder and CEO, Margaret Moore, is also a cofounder of the Harvard Medical School Positive Psychology program, emphasizes that individuals need more than ever to take charge and be the bosses of their own health and wellness, developing a personal wellness plan. Wellcoach coaches work with individuals and with companies who allow for wellness coaching through their employee assistance programs. The diverse areas of well-being covered include the following:

- overall health and well-being,
- energy,
- regular physical activity,
- physical injury management,
- healthy eating habits,
- healthy sleeping habits,
- weight management,
- medical condition(s) management,
- work issues,
- work and life issues,
- family or relationship issues, and
- quitting or reducing smoking.

Certified wellness coaches have diverse credentials, including being social workers, physicians, physical therapists, nurses and nurse practitioners, health educators, dieticians, psychotherapists, exercise physiologists, personal and athletic trainers.

My Wellness Vision

- Being vigorous and youthful
- Being a great role model for my family
- Being at my best energy at least 50 percent of the time
- Being as physically active as long as I can
- Making weight management and stress management part of my everyday life

My main motivators are to set a great example for my children and to feel physically strong and energetic so that I can handle my life's demands.

My main obstacles are the long hours and heavy demands of my work life.

My strategies to overcome my obstacles are to schedule my exercise routines and relaxation activities on Sundays for the following week, and to shorten those activities (rather than miss them) when I hit crunch times.

Clients are encouraged to create a wellness vision and plan. The vision might look something like the "My Wellness Vision" box on p. 150 (for a sample wellness plan, see http://www.eac-wellcoaches.com/images/Sample.Wellness.Plan.pdf).

A typical wellness plan might include a list of activities one will be engaged in consistently three months from now, such as "do aerobic exercise three times per week," and a list of first week's goals, such as start an exercise and food log. These interventions may seem simplistic, yet few people do them on their own, and the wellness coach provides accountability along with the health expertise to move people in the right direction.

Research on Coaching for Disease Management

I am pleased to have been included as the proposed trainer in the first National Institute of Health grant to study the impact of coaching on the management of Type 2 diabetes. Inspired by my one-day coaching workshop, Eileen F. Hayes of the University of Massachusetts Nursing School, who had long been interested in mentoring of nurse practitioners as well as the management of adult diabetes, saw the potential of a study (Hayes, McCahon, Panahi, Hamre, & Pohlman, 2008). Recognizing that of the many complexities involved in managing diabetes, motivating patients to change behavior may be the most challenging, Hayes suggests the use of coaching in the primary care encounter between patients and nurse practitioner. The study proposes training nurse practitioners in coaching skills and comparing their patients' results with those followed in traditional "command and control" practice. The significance of the study is that past life style change programs tested and found to be effective in controlled clinical trials are time and resource intensive. Coaching can be integrated into regular office visits without additional charge. To effectively implement the approach, nurse practitioners will need to participate in coach training, making them pioneers in developing a body of knowledge needed to validate coaching effectiveness.

The long-term implications that coaching holds the promise of being more time and resource efficient in the management of many chronic diseases requiring patient lifestyle changes, and that self-coaching skills can be taught to patients for long-term disease management. We have seen informal results with HIV-positive teenagers and diabetic children and are excited about the possibility of being able to bring coaching to actual clinical trials for disease management.

Corporate Wellness

American Specialty Health (ASH), a 20-year-old, a San Diego based "health improvement organization" offers its Healthyroads Coaching for Weight Management, Tobacco Cessation, and Healthy Living to its own employees at no cost. ASH Employees are encouraged to participate in group wellness activities such as group walks and each year the employee who makes the most progress on their personal health plan gets one week of paid vacation. This model is one I expect will be adopted by more companies over time, as it is well-known that medical expenses are one of the highest costs of labor.

Business Coaching

Business coaching, according to the Worldwide Association of Business Coaches (http://www.wabc.org) is "the process of engaging in meaningful communication with individuals in businesses, organizations, institutions or governments, with the goal of promoting success at all levels of the organization by affecting the actions of those individuals."

Business coaching enables the client to understand and enhance his or her role in achieving business success. The business coach helps the client discover how personal characteristics, including a sense of self and personal perspectives, affect personal and business processes and the ability to reach objectives within a business context. With this method, successful coaching helps the client learn how to change or accommodate personal characteristics and how to create personal and business processes that achieve objectives.

Business coaching establishes an atmosphere of trust, respect, safety, challenge and accountability to motivate both the coach and the client. In turn, this requires that the business coach conduct an ethical and competent practice, based on appropriate professional experience and business knowledge and an understanding of individual and organizational change.

Note that the definition offered here includes a range of practices (for example, team and individual coaching) within business coaching. But throughout, there is a clear focus on achieving business objectives. It is this focus that distinguishes business coaching from other types of coaching. Business coaching addresses the client's development for the purpose of achieving business outcomes rather than achieving personal or career goals.

Business coaching is a broad area that can be broken down in various ways:

- business size (by employees):
  - small office (fewer than 10 employees),
  - small (fewer than 100 employees),
  - medium (fewer than 500 employees), and
  - large;
- business size (by capitalization):
  - large-cap (over $5 billion),
  - mid-cap (between $1 and $5 billion), and
  - small-cap (under $1 billion);
- for and not-for-profit;
- public versus private or closely held; and
- type of ownership (sole proprietor, partnership, family business, or corporation).

Within businesses, we tend to look at similar issues, however, regardless of the type of business or industry:

- how to set and achieve business goals or solve business problems;
- how to motivate, get the best out of people, and boost morale;

- performance improvement (how to do it better and faster with fewer errors);
- creating more profit by looking at areas of the business such as sales, marketing, advertising, profit growth, business systems, time management, and team building strategies;
- leadership development (particularly for future or emerging leaders);
- building a team of motivated, passionate performers;
- succession planning;
- life balance and revitalization—particularly of leaders—and burnout prevention;
- helping business leaders rediscover their passion for their business or chosen career;
- navigating changes in the economy and particular markets;
- causing business breakthroughs (fostering creativity, "out-of-the-box" thinking, and problem solving on new levels);
- "remedial" work with individuals deemed important to the organization who have issues that limit their effectiveness;
- providing a trusted sounding board who will help individuals take steps and implement business choices; and
- creating accountability for producing results.

An online survey conducted by Clear Coaching from October to December 2006 with a wide range of companies that have employed coaches (including Tesco, Coca Cola, Ogilvy & Mather, and others), reported the following results:

- increasing perception (63 percent),
- acquiring a new skill or improving on an existing one (50 percent),
- improving work relationships within a team (50 percent,)
- being able to see other perspectives (47 percent),
- applying some clarity to work life (43 percent),
- increasing motivation (43 percent),
- performance approved (43 percent),
- coachee seemed happier (40 percent),
- enjoying a better atmosphere (40 percent),
- growing into a new role (40 percent),
- changing approaches to work situations (37 percent), and
- agreed goals were obtained (20 percent).

Several large coaching firms such as the Ken Blanchard Companies (https://www.coaching.com/), Marshall Goldsmith Partners (http://www.marshallgoldsmith.com), Stephen Covey, and Franklin Covey personal coaching (http://www.franklincoveycoaching.com) dominate the landscape, along with numerous individuals who bill themselves as business coaches. Current trends in business coaching, according to Sabine Dembkowski and Fiona Eldridge (2003), include six key trends:

1. Driving for professional standards: There are currently no universally accepted standards for business and executive coaching which leads to confusion in the marketplace. Currently, anyone can use the title of "executive coach"—something the authors feel will need to change.

2. "Coming of age"—more professional services: Over the last several years there has been a marked growth in the professionalism of companies and individuals providing coaching. This move towards adopting professional practices seen in other professions ranges from providing formal contracts setting out roles and responsibilities and clarifying expectations about intended outcomes/results to well-produced websites and other marketing materials. Less immediately visible, but equally important, is a continuous intellectual debate in academic and professional journals.

3. Initiating corporate coaching cultures: Some organizations are fully committed to developing a coaching culture to create a new management style. However, many others are still in the process of working out how to move away from old "command and control" cultures. The benefits of changing to a coaching culture are many and in line with the trends towards flatter organizational structures with clear accountabilities. The benefits include creating a more open and honest climate, increased perception of organizational commitment to individual development and career advancement, a more rapid spread of behaviors that support organizational values, and a decrease in expenditure on external support.

4. Growing your own—internal coaching activity: Cost control has contributed to the trend within some large organizations to develop their own internal coaching capabilities. Internal coaches are generally developed through human resources, and programs tend to fall into two main types:

   - In some, individuals take on coaching responsibilities in addition to their existing day-to-day activities.
   - In other programs, individuals are trained as coaches and then devote all their time to providing coaching across the organization.

   Internal coaching activities are perceived to be a cost effective option for organizations especially for entry, lower, and middle-management levels and, hence, this is a trend which is likely to spread more widely.

5. The growth of differentiation: These market forces are leading toward more differentiated coaching services tailored to the level of the individual client. In particular there is a small premium market emerging for senior executives with some coaches to CEOs earning $2,500 per hour.

6. Meeting the demand for integrating methods: The trend is for buyers to demand a greater breadth of techniques, experience and training from their coaches and for coaches to integrate material from multiple disciplines to have a great breadth of techniques in their toolkit.

Coaching the Changing Organization

In the life cycle of every business, new needs and challenges continuously arise. At different times, there are different needs: growing pains, stagnation, resistance to change, rapid change, mergers and acquisitions, regulatory changes, technology advancements, and staff morale—all of which affect leaders, managers, and employees.

Coaching Managers

A key contribution of coaching in organizations is the move towards improved work performance through management development techniques. The goal in training managers is to help them help employees learn and be more productive on a day-to-day basis and to take interest in and promote employees' long-term development and overall work–life balance.

The coaching model encourages employees to take greater responsibility for their own learning and development while forging a positive relationship with the manager. OnTrack Coaching has had the opportunity to train managers as well as human service professionals in coaching, using the same principles but with a different emphasis. We strive to help managers learn to coach employees on how to think better and make better decisions—not to think for them. In the process, we ask the manager to look at his or her own style of getting things done, not infrequently leading the manager to make adjustments in the service of those they manage (for example, giving up the idea "if I do it myself, I know it will be done right"):

- What coaching is, what is isn't, and how it makes a difference in the workplace
- The coaching mindset—a strengths perspective, how to internalize it
- "Coachability"—knowing when it is present and what to do when it isn't
- Three types of coaching
  - Developmental/performance based
  - Remedial
  - Leadership development
- The role of 360s and other assessments
- Key coaching skills
  - Committed listening
  - The coaching "contract"—how to establish workability in the coaching relationship
  - Knowing what to coach
  - Turn goals and commitments into sustainable action
  - Accountability
  - Understanding breakdowns and how to manage them
  - Causing performance breakthroughs
- Shifting into a coaching relationship
- The reluctant coachee
- The reluctant coaching manager

- Coaching conundrums
- How to turn around a stuck coaching process

In addition to specific practical skills to use with employees, managers have an opportunity in their personal development, which may include

- clarifying their values,
- creating or expanding a vision for their management role,
- learning to strengthen their personal foundation to achieve balance and greater fulfillment in their role,
- identifying places they may be stuck and developing new tools to improve their own performance, and
- increasing effectiveness at turning goals and commitments into action.

Stephen Covey's Famous "Seven Habits"

Stephen Covey is the author of the international bestseller *The Seven Habits of Highly Effective People*. Published in 1989, it is his most well-known book, selling more than 15 million copies worldwide, and has changed the lives of many, many people.

Covey got many of the ideas and language for *The Seven Habits of Highly Effective People* from Peter Drucker's (1966) classic *The Effective Executive*. Covey promotes "the character ethic," which is about aligning your values with "universal and timeless" principles.

Covey described "principles" as "external natural laws," whereas "values" are "internal and subjective." He discovered that values govern people's behavior, but it is principles that ultimately determine the consequences of their actions. Covey presents his teachings in a series of seven now well-known habits:

- Habit 1: Be Proactive: Principles of Personal Choice
- Habit 2: Begin with the End in Mind: Principles of Personal Vision
- Habit 3: Put First Things First: Principles of Integrity and Execution
- Habit 4: Think Win/Win: Principles of Mutual Benefit
- Habit 5: Seek First to Understand, Then to be Understood: Principles of Mutual Understanding
- Habit 6: Synergize: Principles of Creative Cooperation
- Habit 7: Sharpen the Saw: Principles of Balanced Self-Renewal

Team Coaching International (TCI)

The work of Team Coaching International (http://www.teamcoaching.international.com) derives from some of the work of the Center for Right Relationship but is uniquely focused on coaching business teams versus training. TCI uses a unique team assessment that measures the team as an entity. Two dimensions are focused on:

1. the productivity continuum: the factors that support the team's ability to be productive; and
2. the positivity continuum: the factors that create a positive environment.

Productivity strengths include the following:

- alignment,
- accountability,
- resources,
- decision making,
- proactivity,
- team leadership, and
- goals and strategies.

Positivity strengths include the following:

- trust,
- respect,
- camaraderie,
- optimism,
- values/diversity,
- communication, and
- constructive interaction.

Teams can be assessed in four quadrants:

	Low team productivity	High team productivity
High positivity	• Collegial, friendship based • Lack of effective focus • Insufficient sense of urgency • Not results oriented • Incompetence tolerated • Sense of connection and fun	• Successful, fun • Synchronicity, flow • Challenging goals, inspiring vision • Change proactive • Open communication • "Good" teamwork
Low positivity	• Atmosphere of criticism, • Blame and cynicism • Overwhelm • No fun • Fear of job loss or failure • Fire-fighting • Turf protection • "Poor" teamwork	• Focus is on efficiency • "Just do it" mentality • Clear objectives • Retention problems, burnout, high turnover • Driven • Competitive

TCI's Team Diagnostic assessment measures these levels. Coaching, based on the assessment, is guided by four principles:

1. Teams exist to produce results.
2. The team is a living system.

3. Team members want to be on high performing teams and want to contribute.
4. The team has within it the means to excel.

The job of the coach is to

- reveal the system to itself,
- pay attention to the energetic field in which the team is operating,
- highlight and celebrate "deep democracy,"
- listen for the urge (what is trying to happen?),
- reinforce coresponsibility, and
- increase positivity/reduce negativity.

Although the "client" is the system, the coaching skills one practices with individual clients can still be applied:

- model transparency,
- normalize the current state,
- name the energetic field, and
- be enormously curious. Be fascinated!

Important questions for the team in forming the coaching contract might be the following:

- What culture do we want to create?
- What will help this team to flourish?
- What will we do when there is conflict and/or pressure to perform?
- How will we know the process is working? What behaviors will we observe?

Here are some typical opportunities for team coaching:

- *Due diligence:* Venture capital and private equity firms want to know the likelihood of making a good investment and the management team of a company is critical to success.
- *Restructuring and onboarding:* Reducing manpower while maintaining the same workload places stress on a team. Changing the team by adding personnel is always risky. When teams blow apart, failure often follows.
- *Mergers and acquisitions:* Merging two different cultures often instigates counterproductive turf wars and personality clashes. Team coaching can speed the integration, lower the risks, and improve morale.
- *Project teams:* Improve productivity and positivity in cross-functional teams, encourage cohesive relationships among internal and external team members, and demonstrate how to navigate through sticky problems such as competing resources.
- *Any change-driven mission:* Minimizes risk of helping teams manage transition and avoids failed projects, which can be both costly and demoralizing.

Team coaching is widely used in healthcare industry. TCI has worked with groups in Minnesota, Washington state, the United Kingdom, and Canada. The healthcare world is already organized around teams. Teams are a natural structure and an essential way to fulfill the mission. According to Phil Sandahl, CCO (chief coaching officer) of TCI, unlike in private industry, where teams are created around projects and there is often competition over resources, in healthcare organizations members of teams are all nominally dedicated to the best outcomes for patients' health and welfare. Although teams are a natural structure in healthcare, Sandahl has said, most healthcare organizations have little understanding, apart from role differentiation, of how teams work. Physicians have less and less time for patients and it matters to everyone in the healthcare system that patients are not getting the care they deserve.

Angie Snell, "process improvement specialist and team coach," worked with a team at a hospital system in Minnesota that has since been rated as highest in employee satisfaction for the state. She used TCI's Team Diagnostic Assessment, which measures a team's productivity and positivity in fourteen specific categories. Upon delivery of TCI's team coaching process, overall productivity scores increased by 30 percent, and positivity scores increased by 31 percent. These results positioned the team high on both the productivity and positivity scales—the ideal for teams. Some categories, such as resources and optimism, increased by as much as 47 percent. Although the quantity of resources and challenges did not improve, the team's perspective and attitude about what was available to them certainly shifted during the coaching process, enabling them to work together in more efficient and effective ways.

These results also correlate to business measures. One of the best indicators of an overall experience is a patient's or family's "likelihood to recommend" a clinic to others. A higher likelihood to recommend strongly relates to greater patient loyalty and overall satisfaction.

After the team coaching process was delivered, there was a 12 percent increase in positive responses to a question measuring the "likelihood to recommend," putting this clinic in the 85th percentile in the nation, as measured by the Press Ganey Patient Satisfaction survey. The average number of patients seen per day (productivity) in this clinic also increased significantly. As this clinic began to see and experience itself as a high-functioning team, so did its "customers."

In reimbursement systems, patient satisfaction is frequently a factor in how reimbursement is calculated. The original survey rated this clinic below the desired threshold. The postcoaching survey raised patient satisfaction to the highest level.

At Johnson & Johnson, Sandahl worked with a dozen engineers to deal with "team toxins." A highlight of the engagement was when one of the team members noted that not only was it invaluable to his work but he could also use the principles at home in relating better to his family.

Teams are also used extensively in government work—particularly in the military where mission is everything and "command and control" is the order of the day. TCI worked with a group of U.S. Navy six sigma black belt specialists and their trainers—world experts on process, measurement, and productivity who could, at the end of the day, design "any process" yet their manager recognized all processes need to be implemented by people and wanted this group to be more cohesive. The team found more of an identity ("we are the Black Belt team!"), which contributed to their conversation around best practices. A similar group was trained at the Charles Schultz Foreign Affairs Institute in Virginia to use within the State Department.

Group Coaching

Ginger Cockerham is on the ICF board of directors, a master certified coach (MCC), and a senior faculty member for Coach University whose specialty is coaching groups. Her niche areas are leading groups within financial services companies, with certified financial planners, and with coaches to achieve specific and measurable results. She also teaches group coaching at Columbia University Teachers College coaching certificate program.

Examples of coaching groups include the following: executive peer groups for encouraging innovation and change, independent sales professionals within an affiliated company, executive women leaders in international organizations, and managers integrating coaching skills for effective team supervision. Examples of teams include sales teams, leadership teams (CEOs, division heads) for setting strategies, and global work teams (often virtual).

"Advanced coaching skills are similar and central for a coach working with groups and/or team members," according to Cockerham, except individuals need to be recruited from different teams of areas of the same organization. She differentiates group coaching from team coaching using four distinctions:

- Choice versus enrollment (selection): This usually involves the leader (sponsor) being able to share how he or she has benefited from coaching.
- Cocreation (with group) versus collaboration (team leader): The group forms its goals out of the group process but, as in group therapy, the gains are individual.
- Environment of confidentiality versus transparency: Where team coaching must be transparent, group coaching requires confidentiality amongst participants and the coach must be careful to promote this.
- Personal commitment versus team accountability: Team coaching requires all be accountable to the group for success, but in group coaching participants' goals are personal and individual. The power of a group is that when individuals make a commitment to their group members to take specific action, they are much more likely to follow through and do it.

As coaching matures, models are evolving. Sophisticated group and team coaching models accomplish what was once considered unattainable: scaling the benefits of coaching to an organizational level.

Your Best Year Yet

The Best Year Yet personal and team strategic planning process is the one I have personally adopted in my coaching work. Not only did I find it invaluable for my own development

> **The Casey Family**
>
> One of the most dramatic coaching results I had was bringing together five adult siblings and their recovered alcoholic father with whom my client, as businessman, had not spoken since discuss their mother's suicide 20 years earlier. Using the structure of the Best Year Yet program, the family was able to create a new paradigm and design a new future of a "family in communication." Once the children listened to their father's side of the story, they were able to forgive him. They created a Best Year Yet plan that gave them each specific tasks to facilitate their staying in touch. My client, the "responsible" one in the family, felt unburdened and his present home life improved dramatically. He was also grateful his children could have a relationship with their only living grandparent.

as a successful coach, but I saw the impact a simple, replicable program could have consistently with individuals, families, for and nonprofit organizations.

The Best Year Yet is structured on "action and mindset." It has elements of the "one-page business plan" design but adds the critical component of calling participants to create a "paradigm shift" in their way of thinking of themselves and their situation. Action without mindset is insufficient to cause transformational change. One executive who was in danger of losing his job made a complete turn-around. He made a plan in which he committed to taking charge of his circumstances and to being a "leader and good communicator." Within several months he solved the problem that had brought attention to his so-called poor performance, and shifted the nature of communication with his boss to emerge as a hero within his organization. He also began holding town meetings with members of his staff of over 350 and received amongst the highest ratings in the organization.

Birthday Wishes, a nonprofit organization dedicated to providing birthday parties to children in homeless shelters, similarly used the Best Year Yet to declare a growth objective for their organization. They went from serving two to now over 60 homeless shelters in Massachusetts, and the year they made their Best Year Yet plan, they received a grant from the Ronald MacDonald House, the first of many they have received since.

For more information, go to http://www.bestyearyet.com.

Carl Kaestner and the Framework for Exceptional Leadership

Carl Kaestner is an executive coach with 20 years of experience developing senior executives of multinational companies. He acts as a "thinking partner for leaders who seek a powerful catalyst to accelerate business growth by developing a core of leaders who can out-think and out-perform their competitors." Kaestner's experience reaches across industries and world cultures, and uniquely positions him to offer new perspectives to today's most complex and challenging business issues. The basis of conscious and effective leadership, according to Kaestner, is the product of "how you are being" in relation to these values. He has been coaching since the 1980s.

I first met Kaestner in 1999 when he was teaching a summer institute course on executive coaching for mental health professionals. I was immediately struck by the fact that he was not only the "real deal"—having worked with clients including Motorola, IKEA, and the Dalai Lama's nonprofit organization—but that he also had a big heart and a very personal and passionate commitment to the success of each one of his clients and students. He is down-to-earth and easy to talk to, with a sense of humor that immediately puts people at ease. In his characteristically modest style, he has stated that to take coaching beyond "tips and techniques," he "had to learn [business] coaching by creating it." He describes the process as one of "pulling" for versus "pushing" for change. If we get to the core of who we are and get out of our own way, we can "unleash the human spirit." The journey is one of developing mastery in getting people past their "history and drama."

Kaestner came to coaching from business school and a background in corporate higher education finance with undergraduate studies in psychology and organizational development. After working in an early coaching organization in the 1980s, he came to coaching, like many, through his own personal development. A fortuitous connection with a California-based coach who was on the board of a philanthropic organization of the Dalai Lama introduced Kaestner to that group and he had the opportunity to coach leaders from 180 centers (hospitals, schools, meditation centers) around the world.

The values he brings to the process are these:

1. integrity (being true to oneself and to one's organization),
2. caring about people and wanting them to be happy and successful,
3. deep connection (both with the client and within the client in
4. relation to his or her own spirit),
5. caring (about people . . . and people who are caring),
6. drive (making it happen),
7. reciprocity (learning from our clients), and
8. agility (fostering the ability to open up and shift one's thinking).

Kaestner's model places who you (the coach) are—defined by integrity, drive, agility, and contribution—squarely in the middle of a triangle defined by knowledge and skills, functional competencies, and leadership competence.

Coaching Entrepreneurs, Solopreneurs, and Family Businesses

Usually small businesses, these represent a good portion of business coaching clients. A large number of small businesses fail within the first three years. Similarly, few family businesses successfully pass through to the second much less third generation. In the majority of cases, the reasons are personal—the entrepreneur or "solopreneur" (sole proprietor) who gets stuck working "in" rather than "on" her or his business; the family that allows either transgenerational or couples dynamics to interfere with the business of doing business. The coach's role, similar to large organizations, is to be a sounding board, brainstorming and accountability partner and, on some occasions, to confront the owner or family members with behaviors that are getting in the way.

Many entrepreneurs also happen to have ADHD. They are usually extremely creative but despite their tremendous talent lack understanding of how to manage their challenges and capitalize on their strengths. They have little or no idea how their unique challenges negatively impact the success of their business or the quality of their lives, much less the lives of those who work with them. A coach will often be the only one they allow to see the extent to which they are in trouble or way out of balance.

According to David Giwerc, MCC, the entrepreneurial coach is one of a

> growing number of specialized personal performance coaches that includes executive coaches who work with CEOs, writing coaches who help writers meet their deadlines, and personal coaches that help people improve the quality of their relationships and other areas of their personal life.

The ADHD entrepreneurial coach, he states, is even more specialized, combining the necessary skills of an entrepreneurial coach with an in-depth understanding of what it is like to live with ADHD. This is an important distinction because so many entrepreneurs seem to have ADHD, and "to some extent, all entrepreneurs share the same risk-taking, novelty-seeking behaviors that are found in people who have been diagnosed with ADHD." The ADHD entrepreneurial coach understands those character traits and can individuals use them to their advantage.

Family business can be very complex with three different systems interacting with each other—the business, the family, and the nonfamily employees. Traditionally, family businesses experiencing difficulties have sought the help of family business consultants—a unique consulting specialty that interfaces with attorneys and accountants as well as the business owners. Family business coaches may connect with those outside systems but their work is more likely to focus on balancing family dynamics and sound business practices.

13

Personal Self-Development

We cannot have deep and enduring satisfaction unless we have self-worth. We cannot have self-worth unless our lives are an earnest attempt to express the finest and most enduring qualities that we are aware of. Purpose is an important condition for an enduring satisfaction with life.

—Richard J. Leider

Is Self-Employment a Good Fit?

For those who have never had a private practice, this can be the greatest challenge to becoming a coach. Self-employment is challenging in and of itself. It is not secure. It is all up to you and you cannot always predict what will come your way. You need to put yourself out there or people won't know you exist so you need to market and sell yourself—something many people who work in healthcare and human services are reluctant to do—as well as familiarize people with what this new modality is and how it can work for them. I have been self-employed for almost 20 years and, although, it provides great freedom, it can be a roller coaster ride at times. I personally wouldn't have it any other way, but I would never suggest quitting a day job to become a full time coach if you need the income. (The average salary of coaches according to a 2007 International Coach Federation survey was $82,671 for full-time coaches and $26,150 for part-time coaches.) Coaching can, however, be a great fit at the right times in one's career cycle. Many coaches, for instance, have had successful careers and are now looking to coaching as a next step. For others, who have been given no choice, coaching provides a way to use one's strengths in an inspiring way and gain support from a community of people whose purpose is to help others do just that. And, as is the case with almost every profession, if one is creative, ambitious, hardworking, and not afraid to market oneself, speak, write and connect with others (or some combination of the above) it is possible to do quite well.

Appendix H is a simple questionnaire from the Small Business Association. Take the self-test, but do not be discouraged if your score isn't very high. Instead, use this information to be aware of your "growth edge." Put yourself into an inquiry. Here are a few questions to ask yourself:

> **Self-Exploration**
>
> - Is my obstacle internal or external?
> - What would it take for me to overcome this obstacle?
> - Am I motivated to make the necessary changes?
> - Do I need a (business) partner who is comfortable in those areas because I know I am not motivated to make those changes?
> - Will my family support me if I take this path? Emotionally? Financially, if necessary?
> - What other resources do I have? Connections? Intellectual property? Financial?
> - Do I need to consult with someone more experience to brainstorm ideas so I can make it work?

Professional Values and Challenges

Beyond the challenge of adjusting to self-employment, the actual mindset shift transition from therapist or other human service professional to coach can be a challenge. It involves embracing a new set of values, broadening our learning base, learning completely new skills and experiencing potential discomfort in trying on new ways of being and doing. Coaching also asks us to pay better attention to our own self-care—something many human service professionals do not necessarily do well. I remember one of my social work colleagues once saying, "When did we ever vow to take an oath of poverty?" I am not just thinking about financial reward, but also about our failure as a group of professions to protect ourselves from the energy drain of working with seriously ill and often destructive individuals as well as unreasonable demands on our time and personhood by clients, agencies and institutions we work for.

Patrick Williams refers to coaching as an *interdevelopmental* process in which living a great life or moving on that path for ourselves is an integral part of the joy of coaching: "Your life cannot be a mess if your coaching business is going to thrive or if your coaching is to be truly effective." My biggest personal challenge was embracing what I wanted in life, and having the courage to turn a few things upside down.

Self-Care and Personal Renewal

There are several tools that can help you align your personal life in this process. The areas that deserve the most attention are the following:

- *Eliminating "tolerations"* or energy drainers—situations *and* people (or, at least, contact with the people that drain your energy).
- *"Completions" or decluttering*, including relationships as well as the "stuff" that doesn't support one's goals and dreams. Getting "complete" with one's parents and even

ex-spouses can be very liberating. Coaching approaches this not from a psychodynamic perspective of understanding the relationships and "working it through" but rather from a more practical perspective. Does holding on to past grievances serve you or forward your dreams and desires? Usually it doesn't. Completion, which may in some cases, involve forgiveness of even difficult or egregious circumstances, is about seeing ones self-interest clearly. "Getting complete" with people who hurt us in the past does not mean condoning; it simply means agreeing within oneself to let go of anger and resentments that don't support one having a peaceful and meaningful life.

- *Authenticity and personal integrity*—being true to oneself, being "whole and complete." In *An Invented Life*, Warren Bennis (1994) wrote "To be authentic is literally to be your own author . . . to discover your native energies and desires, and then find a way of acting on them" (p. 2). Personal integrity, he says, might entail making amends to others or cleaning up past problems that impact one's self-confidence or create unnecessary noise in our minds. "When you've done that, you are not existing simply to live up to an image posited by the culture family, tradition or some other authority. When you write your own life, you have played the game that was natural for you to play. You have kept covenant with your own promise" (Bennis, 1994, p. 2).

- *Creating a strong financial foundation* from which to operate. For some, this may involve an major financial overhaul; for others, it may involve simplifying one's life; for others still, simply taking charge and becoming a good "steward" of one's resources. Recently, most of us have seen a decline in our incomes and begun to reevaluate our financial futures and the very values we attach to money. A strong financial foundation is more important now than ever.

- *"Extreme self-care"*—arranging one's life to have good balance and gain energy. This involves creating a schedule that works, adequate vacation time, time to do the things one loves to do, be with the people we enjoy being with, eliminating unhealthy patterns of smoking and drinking, health diet and exercise, and time for pampering (massage, yoga and personal body care). Cheryl Richardson, who first coined the term "extreme self-care," has also used the phrase "Be incredibly self-ish." By hyphenating the word in this way, she indicated that we need to take care of ourselves in order to do our best for others. Using the example of the sign above the seats on airplanes (first, use the oxygen yourself before helping the child or person next to you), she gives permission to focus on self-care. Self-care also involves creating good work– life balance—something often very difficult to maintain. Life balance is dynamic—it constantly shifts—so it is important to keep revisiting this area.

There are a number of ways to build this foundation. I personally have found the Landmark Forum to be a particularly useful program for dealing with completions and integrity issues (see the interview with David Cunningham in chapter 15 to learn more about how it works). Cheryl Richardson's (1998) *"Take Time for Your Life* and CoachVille's "Clean Sweep," a self-administered program involving 100 questions regarding your whole life, are also valuable tools. Debbie Ford's (1999) *The Dark Side of the Light Chasers* is an excellent book that can connect you to your Gremlin side. Ruiz's (1997) *The Four Agreements* is also extremely useful in aligning one's integrity. *The 28 Laws of Attraction* (Leonard, 2007) is an excellent template for becoming more attractive and naturally drawing clients to you. And, finally, Jinny Ditzler's (2000) *Your Best Year Yet! Ten Questions for Making Your Next Twelve Months Your Most Successful Ever* is a wonderful personal strategic planning process that aligns your core values with your personal purpose, mission, and life roles.

Jim Loehr and Tony Schwartz (2003) have told us we are a "world hostile to rest" and advise focusing on energy management instead of time management. What they have described as "full engagement" requires drawing on four separate but related sources of energy: physical, emotional, mental, and spiritual. They also caution readers that to build capacity, we need to push beyond our normal limits, but overuse can be as dangerous as underuse. Like athletes in training, we need systematic ways of building our energy reserves. We need to balance energy expenditure and energy renewal.

Regardless of the system one uses, they all point in the same direction. Life is complex and multifaceted. We cannot do our best unless we pay attention to all of the arenas. The do interconnect. We are the common denominator.

Of course, the best way is to have your own coach. In the same way that many therapists go through therapy to experience the process as well as deal with their own life issues, working with a mentor coach is essential. It is actually even required for certification.

Money

Money is a source of struggle and conflict for many. Human service professionals traditionally have operated from a position of self-sacrifice regarding their finances. I have, for example, worked with several practitioners in their fifties who have little or no retirement money set aside. Some were working in fee-for-service in settings where they only paid if clients show up, so on days when they have many cancellations. Frequently, one only needs permission to know one can be good, do good, and earn decent money too!

Self-Exploration: Extending the Boundaries

- Where will you extend the boundaries in your life?
- What new playing fields and world of possibility are you willing to
- create?
- What, where and with whom will you be creative in new and unpredicted ways?
- What unpredictable, even impossible outcomes are you willing to produce?

Barbara

Barbara was a therapist in dire straits financially. A divorce and difficult parenting situation had put her deep into debt. A shifting demographic in the town in which she had her private practice, managed care and her own crisis-ridden life, all had created the perfect storm for her once six-figure income to dwindle to next to nothing.

When we met, she told me she had worked with a very reputable group practice and could probably go back there at any time. She seemed surprised that I asked her if she would consider doing that given she hoped I would instead encourage her to develop a business idea she had.

When I discussed the basic principle of having a strong financial foundation, she wept and told me she knew that but had convinced herself she "should" follow her dream and it would all work out. She returned to the practice and worked feverishly for one year, gleefully emailing me that she had paid off all her debts. She is now solvent again and has started to work on her dream business in her part-time. It turns out it was worth waiting to do that because the tools available to her online now are making it much easier to do.

14

Clients

The meeting of two personalities is like the contact of two chemical substances;
if there is any reaction, both are transformed.

—Carl Gustav Jung

Clients tend to come from many places but a common thread is their desire for something more—more meaning and purpose, more passion for what they are doing, more money or business, more of a sense of making a difference. Not infrequently a life change propelled them to take action—a milestone birthday or anniversary on their job, a layoff (sometimes welcome, sometimes not), external inspiration from reading a book or seeing a movie.

Others have an "issue" they are concerned about. They know they aren't performing adequately at work or that their job is not a good fit for them.

Ken was one such client. A tax attorney, he was unhappy in his law firm. The long hours were not compatible with his family values. He resented his work and was not progressing in his firm. He did not see himself as starting a solo practice. I encouraged him to take stock of his whole life and to do a life-planning exercise with his wife, whom I never met. Within months, it became clear they both shared a vision of emigrating, and it didn't take long for him to find a new position. The family relocated and are all happier now.

Another attorney participated in a "Results Group" I led. Participants met 15 times over a course of six months, with meetings centered on each having a specific goal in the area of work, relationships, creativity, health, or community. Randy liked law but was adverse to any form of controversy. When I met him, in fact, he was not, to his wife's chagrin, working in the law and was underemployed. With the help of the group who discovered a family member had written his law school application for him, he "reinvented" himself. He loved to write and do research and began by doing a small project for a historical society while in the group. Later, he obtained his masters degree in library science. He now heads a major university law library.

Many coaching clients are "stuck." They don't see themselves as having mental health issues but they are aware of hitting a wall. Cheryl had hit a wall with her health. Despite being very satisfied with her life and, with her therapist's blessing, having completed psychotherapy, she was unable to lose weight. She was highly motivated, but she lacked accountability. She had joined just about every weight loss program that existed. Her complaint about each was the same—none were personalized to her. She literally wanted someone who

Ruth's Leap Of Confidence

Ruth Hegarty came to see me in late 2005. She had just quit her job at a local university where she worked as an executive assistant in the Department of Communication and Journalism. She had been hired to stay on as an adjunct faculty member teaching public speaking and wanted to start her own business as a confidence coach. I was struck by her enthusiasm and commitment but confess I found her to be a bit quirky when she told me she had a pet rat. Could she pull it off? We worked together for a few months which was all her budget would allow and during that time she launched her business, Leap of Confidence: Personal Confidence and Empowerment Programs for Women (http://www.confidencementor.com).

Periodically, I would receive her e-mails, and recently my interest was piqued when her newsletter announced her *Art of Joyful Living* Internet radio show, three blogs, and a "Law of Attraction Starter Kit," so I called her up. What I learned was incredibly moving. She had "gotten by" for several years but in the past year, after getting certified in Law of Attraction coaching, moved from "being an employee" to "being an entrepreneur." The catalyst was the death of her mother last year, leaving her with the care of her handicapped father. She had already decided to adopt a special needs child and she put those wheels in motion, despite "pushback" from friends and relatives. She knew, however, that to make her dream realistic she needed to make big changes in her life. She knew she wanted to make six . . . maybe even seven figures and only work from 9 to 2 every day.

What she did was counterintuitive. She started to focus on herself. She cut back on teaching, began getting regular massages, hired a maid service and invested money in her business, hiring a VA and a business coach who helped her develop her new products. She knew she needed to give herself permission to be bold and strategically position herself in her field (working with female entrepreneurs) and hit upon the idea of "Effortless Success for Women Entrepreneurs." She is actively using Facebook and Twitter, which she initially hated but she gave herself 90 days and saw it pay off. She already built an online community of 1,000. Best of all, she found she could be authentic and even discuss her pet rat and attract others to her pages as a result. At the time of writing, I asked her if she had yet reached her six-figure goal. She had not but stated she was "on track" reach it in the next year.

would be more or a personal trainer to her health and well-being. When we began working together, it became clear the pattern extended beyond food. She was tolerating a number of personal situations that drained her and left her frustrated so she ate to compensate. We worked together systematically on a plan for eliminating her tolerations.

We began by her categorizing them—which could and would she act on and thereby eliminate, which would she postpone and act on at a later date once certain conditions were met, and which would she agree to move into a new category called "I can't change this, so I chose to live at peace with it." Within six months she had addressed all of the issues she could act on and successfully moved all but one of the others to the "live with and be at peace" category. At our weekly sessions, we would count the number of items left and I would ask her to self-rate, on a scale of one to 10, her feelings of satisfaction with her handling of her tolerations. She lost over 30 pounds in 10 months.

Sue was a dental hygienist who struggled with a long-term eating disorder. A mother of three and successful in her field, she was unable to stop the destructive cycle of self-abuse. She participated in several cycles of dialectic behavioral therapy (DBT) and would improve for a time, only to return to her "bad" behaviors. I saw coaching as complimenting the DBT work, which she seemed to value. I gently began bringing some coaching questions into our therapy sessions. What would it be like if she got past her eating disorder? What would she wish for if she could be free? To my surprise she readily answered that she wanted to run without it becoming a symptom. She loved running for the sake of running and felt peaceful while she did it but her eating disorder voice would kick in and tell her to count calories burned. My coaching intuition responded by saying, if there was only something else you could count instead! At that point, she had an inspiration. What if she could count money to run for? She came up with an elaborate but doable plan. She would raise money by putting change in a jar when she succeeded in freeing herself of counting calories, then raise money directly when she ran races by asking for donations. She realized if she collapsed during a race from poor self-care, the donations would be less, and this added motivation. She chose to raise money for a major disease that had affected several members of her family. Some time after terminating therapy, I continue to receive letters announcing her next race, and I am always happy to donate!

Adam worked for a major food company in the New York/New Jersey area—the largest market in the world for their products—but came to me on his own because he did not like how he was managing his job. His position involved being an intermediary between the wholesalers who placed product in the supermarkets and the corporation. He had moved there after getting a divorce and was concerned the only way he could get the wholesalers to partner with him was to "break arms and legs," which he didn't want to do. He realized the way he had dominated his wife was a major factor in the demise of their marriage and that his training as a marine didn't make it easier for him to be flexible in his approach. We brainstormed things he could do, and in an "aha" moment, he saw he could "coach" the wholesalers. He began immediately and soon saw a complete turnaround in their attitude toward them. Instead of literally running away when they saw him coming, they began to approach him. Within six months, his numbers had increased by 12 percent—a huge gain in that business, especially given that no new products were introduced. He also began a new personal relationship and was able to bring a "new way of being" to it. He contacted his former wife and made amends with her as well and stated he "felt like a new person."

A senior auditor for a large and innovative accounting firm, Rick was having difficulty in a number of areas. His firm hired me to "straighten him out." He was seen as competent at his work but failing to delegate well or complete work in a thorough and timely manner. His affable nature actually won the firm new business, making him an asset, but that was counterbalanced by some inaccuracies in his work and the perception that he spent too much time on site with clients "schmoozing" instead of auditing. This kind of "remedial" coaching can be problematic but, fortunately, Rick was very amenable to coaching. He was unhappy with his performance as well, and was spending much too much time at the office which was causing tension at home. He welcomed the opportunity to learn some new skills for managing himself better in his position, and was interested in eventually making "partner," which he did not see as likely to happen if he continued on his present path.

I gave him a DiSC styles assessment and went over it with him line-by-line. We were quickly able to identify his strengths and weaknesses and form a plan. I also did a 360 assessment, speaking with his peers, his manager, and one person he managed. The picture was consistent among all of them. He was seen as competent but disorganized and inefficient. Together, Rick and I created an action plan—one that also included his personal agenda. His wife had just given birth to a third child, and with his increased responsibilities at home, he wanted to see more of his family. This entailed planning a move—he had a one-hour commute—to be closer to the firm. That meant he needed to feel secure in his position and certain he wanted to remain there. One of the first changes he made was to request his desk be relocated to a quieter space within the firm. He knew this would help him set limits on personal interaction with other staff, and be a good practice ground for when he was onsite at client companies. We then discussed how he could be more effective at delegating responsibility to the accountants who worked under him by becoming a coaching manager. This one shift produced dramatic results. Instead of having to know all the details before assigning work to them or trusting they would come to him with problems, he was able to build a system of accountability that allowed them to think for themselves and keep him informed. Within four months, he received two promotions, and he and his wife purchased a home from a family member within 20 minutes of the office. His manager, impressed by Rick's results, expressed interested in being coached as well.

Entrepreneurs wear many hats, but mediator is not one they are trained in. A local business owner was tearing his hair out because his three in-house employees could not be in the office at the same time. The knot of complicated feelings among them was impossible to disentangle, and it was having a direct effect on the business. The owner got my name from a friend and called because he wanted a business coach who knew about therapy. I agreed to do what I could, although I was not optimistic, but he did not want to let any of them go and thought it was worth trying.

I interviewed each of the four of them and learned from the three employees that the owner played a part in fueling the fires by being vague and indecisive and taking both sides on many issues. They all liked him personally but did not find him to be an effective leader. Each was also critical of the other two but felt they could work it out. One wanted a simple apology for a small incident; another just wanted to feel a "thaw" in the atmosphere; the third wanted to see some big changes. I spoke to the owner who then agreed to a half-day coaching session that I set up as a form of "appreciative inquiry." During the discussion that afternoon, the apology was given, the feelings in the room relaxed, and the desired changes were discussed and subsequently implemented. Business improved after the meeting, but the staff person who wanted the big changes ended up resigning. In his exit interview, he told the owner he had gotten a boost in confidence from seeing his ideas being successfully used, but, even better, since he had set up some excellent new systems in the company, felt his salary could be reinvested elsewhere to help the business grow.

Another entrepreneur was a busy mother of two young children and running a successful company, at her "wit's end and losing motivation for my business." I guided her to figure out what would get me back to loving my business. Through thoughtful inquiry and committed listened, I helped her reconnect to her vision and to an idea to expand the business in a market that really excited her. In record time, she opened a new office in Washington, DC, and felt reenergized about her business and the future of her company.

As a family-systems trained family therapist, I enjoy working with family businesses. In contrast to family business consulting, which uses an expert approach, I focus on being the coach "on the court" with the family and key employees. Coaching a family business is delicate work, to say the least.

Founded by the parents more than 30 years earlier, a consulting firm I worked with was award winning and one of the top firms in its industry—the only one not based in New York City. Their clients were major corporations, and their business was worldwide. The older parents wanted to retire but were not confident in passing the business on to the one son who worked in the business, despite his loyalty. (Their other children wanted nothing to do with it.) To make matters worse, that industry went through a major decline after the dotcom bust, and big changes needed to be made. The son, as in many family businesses, had modern ideas that the parents were reluctant to accept. They wanted to preserve the integrity of the business they created. I worked with the family and staff in various combinations over a period of more than two years, during which time the business downsized, the parents "retired" to a warm climate, and most of the permanent staff were let go in favor of subcontractors; however, the son not only has maintained the excellent reputation of the business, but financially it remains sound and continues to attract major clients.

The last example is team coaching of a group I mentioned earlier. I had worked with a professional whose wife attended a presentation I gave in the Washington, DC, area. After many months of listening to him discuss his boss, whom he both feared and admired, I saw an opportunity to offer a solution to some real issues in the workplace. My client facilitated the introduction, and I was hired to do a Best Year Yet team strategic planning and coaching program with eight software engineers. When I arrived, however, the sponsor had invited a second team to join in. It happened that a good friend's (also a social worker) brother was in the group. I did not know she had a brother in another state, but he looked remarkably like her son and quickly the connection was made. Over lunch, he informed the entire group that I was a therapist. After reassuring them that I did not think they were "any crazier than any other group" I had worked with, we had a very productive two days. The plan the group created was effective, and the monthly follow-up meetings kept them on track as they went through some major changes in their business. Throughout, I received e-mails with all sorts of personal sharing. One man shared his plans to retire and become a lay minister. One of the women poignantly shared her feelings about her mother who died suddenly. My client's boss, who did not see himself as being good with people, watched with curiosity as they opened up to me and as I was able to cajole them into following through on their commitments through the "power of positive peer pressure." We had to stop the program a few months earlier than planned when the company was sold to a major multinational corporation, but I kept in touch with the team sponsor, who eventually left and bought his own consulting company. I helped him hire his management group, and eventually he and I started a new company together, focusing on the IT industry.

Unlike many coaches who are highly specialized, I have enjoyed working with a variety of individuals, for- and not-for-profit businesses, and teams. The common element is that most of my clients are "up to something big." They want to be better, more effective, improve their organization, and, frequently, create something new. If they work within corporations, they are frequently what I call "heroic" leaders who will stick their neck out to make things better. If they are individuals, they are generally unusually creative or passionate about what they are doing or would like to do. If they happen to be patients, struggling with a mental health issue, I can still use coaching skills and help them become inspired by some aspect of our work together that focuses them on their strengths.

The most important thing to remember is that coaching is not a "one size fits all" venture, and by being creative, one can benefit a broad cross-section of individuals.

15

Making a Difference

We can do no great things, only small things with great love.

—Mother Teresa

The past 10 years have seen growth in the number of nonprofit organizations throughout the country at a tremendous rate of about 80 percent. According to Andrew Wolk, CEO of Cambridge, Massachusetts–based funding organization Root Cause, 115 nonprofits were started per day before the economic downturn. In private industry, he has pointed out in his blog (http://andrewwolk.com), a company generally wants to hold onto a monopoly for as long as it can. By contrast, in the nonprofit sector, no one organization can solve the social problem it is working on.

With perspective, Wolk went on to ask the following questions: What are the unique roles of a direct service organization, an advocacy organization, a coalition, or the government? How do they all fit together to ensure lasting social impact? How can each organization, concerned with its own sustainability and impact, look at its role within a collective purpose? Bringing those worlds together will, perhaps, constitute the signal "social innovation" of the decade to come—*social movement innovation*. President Obama's launch, in February 2009, of a yet-to-be-described Office of Social Innovation will seek to provide federal assistance to innovative nonprofit groups that are working on the country's most pressing problems.

When we look at the large arena in which we can make a difference, what role does coaching play? How can coaches help? Does coaching have new and innovative contributions to make? I believe it does.

Following are a number of examples—first of social worker coaches making a difference; next of social agencies in which coaching has been used to make a difference, both to staff and to constituents; and, finally, of organizations founded by ordinary individuals who have benefited from being coached to bring a passion or dream of making a contribution to society to fruition. You will see new theoretical approaches grounded in coaching; new ways that organizations are working together, based on programs that bring nonprofit leaders together through coaching; and the effect of coaching on people with a mission and vision they have brought from nothing into making a big impact, both domestically and around the world.

Coaching for Nonprofit and Human Service Organizations

Proven very successful in helping individuals and corporations achieve their goals, coaching can also address some of the unique challenges of the nonprofit and human service world. Nonprofit and human service organizations attract caring professionals who operate under rewarding yet often stressful conditions:

- heavy workloads;
- little time and resources for reengineering work for greater efficiency and effectiveness, even when sorely needed;
- burnout and "service fatigue," which can lead to a lost sense of mission even for the most dedicated professionals;
- tight budgets, particularly in these difficult times, meaning priority and resource allocations are constantly in flux, leaving organizations in a nerve-wracking state of constant uncertainty;
- wearing "too many hats" and, thus, not having time to communicate with teammates, which can result in confusion, inefficiency, and sometimes even mistrust;
- lack of business or management training (historically the norm for leaders of nonprofits); and
- safety issues.

Coaching Nonprofit Leaders

California-based CompassPoint Nonprofit Services embarked on a 12-month demonstration project of executive coaching with 25 executive directors in the San Francisco Bay area. A longitudinal evaluation by Harder + Company studied new executive directors who worked one-on-one with executive coaches who helped them navigate both personal life issues and organizational leadership matters. Some of the questions, they looked at were these: What promise does coaching offer to nonprofit leaders? What effect can coaching have on developing and sustaining effective leaders within their organizations and the nonprofit sector? Key findings were as follows:

- leadership:
  - increased confidence in exercising leadership,
  - improved ability to connect with the organization's vision, and
  - increased confidence in leading the organization toward fulfilling the vision; and
- management:
  - increased task completion and productivity,
  - improved personnel management skills, and
  - better relationships with staff and board of directors (for example, improved communication skills).

The complete results can be found here: http://www.compasspoint.org/content/index.php?pid=199.

On the other side of the coin are unlimited opportunities to "make a difference." There is a crying need for more innovative programs that bring the skills that coaching can provide to communities around the globe. Professionals who know the field—be it human services or healthcare—are best equipped to coach in this arena. Some of the areas of intervention that have been defined are as follows:

- Guide organizations in defining their mission definition; analyzing their strengths, weaknesses, opportunities, and threats (SWOT analysis); and develop appropriate strategic plans.
- Guide organizations through transitions in mission, leadership, or management; adoption of new values; or reinvigoration of old ones.
- Develop leadership skills among executives, managers, and volunteers.
- Coach individual professionals to develop the personal skills that enrich the organization and contribute to fulfillment of its mission.
- Train human service professionals in coaching techniques for management or as a supplement to individual service practices.
- Launch new 501(c)(3) organizations.
- Provide keys to balance and fulfillment to staff through onsite "balance workshops."
- Develop or help executive directors, program managers, and clinicians to develop new and innovative programs for specific populations (HIV-positive individuals, diabetes patients, heart patients, people with weight issues, cancer survivors, prisoners, veterans) or entirely new initiatives (Birthday Wishes, WE CAN) or to bring innovation to existing systems (coaching and positive psychology, Wellcoaches).

I have had the pleasure of participating in the development of two new programs in addition to working with executive directors of several existing philanthropic organizations.

WE CAN (http://www.wecancenter.org). WE CAN (Women's Empowerment through Cape Area Networking) is a mentoring organization on Cape Cod, Massachusetts. Known for its pristine beaches and National Seashore, Cape Cod is the summer home to many well-known people and an increasingly popular retirement location for middle- and upper-middle-class individuals. With little year-round industry, the Cape has significant unemployment and underemployment problems, high rates of alcohol and substance abuse, and large population of poor women (many on public assistance). Jacqueline Scarborough, a year-round resident, wanted to make a difference for those women.

Since my work with Jacqui, WE CAN has been incorporated; it is now a sizeable nonprofit, supported by the United Way, whose mission is defined as "recognizing that every member of the community's well-being contributes to the whole community [and] support[ing] Cape Cod women in life transitions with services that bring increased opportunity, self-sufficiency and stability." WE CAN's programs include offerings in the following areas:

- options (career services, Divorce Boot Camp, and referral services),
- "Pathmakers" (a mentoring program consisting of one-on-one mentoring and monthly meetings of the entire mentor–mentee community),

Case Study: Starting a Nonprofit

I met Marilyn at a seminar on "masterful coaching" I attended last year. She was a guest speaker and addressed using coaching in human services. I had gone to the coaching seminar to learn about coaching for WE CAN, a new nonprofit I had just founded. Although I didn't know much about coaching, I knew enough to know I wanted to learn it to use there and thought it would be useful within the organization. My belief was validated. I immediately recognized coaching as an invaluable professional practice for human services professional and Marilyn as terrific resource for an inspired entrepreneur.

In just a few months of training with—and being coached by—Marilyn, I was able to take a the organization that had already been formed and build out our infrastructure, engage wonderful administrative staff volunteers, launch a legal clinic to assist women entrepreneurs, match up 20 mentoring pairs, start three mentoring groups, and get our first financial grant. Our first educational event, a women's financial fair, held just nine months after I began working with OnTrack, is being sponsored by five major financial institutions, reached an estimated 200 women on Cape Cod.

Accomplishing so much in so little time would have consumed me if I hadn't had a coach to help me chart my course. In our weekly coaching sessions, Marilyn helped me take stock so that my actions were focused and purposeful.

At the start, she helped me to clarify my vision for WE CAN through conversation, analytic exercises, and formal planning procedures. As the organization started to take shape, she helped me overcome my fear of business and finance, delegate authority, and learn to say "no"—all skills that have made me a stronger, more professional leader. She also offered many concrete suggestions—contacts, articles, and other resources—that were tremendously helpful in solving immediate problems and sparking new ideas.

As we worked together, Marilyn also trained and mentored me as a coach. I've used the technique to help clients, to get the best performance out of my staff, and to generate new ideas for programs. The result is an inspired team that is humming with excitement and productivity. Accomplishing as much as we have in so little time would have been impossible without OnTrack and Marilyn's coaching expertise.

—Jacqueline Scarbrough, Founder and Director, WE CAN, Harwich Port, MA

- legal clinics (free services volunteered by 18 members of the Massachusetts Bar),
- computer classes for women with little or no prior computer experience (covering introduction to a variety of common Microsoft programs—Word, Excel, Powerpoint, and Publisher—as well as use of Internet, research, sending attachments, and using charge cards online), and
- workshops and the annual "Women's Words of Wit and Wisdom" fundraiser (featuring female authors, both permanent and summer residents).

Birthday Wishes (http://www.birthdaywishes.org). The Birthday Wishes mission is simple: To bring birthday parties to the more than 3,000 children staying in homeless shelters in Massachusetts. Birthday Wishes recognizes the importance of a birthday in a child's life and believes that the gift of a birthday celebration will provide normalcy, joy, and hope in these children's otherwise unsettled lives. The organization's grassroots philosophy fosters the spirit of volunteerism and community service in the adults, children, and families who donate their time and resources to its mission.

Birthday Wishes was founded in November 2002 by Lisa Vasiloff, Karen Yahara, and Carol Zwanger—three friends and colleagues who wanted to help homeless children build self-esteem. Having volunteered in several homeless shelters, it occurred to the trio—as they attended one of their own children's birthday parties—that at the shelters, children's birthdays often came and went uncelebrated. Their subsequent research indicated that no organizations existed exclusively to provide birthday parties to children living in homeless shelters. After speaking with local shelters and state advocacy groups, they found that most homeless shelters do not have the personnel or resources necessary to hold birthday parties for the children who stay there. Furthermore, the parent (usually a mother) is often unable, both economically and emotionally, to organize a party for the child. Some parents, embarrassed that they do not have money for cakes and presents, don't even tell their children that they have a birthday. For homeless children, birthday parties are a luxury that neither the parent nor the shelter can afford. Yet a birthday is an important event in the life of a child. Birthday Wishes was founded on the belief that every child, regardless of their living situation, should have their birthday recognized and celebrated. Birthday Wishes has found that something as simple and "normal" as a birthday party has the power to make a child living in a homeless shelters feel special and, perhaps more important, like a "regular kid."

The first parties were held at the Second Step shelter in Newton, Massachusetts. Within a few months, eight more shelters were added, and within three years growth had doubled. Today, Birthday Wishes serves over 1,000 children in more than 65 shelters in eastern Massachusetts and Worcester. Birthday Wishes hopes to reach all children living in homeless shelters in the state of Massachusetts within the next five years and to serve as a model for Birthday Wishes branches in cities throughout the United States.

The rapid and continued growth of Birthday Wishes is due in large part to community involvement. Everyone can relate to the importance of a birthday, and this has meant much grassroots support. Birthday Wishes volunteers number over 400 and include local teens, adults, and children (participating as individuals or as part of a family); scout troops; church groups; sports teams; and school programs. The volunteers are a diverse group, representing scores of communities in Massachusetts, and they range in age from toddlers to senior citizens. Volunteers help to provide the party supplies needed for monthly parties, and, most important, they attend and help to run the birthday parties. The various ways in which volunteers can contribute allow for many levels of participation and provide a wonderful opportunity for families to volunteer together.

Social Worker Coaches Making a Difference

Marita Frijohn: The Center for Right Relationship
(http://www.centerforrightrelationship.com/)

Marita, is co-owner and president of the Center for Right Relationship. She is a faculty member of the Coaches Training Institute (CTI), consultant to several large organizations, and mentor to a large number of practitioners in the field of relationship systems work. She designs curriculums and operates training programs in relationship systems work for coaches, executives, and teams. She came to this work with an extensive background in clinical social work, community development, process work, family systems therapy, business consulting, and alternative dispute resolution. She has an international mentor coaching practice of individuals, partnerships, and teams. Her primary focuses in coaching are on systemic change, leveraging diversity, creative communication, deep democracy in conflict management, and the development of learning organizations.

Marita and her business partner Faith Fuller have created a unified field theory of relationship systems work combining contributions from the co-active coaching model, alternative dispute resolution, process work, general systems theory, and Taoism, with strong influences from John Gottman (a pioneer in the use of positive psychology in the realm of relationships; see Gottman & Silver, 1999) and Arnold Mindell (specifically his notion of "deep democracy"; see http://www.aamindell.net). The Center for Right Relationship operationalizes complex theory in easily applicable skills. It brings a depth of experience in working with relationships for the past 16 years and provides a very innovative model of relationship systems work.

Deep democracy, according to Mindell (1992), is "our sense that the world is here to help us to become our entire selves, and that we are here to help the world to become whole" (p. 13). Deep democracy, or "multileveled awareness," is typified by acceptance of the simultaneous importance of all voices and roles and the three levels of experience:

- consensus reality (where status, hierarchy, and "rankism" and other "isms"—such as racism, sexism, ageism, and nationalism—live),
- dreams, and
- essence or sentient reality.

Everyday reality and its problems are as important as those problems and figures reflected in dreams and are also as important as any potential oneness or spiritual experience at the essence level of reality, where rank no longer exists.

Deep democracy provides an integrated structural framework for working with and including marginalized experiences, roles, and voices. Unlike "classical" democracy, which focuses on majority rule, deep democracy suggests that all voices, states of awareness, and frameworks of reality are important. Deep democracy also suggests that all of the information carried within these voices, awarenesses, and frameworks is needed to understand the complete process of a system. Deep democracy is an attitude that focuses on awareness of voices that are both central and marginal. As long as there is a sense that one person or level is more important than another, deep democracy is not at hand.

Deep democracy is a psychosocial–political paradigm and methodology. Mindell initially called his paradigm "processwork," which formulated these principles and demonstrated how they could be used in psychotherapy. In the late 1980s, he started to formulate them as the political principle that he called deep democracy, and the term first appeared in his book *The Leader as Martial Artist* (Mindell, 1992). A physicist and a Jungian analyst, Mindell had researched and written extensively on how awareness creates reality and how we perceive it on different levels, creating different frameworks of reality. An example for this is how we perceive time: the measurable reality of the seconds ticking in a clock; the dreamlike "subjective" perception of time as it passes during an encounter with a lover; and the sentient essence of timelessness as we catch the moment of a sunrise, which goes beyond time as we know it and replaces, for a moment, the concept of future with hope.

This type of awareness can be focused on groups, organizations, one's own inner experiences, people in conflict, and so on. Allowing oneself to take seriously seemingly unimportant events and feelings can often bring unexpected solutions to both group and inner conflicts.

Although the term and the concepts of deep democracy are now being used by various groups in different ways, they have a common denominator that Mindell has described very well: An experience of deep democracy is a process of flow in which all actors on the stage are needed to create the play that we are watching. This is the level of engagement that Marita seeks to produce within client systems.

Interview with Marita. Born in South Africa and trained during the late 1960s and 1970s at the University of Stellenbach during the height of apartheid, which affected her deeply, Marita did a year of postgraduate medical social work in Capetown. There, she was fortunate enough to be on the team of Christian Barnard, who successfully performed the first heart transplant in 1967. While at Groote Schuur Hospital, where Barnard worked, she met a senior family systems student of Salvador Minuchin and "the whole world opened up," laying the groundwork for who she is now. In Cape Town at that time, anything seen as being against the government was perceived as "communist." Marita experienced being dragged out in the middle of the night to be interrogated, and frequently classrooms were empty because her fellow social work students were very politically active. Finally, the death of fellow student activist Stephen Biko "catapulted" her out of South Africa in 1978.

She came to the United States with the idea of doing a cross-cultural study of death and dying to complete her doctoral dissertation on terminal care. She spent two years in the Amazon, but, due again to political unrest, it was a traumatic experience. By the time she got to San Francisco in 1989, Marita had become very involved in work of Mindell and began practicing as a hypnotherapist, which brought her a large population of sexual abuse and multiple personality disorder clients. She eventually "burned out" again and discovered first Coach University and then, in her own backyard, the CTI in the late 1990s. She became involved with the CTI model because it was "face-to-face" training.

Marita explains the distinctions between Coach U and CTI very clearly. Thomas Leonard, founder of Coach U—who "pioneered" the whole online existence of coaching with a tremendous amount of collateral, "handy-dandy" material—came very clearly from an organizational and business environment. CTI approached coaching from strong personal development perspective, which is what was very attractive to Marita, who was "ready for personal transformation" for herself.

At time she attended CTI, Marita was already doing conjoint work with partner and Center for Right Relationship cofounder psychologist, Faith Fuller. Smitten with the CTI work, she became a trainer and faculty member within two years; however, she missed the group work and organizational focus of the consulting she had been doing before. Around 1998, she and Faith began to look at whether what they were doing was trainable. Using a consultant who discerned a distinct and unique methodology that they were able to "pour into a coach training vessel," they brought their "relationship coaching" model to CTI as an already approved International Coach Federation (ICF) course in 2003 and licensed it to CTI. The model eventually became the basis for about one-third of CTI's course work—simply too big—so in 2007 they took it back in house to develop and expand it as they wanted. The ORSC (organization and relationship systems coaching) program and the Center for Right Relationship have since doubled in size, making it the most successful relationally oriented coach training program in the world. Marita and Faith have created an 84-hour certification program and are in the process of becoming fully certified as a full training program, which would make them the first business certification program through the ICF. They launched the program in March 2008 and have already certified 60 graduates. There are approximately 2,500 to 3,000 students who have done some or all of the ORSC program, with trainings in 12 countries and graduates in 27 countries. Of Marita's personal work now, approximately 80 percent is teaching (training, mentoring, and curriculum design) and only 20 percent is coaching and consulting.

The ORSC Model. The ORSC model is based on the notion that

> relationship is the fundamental bond that defines living things. Within each relationship is the power to heal and the potential to harm. The impact of relationship is at once intimate and global in scale. Given current world events there is no time to waste.

ORSC shifts the focus from the individuals in a system to the relationship itself: an important player called the *Third Entity*. ORSC provides relationship systems practitioners with a model for working directly with a system rather than doing individual work with members of the group. This subtle shift, it is maintained, has a profound effect on the results that are possible in systems coaching; it requires a very different skill set than that of facilitating individual work within a group setting (for more details, see the discussion of ORSC in chapter 6).

The Social Work/Therapist Influence. Marita is very clear that what social work gave her is a "client-centered model"—one that begins "where the client [in this case, the system] is" and follows the same with deep curiosity. The moment people come together—friends, family, work—there is conflict. Her work is focused on motivational issues and "adapting and becoming resilient in a complex world." Although, she states, coaching can "look and feel similar to therapy, if anything looks like a psychological issue, coaching is not the place to deal with it, and clients are referred back to therapy." She asserts that the differences between the two professions rest more in the "stances" than in the techniques used. Some of the questions she believes worth considering are these:

- How is the client viewing the professional?
- What is the client coming for?
- How is the professional viewing the client?
- What is the role the professional sees for him- or herself with this client?

Key to the ORSC model is imbuing students, many of whom have experienced coaching as a "feel-good" model but have trouble relating to the psychological savvy and emotional intelligence needed to be truly effective, with a strong outer, evidence-based knowledge as well as a deepening sense of their inner work.

Rosamund Zander and the Art of Possibility (http://www.rosamundzander.com)

Roz Zander is a pioneer in the field of leadership and relationship. She has created a leadership model that coaches individuals to create a life of vision, passion, and contribution. Her work, in all its capacities, is about growth. Her writing, teaching, and coaching create pathways to lives that are authentic and meaningful.

As a social worker, family therapist, and executive coach, Roz develops models for leadership and effective action. Her work is detailed in *The Art of Possibility* (Zander & Zander, 2000), which presents a synthesis of her work and the leadership practices of Boston Philharmonic conductor Benjamin Zander.

The Art of Possibility is a *New York Times* bestseller that has been translated into 15 languages and sold over 500,000 copies worldwide. Presenting 12 breakthrough practices for bringing creativity into action, it combines Benjamin Zander's experience as an orchestra conductor and his talent as a teacher and communicator with Roz's ability to design innovative paradigms for personal and professional development. The authors' interwoven perspectives provide a deep sense of the powerful role that possibility can play in every aspect of life. Roz is a wonderful painter as well, and her work is based on the idea that creativity is an innate adult capacity. She offers intuitive, inventive coaching for effective personal and professional relationships.

In addition to working with corporations, institutions, and teams—including Hampton/Hilton Inns, IBM, Whirlpool, the Bureau of Public Debt, Harvard Medical School, and Carnegie Mellon University—Roz conducts a long-term accomplishment program for individuals and groups committed to completing major projects. I was introduced to coaching in a classroom a decade earlier by Frederick Hudson, but Roz was my first personal coach, for which I am incredibly grateful.

Randy Nathan: LEAP

Randy Nathan, MSW, founder and director of LEAP (**l**ead, **e**xcel, **a**ct, **p**ersevere) in Livingston, New Jersey, is a certified "empowerment coach" who works exclusively with high school and college-age students. He discovered coaching accidentally when searching on excite.com to learn about drills after agreeing to coach his 8-year-old son's basketball team. He "devoured" books on the subject and began training with the Institute for Professional Excellence in Coaching. Two weeks into his second coaching module, it became evident to him that he needed to leave his position as executive director of a synagogue in New Jersey. A two-month transition helped him start his coaching practice with teens. After one year, he had what many considered a full coaching practice of 12 to 14 regular clients, all teenagers who had come to him through parents, friends, and occasionally teachers. He loved what he was doing but realized he could not reach enough kids to make a significant enough impact, so he founded LEAP.

Among the challenges Randy sees facing teenagers today are these:

- tremendous amounts of stress;
- complicated choices;
- parental expectations;
- a sense of entitlement and desire for immediate gratification;
- low levels of self-esteem and confidence;
- insurmountable pressures to fit in;
- bullying and violent behaviors;
- increasingly severe consequences;
- fear of failure and making mistakes; and
- the ubiquity of alcohol, drugs, smoking, sex, and explicit internet images

Randy's intention was to move from coaching a few kids to coaching many, but others were interested in what he was doing and began asking him to train them. He has since trained 19 coaches, 10 of whom are actively working with kids. He requires the coaches he trains to have some basic form of coach training first so he can concentrate on training them specifically in working with young people.

Randy's other accomplishments include coaching the entire freshman class of 300 of Teaneck High School when a new principal became concerned that 60 percent had a least one F in their first semester. Randy also started LEAP Expedition, a five-day outdoor program using his 10 years as a camp director to integrate his coaching with nature study and survival skills programming. LEAP Challenge is a one-day, school-based program. Recently, Randy took on a business partner to take LEAP to the next level, which might include expanding outside of New Jersey (they have already have spoken with a potential partner in Korea about bringing the program there).

Their newest program is Project NextGen, aimed at addressing "the quarterlife crisis," a period of anxiety, uncertainty, and inner turmoil that often accompanies the transition to adulthood. This term was coined by Abby Wilner, coauthor of Quarterlife Crisis

(Robbins & Wilner, 2001), in 1997 after she graduated from college, moved back home, and could not figure out what to do with her life. Essentially, on the basis of traditional markers such as financial independence and starting a family, it is taking longer to become an adult today. The average American changes jobs eight times before the age of 32; the average college graduate accrues $20,000 in education loan debt; and the average age at which people get married is now 27. Project NextGen is designed to help young people grapple with questions such as these:

- What if I don't get into a good college? Am I a failure?
- What am I supposed to be doing with my life?
- I picked a major in college that I hate. Am I stuck in this field for life?
- Should I move out of my parent's house? Should I rent or buy?
- I couldn't imagine coming to this job every day. What are my options?
- Where do I take my career next?

With a focus on the 13- to 28-year-old age group, Project NextGen has created three flagship programs directly related to each subgroup in the millennial generation:

- *Pre-Crisis* (ages 13 through 17) helps youths and teenagers identify their purpose, overcome their limiting beliefs, enhance peer relationships, and develop a plan for reaching their true potential. Using a strategic coaching process, the LEAP program teaches youths greater respect for the choices they make, increased confidence in themselves, better problem-solving skills, greater personal strength, and more commitment toward their future.
- *Near-Crisis* (ages 18 through 22): This Career Jumpstart Program focuses on students at the college/university level who are learning to examine their priorities, determine their goals, and leverage their education into a career they are excited about entering in the near future. During this period, most students are confused as to their future and the decisions they have made regarding their "career." Providing them with the best tools available to understand their skill sets and create a clear plan is essential to their continued success.
- *In-Crisis* (ages 23 through 28): The Workforce 2.0 program focuses on young professionals transitioning into the "real world."

Although his new business has been much more demanding than he ever imagined, personally Randy could not be happier. Although working harder than ever before, he says, "It doesn't feel like work. . . . I am living my purpose."

Reggie Odom: Mindfulness and Coaching in a School to Work Program (http://www.reggieodom.com)

Reggie was one of the early pioneers of coaching in social programs. Around 1999, she received two years of grant funding to provide coaching and mindfulness meditation to Boston high school students in a school-to-work program. The program, whose participants ranged from honor students to dropouts, was not only popular but made a clear impact. This was brought home one icy December evening when you could take a step and end up on the ground: There was perfect attendance—kids and parents—for parent–teacher meetings.

Marcus and Richard Games: Sojourners (http://www.sojourners.org)

Sojourners Care Network is an asset-based youth development organization serving Appalachian Ohio, Kentucky, and West Virginia. A nonprofit organization founded early in 1999 by two brothers, Marcus and Richard Games, Sojourners fosters positive development opportunities for children and young adults living in the most distressed counties of Appalachia.

After six successful years, Sojourners has been involved in deep reflection and strategic planning on the future of the organization. Through this reflection, Sojourners has made a decision to focus its efforts intensively on ensuring that foster care youths successfully transition into adulthood, through implementation of the Age Up Initiative.

The term "age out" is often associated with youths who turn 18 and leave the foster care system. What is also associated with "aging out" for many young people is homelessness, poverty, and involvement in crime. Sojourners has seen firsthand how young people, if not fully prepared, can return to dire situations after they turn 18. Sojourners is dedicated to helping young people "age up" instead of "out" of foster care:

> While a young person may "age out" onto the street, those supported by Sojourners will "age up" into something bigger and better, whether that be a job or college. We believe that by focusing our mission, vision, values, and programmatic strategies on ensuring the successful transition of foster care youth into adulthood, we can change the lives of these young people forever.

Marcus's background is in nonprofit management, whereas Richard has an MSW. The brothers started Sojourners with a $180,000 personal loan they were able to pay off in one year. The agency serves approximately 1,000 youths per year and has a $3 million budget. In addition to integrating coaching principles into direct work with youths for motivation, building positive peer relationships, and teaching youths how to be role models for the younger children, Richard has also used coaching skills with his senior management in helping them "live more balanced lives" and come to grips with their own values, which he recognizes as critical in working with young people. He has also brought the model to Sojourners' training for foster caregivers and involved youths in leading the trainings.

Coaching Other Social Workers and Social Work Leaders

Christine Coward has been a master's-level social worker since 1991 and has worked primarily in child welfare organizations. Since her coach training, she has applied coaching techniques and skills in working with leaders in social work organizations. There are unique stressors to being a manager in social service organizations, such as high staff turnover, poor funding, staff safety issues, and burnout. Christine knows this intimately and helps managers deal with their stress more effectively, engage and retain their staff, and help staff improve their awareness (this includes teaching techniques to increase safety). Her clients include family support services; child welfare services; and PCVS, a credentials verification organization for hospitals, physician practices, health plans, and other healthcare organizations.

Others Making a Difference

Maya Balle

Not all coaches making a difference are social workers, health care providers, or human services professionals. For instance, Maya Balle, a coach with a long history of nonprofit involvement, teamed up with Liz Walker, former Boston-based CBS news journalist and ordained Harvard Divinity School minister, to make a film, *A Glory from the God*, about genocide and rape in Sudan (see http://www.lizwalkerjourneyproductions.org/).

Maya was Walker's coach in the creation of *A Glory from the God*, and together they did some very gutsy things to raise money to make the film. For example, they partnered with the Boston Museum of Fine Arts film program and the ICF to show the first 10 minutes of the film and brought together people who wanted to help. This led to the formation of Liz Walker Journey Productions and creation of a conversation guide that would take the film into community to teach people how they can help. The book and conversation guide are sold on the Web site (http://www.lizwalkerjourneyproductions.org/), and all of the proceeds are going to a school for girls.

This initiative led to founding Navigational Strategies, an organization that provides keynote addresses about how to give and contribute in your community. While raising money for Walker, Maya saw that other nonprofits needed help in this area, realizing that many nonprofit leaders needed to learn about "social entrepreneurship" (use of entrepreneurial principles to organize, create, and manage a venture to make social change *and* money)—looking at product and services "for the greater good"—to make money for their organizations.

Virginia Kellogg

Virginia Kellogg, one of the early leaders and trainers at CTI and one of Maya's mentors, does the majority of her work with nonprofit organizations. She began with the Laura Whitworth Prison Project at the Federal Correctional Institute in Denver, Colorado, where she and Laura (one of the founders and leaders of co-active coaching) trained 100 prisoners to coach youths at risk. Despite challenges of prisoners being transferred out (a prison routine to prevent close relationships from developing among prisoners), not one prisoner left the program by choice. Several received their coach training certifications and continued to coach in the program after release from prison.

With Reule Hunt, Virginia went on to develop a program for female prisoners in another institution, focusing this time on coaching life skills. Their goal was to coach for personal leadership with a focus on making wise decisions in life—in interpersonal relationships, family matters, work, money, and day-to-day choices. The impact of the program was that participants became "lit up" about possibilities in their own lives. They felt empowered in seeing they had choice in the matter of how their lives went, and they wanted then to "pay it forward" by helping and empowering others.

Virginia's work expanded to the Coaching and Philanthropy Project, an initiative of the Kellogg Foundation (no relationship). The Coaching and Philanthropy Project was created to assess and advance the application of coaching as a strategy for building effective organizations within the nonprofit sector. This project grew out of the recognition that the fields of coaching and philanthropy have much to contribute to one another, and it aims to help nonprofits and funders become conscious consumers of coaching as a means for leadership development and organizational effectiveness and to develop the coaching profession to support the needs of nonprofit organizations. It has three main goals:

1. Help nonprofits become conscious consumers by making the best use of coaching as a means for leadership development and organizational effectiveness.
2. Help foundations understand how coaching "fits" as a strategy for leadership development and organizational effectiveness.
3. Develop the coaching profession to most effectively support the needs of nonprofit organizations, leadership development, and organizational effectiveness, engaging nonprofits in a healthy way so that they want to think about how to use coaching in the nonprofit sector.

Virginia is in charge of what is now "phase 2," looking at the effectiveness of coaching in nonprofit organizations.

As part of the research, a Coach Training Pilot Project was developed to train coaches who work with underserved and underprivileged populations. Trainees include 32 nonprofit professionals and self-identified consultants of color who are being trained in return for information on what is really needed to be relevant to nonprofits and people of color. Michelle Gislason of CompassPoint Nonprofit Services leads the actual training component.

Examples of deliverables for this project include the following:

- tools for screening and selecting coaches,
- a resource directory of programs that provide coaching,
- case studies and articles to inform nonprofits and funders about how coaching relates to leadership development and capacity building,
- a resource Web site for nonprofits and funders seeking information about coaching, and
- affinity groups for coaches working with nonprofits.

Other programs in which Virginia has participated include LeaderSpring, focusing on working with nonprofit leaders in the San Francisco Bay area (with Cynthia Chavez) and the Women's Funding Project, a consortium of foundations that funds women's foundations around the world. LeaderSpring provides a two-year on-the-job leadership training program that includes one week of resident coaching and mentoring at a national respected nonprofit agency. Executive Director Chavez, who brought over 23 years of experience in nonprofit management and community building for social change to LeaderSpring, has stated that coaching has been invaluable to her personally and has made a huge contribution to the success of her programs.

Virginia is also about to begin working with the Gheens Foundation "Bridges to Tomorrow" program in Louisville, Kentucky, training family coaches to help prepare all preschool children for successful entry into the school system.

She answers the question "What are the best uses of coaching in nonprofits?" by distinguishing five areas:

- as a leadership development/support tool for executive directors (how can they use their skills most effectively and prevent burnout?);
- to create coaching cultures in organizations, which leads to less work and greater effectiveness for everyone;
- to develop communication skills;
- to empower clients by helping them to see they have a say in their lives and can make a difference in the world; and
- by helping certain populations use the skills they have developed "working the system" to work on behalf of their own empowerment.

The Landmark Forum (http://www.landmarkeducation.com/)

There is a vitality, a life force, an energy, a quickening that is translated through you into action, and because there is only one of you in all of time, this expression is unique. And if you block it, it will never exist through any other medium and it will be lost. The world will not have it. It is not your business to determine how good it is nor how valuable nor how it compares with other expressions. It is your business to keep it yours clearly and directly, to keep the channel open.

—Martha Graham

Nowhere have the premises of coaching been brought more to life than through the work of Landmark Education. Stemming from its origins in the 1970s controversial est (Erhard Seminar Trainings) programs, Landmark Education's core program, the Landmark Forum, has been delivered to millions of people around the world. I first participated in the Landmark Forum in 1994, at the urging of Roz Zander. The Landmark Forum was key to the personal transformation in my way of working that eventually led me to coaching. I have since completed a number of other Landmark Education programs (including their extremely rigorous leadership training), and I have returned to the Landmark Forum several times. Each time, I have wanted to understand the what they do to cause individuals to transform themselves in only three short days, so I decided to go right to a Forum leader to learn how it really works.

David Cunningham has been a Landmark Forum leader since 1991, but his roots are in social work. Although not degreed in social work (his master's is in education), his social work career which began in the 1970s when he taught profoundly developmentally disabled children, which led him to work with special needs children in schools, Parents Anonymous, and the Connecticut Justice for Children Collaboration (of which he was a executive director). Eventually, he reached the national level as a delegate to Jimmy Carter's White House Conference on Families. In 1984, he joined the National Committee for Prevention of Child Abuse in Chicago and was instrumental in establishing nonprofit child abuse prevention organizations and passing child abuse prevention laws in most states. He had been looking for something he could do to expand the difference he could make beyond the local level, and he credits his first transformational program, an early iteration of the Landmark Forum, in which he participated in 1983, for making that possible. In 1988, after a personal tragedy, he made Landmark Education his career, and he became a Forum leader in 1991.

David has led the Landmark Forum to somewhere between 50,000 and 60,000 people (100,000 in all programs) all over the world—from Bucharest and Bangkok to Tel Aviv—and has seen that the difference it makes transcends linguistic, cultural, and socioeconomic barriers. In Africa, for instance, frequently people walk miles to attend the Landmark Forum.

So, how does the Landmark Forum generate such a big difference for people in such a short period of time? According to David, there are three key elements of coaching involved in how participants are invited to relate to their Landmark Forum leaders:

1. as coaches who are totally dedicated to the players winning the game;
2. as coaches who can only talk—the players need to play to game ("The conversation we're having has to open to door to allow them to win"); and
3. as coaches whose job is to empower people in the areas that matter to *them*.

The work of Landmark Education is "transformation." The definition the Landmark Education Corporation uses is this: "the genesis of a new realm of possibility for oneself and one's life." The commitment of the Landmark Forum is to empower people to "put the past in the past where it belongs" so they can create a new future. This new future

- is informed by but in no ways constrained by the past,
- totally inspires the person and gives them power in the present,
- comes to life in the domain of "being" (versus what one "does" or "has"), and
- once invented then reaches back to and transforms the present.

"Transformation," according to David, is not change. It's only what you make up about the past that predicts the future to begin with—the facts of the past predict nothing. Here, we can hear similarities with Michael White's "narrative therapy" (M. White, 2007; M. White & Eptson,1990). The process involves

- separating the "facts" from the "story";
- acknowledging the story as a story (or interpretation of what happened) and recognizing that, as a story, it is made up and only one of many possible stories one might have;
- taking responsibility for the past, or "being cause in the matter" of the past, which is viewed not as "the right thing to do" but as *a possible way to relate to life* that gets the past complete; and
- allowing people, as a result, to "complete" the past and get to nothing, where
- once complete, one can invent new possibilities for being extraordinary, leaving one loving one's life and living it powerfully.

Recently, David led a program in a prison with a group of about 40 who had been there from anywhere between 3 and 40 years. During the program, one of the prisoners, who had not heard from his family in 15 years, took responsibility for what he had done and called his sister. He acknowledged his responsibility for the crime he had committed (rather than blaming others) and the effect his being imprisoned had had on the family, and he apologized. "For the first time, I didn't have any need to justify myself," he said, "and I felt good." After the program, his sister began to call him, and he was reconnected with his family.

"Integrity," according to David, is the cornerstone personal value of the Landmark Forum. "Nothing in life works as it should without integrity." The next important concept is that of "distinguishing." Distinguishing is "how" the Landmark Forum works. People see things they never saw before. David uses the example of *Highlights* magazine, which, I am sure, most of you remember from your childhood. We see the house, the bird, and the bush, but we must find the fish. What allows people insight is the distinguishing right before them of aspects of their lives that help them see that *who they are being* is causing the results in their life. "Authenticity" is "why" it works (and works so quickly). Trust consistently happens almost immediately, which David maintains is because they are the "real deal."

Landmark Forum leaders do what is consistent with their commitments and the values they express. They understand that the program it is not about them. When participants "resist" accepting the distinctions (which, by the way, are presented as invented, not "the truth," so there really is nothing to resist), leaders bring an extraordinarily accepting response. They are far from pushovers in the process, but they manage to truly convey to participants that they are whole, complete, and perfect just the way they are but perhaps simply have barriers to the full expression of this state. David says, "We're there to 'disappear' what's gotten on them over the years . . . no matter how they are behaving in the moment."

The bulk of the program (2.5 of three days) is about "completing the past." It includes an exercise about fear in which participants are encouraged to separate the experience of fear from the story about what they are afraid of, taking responsibility for the fear they have so they can complete the past about being afraid. Fear, David states, also causes "hiding," and the exercise allows people to stay connected even while afraid and to be able to communicate their fears more openly afterward. Our habitual coping mechanisms are described as "rackets" and "strong suits," the former being how we tend to "be" when we have a complaint and the latter being ways of being developed at different developmental stages of our lives, which were once functional adaptations but have long ceased to leave us fulfilled. "Rackets" and "strong suits" are part of our automatic way of functioning; once they are distinguished, we have more freedom in our ways of being. Unlike psychological interpretations, they are held as the "what's so" about us (like having brown hair) and seem to be accompanied by little stigma.

Some of the specific effects David has seen as a result of programs he has conducted include the following:

- the prison inmate who reconciled with his family;
- a teacher who was physically threatened by a student, had grown to "hate" teaching and mistrust all kids, but was able to return to teaching;
- many individuals able to "complete" various forms of abuse and give up their interpretation of themselves as being "damaged";
- a man who stuttered who is now a public speaker and has spoken to over 500 kids about stuttering;
- a union negotiator who was "at war" with a company over benefits for 100,000 workers and was able, following the Forum, to successful negotiate an agreement; and
- specific programs created out of participating in senior Landmark Education courses, such as the Self-Expression and Leadership Program, including
  - Pachamama Alliance (http://pachamama.org),
  - Awakening the Dreamer Initiative (http://awakeningthedreamer.org),
  - Fight Fistula (http://www.fightfistula.org),
  - Hearts of Fire (http://www.heartsoffire.tv),
  - Homeless Not Toothless (http://www.homelessnottoothless.org),
  - Causes for Change (http://www.causesforchange.org),
  - Special Spectators (http://www.specialspectators.org),
  - Cherish our Children International (http://www.cherishourchildren.org),
  - Where Peace Lives (http://www.wherepeacelives.org),
  - Make a Film Foundation (http://www.makeafilmfoundation.org),
  - Bumpenya (http://bumpenya.com), and
  - StepUp Foundation (http://www.stepupfoundation.com).

A few of these programs are described in detail here:

Pachamama Alliance and Awakening the Dreamer Initiative. The Pachamama Alliance's two-fold mission is (1) to preserve the Earth's tropical rainforests by empowering the indigenous people who are its natural custodians and (2) to contribute to the creation of a new global vision of equity and sustainability for all.

Founded by Lynne Twist, author of *The Soul of Money* (2006), in the late 1990s, the Pachamama Alliance works with seven communities of people that cover 5 million acres of rainforest. The foundation, which began through partnership with the indigenous Achuar people in a remote Amazonian region of Ecuador who were concerned about the growing threat to their ancient way of life, has provided funding for many capacity-building tools, including airplanes (because there is no road access that deep in the jungle), radios, global positioning system mapping, and legal support in the Achuar's stand against oil development. They have gotten 90 percent of the land titled to the indigenous peoples in a region where most square footage had been parceled out to oil companies for development and prevented drilling in those areas.

From the beginning,

> the indigenous partners reminded us [the Pachamama Alliance] that one of the most powerful actions that can be taken in support of the rainforest and its inhabitants is to "change the dream of the North," since it is our dream—our desires and appetites—that is driving the destruction of the rainforests around the world. Ultimately, to assure the long-term survival of our rainforests, and indeed of the natural world and even ourselves, we need to address the core values and ways of seeing the world that are deeply imbedded in our modern worldview. (Awakening the Dreamer, n.d.)

This led to the founding of a sister organization, the Awakening the Dreamer initiative, whose mission is "bringing forth an environmentally sustainable, spiritually fulfilling and socially just human presence on Planet Earth"—the fulfillment of the second part of the Pachamama Alliance strategy. Since 2005 when it was begun, nearly 8,000 people have gone through an Awakening the Dreamer symposium in 11 countries. More than 350 people are trained as facilitators of the symposium, bringing it forward to other countries, translating it into different languages adapting it for use in businesses and with young people in high schools and colleges, and forming alliances with other organizations to bring it to their constituents globally. There have been four major fund raising events in Boston and Philadelphia, both of which are now thriving Pachamama communities.

Hearts of Fire. The Hearts of Fire (n.d.) mission is to bring

> the voice of homeless people to the public through compelling expressions of their art and music. We capture their art and music on site through facilitated art workshops and a mobile recording studio. In partnership with local homeless advocates and agencies, we tap into the vast pool of artistic talent among the homeless. We nurture that talent to not only draw attention to the issue of homelessness, but to begin a fundamental shift in how people relate to the homeless. By facilitating, capturing and publicizing the art and music of homeless men, women and children, we vividly display the face of their humanity to the world.

Bob Ballard created Hearts of Fire in Landmark Education's Power and Contribution course, a senior course in which participants are charged with solving an "impossible" problem. The Ojai, California–based 501(c)(3) organization was founded four years ago. Using a donated recreational vehicle, the Hearts of Fire project has toured homeless shelters throughout the United States for the past several years, bringing art and music into the lives of the homeless.

Ballard, Hearts of Fire's executive director as well as its founder, states, "We want to give homeless people the opportunity to be seen and heard through the expression of art and music to connect their humanity with our own." Projects have included hands-on art workshops with more than 100 homeless men, women, and children at the Ventura County Rescue Mission in Oxnard, California; an outdoor art and music workshop; creation of a music video (Ballard is a musician and composer); and numerous shelter-based workshops. Marika Zoll, a clinical psychologist who specializes in art therapy for the homeless and other at-risk populations, has said that creating art can help raise self-esteem and encourage positive interaction with others. She has pointed out that homeless individuals have intense feelings of being "not good enough," and the process of art-making and expressing oneself creatively has a positive effect on the brain (see Cahill, 2008).

Homeless Not Toothless. Homeless Not Toothless (mission: "Raising the pride and dignity of the underserved through quality dental services") was founded by Jay Grossman, a dentist in the affluent Brentwood area of Los Angeles County in 1992 in the Landmark Self-Expression and Leadership Program. In this program, participants are asked to create a project and "give it away." Jay's mission was to put "bite" into attacking the homeless problem by helping patients smile and raising their self-esteem so those motivated to do so can get back to work. In a world where an increasing number of individuals are one paycheck away from homelessness, he felt that dental hygiene, also related to overall health, can make a big difference.

Since its inception, the organization it has provided approximately 2,000 dental visits, amounting to over 1 million dollars worth of free dental work through over three dozen different dental practices in the Los Angeles area. Dentists volunteer their time and either pay for laboratory expenses themselves or work with labs who donate dental work as their way of contributing to this cause. A former U.S. Navy dental officer who happened to open his dental practice across the street from a Veteran's Administration hospital, Jay noticed many homeless veterans hanging out there and took his effort a step further than dental work. Believing you should "teach a man to fish and not just give him a fish," he asks prospective patients to commit to a sobriety program; be clean and sober for six months when starting treatment; show up on time for appointments, bathed and appropriately dressed; and "pay it forward" by helping others in whatever ways they can. Patients are required to go through an intense screening process at the Venice Family Clinic. Most important, he connects patients with Chrysalis, a nonprofit community-based organization in Los Angeles County dedicated to creating and locating employment opportunities to help homeless and other disadvantaged individuals become self-supporting. Chrysalis (http://www.changelives.org) has had a 92 percent success rate. Homeless Not Toothless has been featured numerous times on local network TV and nationally on CNN, and actress/philanthropist Sharon Stone is a member of their Board of Directors (see http://www.homelessnottoothless.org/).

Special Spectators. "Special Spectators, a Chicago-based 501(c)(3) organization, creates magical days for seriously ill children and their families at college sporting events across the United States" (see http://www.specialspectators.org/). The organization was created in spring 2002 by Blake Rockwell, a big sports fan, while he was a participant in the Landmark Self-Expression and Leadership Program. Blake got the idea to give seriously ill children a chance to attend college sporting events. Since its inception, Special Spectators has grown to include over 40 participating colleges and universities, including 22 Division 1A schools.

Children with serious illnesses who would otherwise not be able to participate in sports or attend games are treated to an all-day event. The day includes special VIP seating, tours of the stadium and locker rooms, visits with the players, and a visit to the field during half time during which the whole stadium cheers for them. Blake has been able to expand the program significantly with the help of Levy Cares, the nonprofit foundation of Levy Restaurants, a Chicago food company that supplies hot dogs to stadium vendors. The project has been covered by various newspapers, television and radio stations, and ESPN.com.

Cherish Our Children International. Cherish Our Children International (COCI) is dedicated to making a difference for the world's most needy and vulnerable children. Around the world, natural disasters, civil strife, war, and genocide have had a devastating impact on millions of children. The very people who face the greatest impact of these events are also the ones that are the most often forgotten. With a need so great, the goal of COCI is to fund, develop, pilot, and replicate local initiatives to serve these children.

Juli Kamin (now Juli Hall) of Houston, Texas, created and developed Cherish Our Children through her participation with Landmark Education's Team Management and Leadership Program. She was moved to ease the plight of Romanian orphans abandoned after the fall of the Ceausescu regime. She established COCI as a nonprofit organization to sponsor and implement model programs that now benefit children around the world, including Romania, Serbia, Kenya, Israel, Mexico, and the United States.

COCI's support and initiatives have aided HIV-positive children in Romania, abandoned children in Serbian orphanages, and children of incarcerated prisoners in the United States, and they have supported a soccer program in Israel that acts as a bridge between Jewish and Arab children. Other COCI accomplishments include the following:

- working with Hurricane Katrina child survivors in Houston to coordinate housing, education, and the location of relatives through a special COCI-designed Web site and providing formula to babies;
- funding a mother/child shelter to prevent the abandonment of more than 100 babies in Bucharest, Romania;
- funding temporary preadoptive foster homes to help children make the transition from institutions to family life;
- funding model family-style group homes in Romania for abandoned children with HIV;

- funding an HIV testing and counseling center in Constanta, Romania, to prevent the vertical transmission of the disease from mother to child;
- establishing a medical/nutritional care model for HIV-positive children with limited resources;
- teaching postinstitutionalized "handicapped" teens the skills necessary for self-sufficiency in a residential environment in Turnu Severin, Romania;
- training pre-school teachers in Montessori methodologies and providing materials to open Montessori classrooms for disadvantaged children in Turnu Severin, Romania;
- supporting art therapy for over 1,000 abandoned children in Romanian orphanages;
- developing a model community-service child development center and providing caregiver training for children with special needs in Iasi, Romania;
- bringing physical therapy techniques to over 300 child caregivers in Eastern Europe;
- providing emergency relief to an orphanage with 100 children in Iaşi, Romania, after government funds were exhausted and there was no money left for caregiver salaries or food for the children;
- rebuilding kindergartens in Sarajevo, Bosnia and Herzegovina, so that more than 1,250 children could attend school; and
- establishing a children's resource center in Belgrade, Serbia, to provide social intervention and transportation services to over 1,400 children from institutions and outlying low income areas.

Make a Film Foundation. The Make a Film Foundation (mission: "Teaming industry professionals with critically and terminally diagnosed youth to help them create short film legacies") is another program created in Landmark Education's Self-Expression and Leadership Program. Tamika Lamison—an accomplished actor, writer, and director—had numerous contacts in Hollywood and decided to draw on those resources. She partnered with Sarah Elgart, who had previously headed the Dream Project, which produced texts and short documentary films about the hopes and dreams of children with critical illnesses, and together they formed Make a Film.

The films they support are not about illness; rather, they are an opportunity for the ill youngsters to be fully self-expressed (a core value of the Self-Expression and Leadership Program). The first film produced, *Put it in a Book*, was created by Jabril Muhammad, a 19-year-old with sickle cell anemia who drew on his own observations of gang violence in the Los Angeles area to tell the story of a young man's choice between pursuing revenge for a murdered brother and the path of a just life. Lamison used her Hollywood connections to bring some talented and famous people on board, including award-winning filmmaker Rodrigo Garcia (*9 Lives, The Sopranos*) as director and arranged mentoring for Muhammad by notables such as Isaiah Washington. None of the cast or crew were paid for their services, and the film has been slated to appear at a number of prominent festivals. For the next project, Make a Film also partnered with the Make-a-Wish Foundation to sponsor a film by Clayton Beabout, an 11-year-old Kansas resident suffering from Vater's

Syndrome. As the organization has become known, grants from companies both inside and outside the film industry have expanded.

Although Lamison had the idea in her head, she has noted that "if I hadn't taken the Self-Expression and Leadership Program, I probably wouldn't have done anything."

Summary. David Cunningham describes the impact of the Landmark Forum as providing the possibility of "transformation showing up in every aspect of life." The key values, most of which are embedded in the culture of coaching on which I believe Landmark Education and its precursor programs have had a profound influence, are these:

- People are whole, complete, and perfect the way they are.
- Anything is possible—anything you want for yourself or your life is available.
- People need to be empowered in what matters to them.
- *Completing the past* needs to be emphasized rather than overcoming the past.
- Making a difference in the world is based on *transformation*, not change (the key insight is "nobody is wrong").

There are no "bad guys" of whom we are victims, and acceptance is the ability to fully be with things exactly as they are. Forgiveness is the ability to love another despite whatever they may have done (as distinct from condoning) so that we can "get to nothing," where it is then possible to create new possibilities for the future. Those new possibilities frequently involve stepping out of our "petty grievances" and, as we have seen, allowing individuals to make a huge difference in the world.

Social Innovation and Entrepreneurship

San Francisco has what is probably the most active social innovation community in the country right now. Not surprisingly, it is the home of CTI and forward-thinking coaches, like Virginia Kellogg, who have caused transformation in the community, helping tie together organizations through both coaching within the organizations and starting a movement to provide coaching to executive directors for the purpose of helping them grow their organizations.

Social entrepreneurship is the work of a social entrepreneur. A social entrepreneur is someone who recognizes a social problem and uses entrepreneurial principles to organize, create, and manage a venture to make social change. Whereas a business entrepreneur typically measures performance in profit and return, a social entrepreneur assesses success in terms of the impact he or she has on society. Although social entrepreneurs often work through nonprofits and citizen groups, many work in the private and governmental sectors.

The emerging field of social entrepreneurism has grown out of a number of fields, including business, social welfare, community development, community service, and international development. Social entrepreneurship has also been referred to as venture development, community wealth creation, social ventures, social entrepreneurs, social entrepreneurship, nonprofit enterprise, affirmative business, social purpose business, and microenterprise.

The main aim of a social enterprise is to further its social and environmental goals. Social enterprises are often, but not always, nonprofits. Social enterprises are for "more than profit." Although the terms are relatively new, social entrepreneurs and social entrepreneurship can be found throughout history. A list of a few historically noteworthy people whose work exemplifies classic social entrepreneurship would include Florence Nightingale (founder of the first nursing school and developer of modern nursing practices) and Robert Owen (founder of the cooperative movement).

The nonprofit sector is quite large and diverse, as are the resources available to it. Social enterprise efforts could be thought of as spanning a continuum ranging from those who engage in fee-for-service activities to those who engage in a variety of corporate–nonprofit partnerships (such as cause-related marketing or "cross-branding" efforts) to those who operate revenue-generating ventures employing particular client populations. Groups like the Roberts Enterprise Development Fund focus primarily on supporting nonprofits engaged in enterprise creation as a way of providing transitional and permanent employment to homeless and very low-income individuals. Other nonprofits are focused on the goal of assisting individuals in launching their own small, for-profit businesses. The practice of assisting individuals who are members of "disadvantaged" communities to start their own businesses is referred to as "microenterprise" or "self-employment." Many of these organizations are turning to coaching to help their constituent groups as well.

Root Cause is a nonprofit organization that works to accelerate the identification of solutions to social and economic problems by supporting social innovators and educating social impact investors through business planning and implementation, leadership development, research, and the creation of professional and funding networks that unite the public, private, and nonprofit sectors.

Founded in 2004 by Andrew Wolk, Root Cause has raised more than $22 million in investment and produced seven publications in its pursuit of advancing social innovation. Root Cause clients address issues like youth development, seniors and aging, and economic development, and the organization has developed a network of over 4,500 nonprofit, business, foundation, academic, and government leaders and engaged almost 250 professionally skilled volunteers.

Root Cause's Social Innovation Forum focuses on creating an "alternative philanthropic marketplace that will encourage social investors to invest and reinvest in the organizations best positioned to chip away at the root causes of our social problems" (Root Cause, n.d.). Social innovators—those demonstrating promising approaches to addressing specific social problems—are chosen annually and provided with strategy consulting, executive coaching, and introductions to a philanthropic investment community made up of government leaders, foundations, and individual donors who are willing to offer time, talent, relationships, and money. The goal is to increase progress in solving pressing social problems by directing resources to "innovative, results-oriented organizations striving for efficiency, effectiveness, and sustainability" (Root Cause, n.d.). Some of the 2008 and 2009 social innovators are the following:

- Cradles to Crayons (http://www.cradlestocrayons.org), equipping poor and homeless children with basic essentials (and supplying some of the birthday "gifts" to Birthday Wishes);
- Access Boston (http://www.accessboston.org), providing free financial aid advice and advocacy to low-income students;
- Hearth Outreach Program (http://www.hearth-home.org), assisting homeless elders in locating affordable housing, health care, and social services; and
- Raw Art Works (http://www.rawart.org), offering free arts programs to disadvantaged youth age 6 to 19 years.

Asset-Based Community Development

Asset-based community development is an approach to community development that advocates the use of skills and strengths that are already present within the community, rather than obtaining help from outside institutions. The Asset-Based Community Development Institute was established in 1995 by the Community Development Program at Northwestern University's Institute for Policy Research and is built on three decades of community development research by Jodi Krentzman and John L. McKnight. The Asset-Based Community Development Institute spreads its findings on capacity-building community development in two ways: (1) through extensive and substantial interactions with community builders and (2) by producing practical resources and tools for community builders to identify, nurture, and mobilize neighborhood assets.

The phrase "asset-based" refers to a positive, "capacity-driven" approach that encourages community members to make progress for themselves, as opposed to a traditional "needs-driven" approach that makes the community dependent on institutional help. The basic principles of asset-based community development are consistent with coaching:

- *Focus on gifts*: Every person and group (and community) has existing gifts and abilities—social capital or assets—that can be identified and used to build stronger communities from within.
- *Associational life*: Groups of people voluntarily coming together to make a difference (versus systems of well-resourced professional services) are more likely to provide a critical sense of care and belonging.
- *Power in our hands*: Sustainable community improvements occur when citizens—not waiting on professionals or elected leaders—discover their own power to act and begin producing their desired future.

Asset-based community development is just one of many innovative approaches that demonstrate the ability of communities as well as individuals, families, and business to transform themselves. The common threads to all of the programs described in this chapter, and all of the approaches to coaching described earlier in this book, are vision, passion, planning, and belief that the client—be it an individual, family, business, or community—is, in "co-active" language, *naturally* creative, resourceful, and whole. From this perspective, whether we fully embrace coaching as a new professional pursuit or simply use coaching skills and techniques in our existing work, we can *all* make a difference.

Epilogue

I firmly hope that this book has provided a balanced view of coaching that has exposed readers to the breadth, depth, and unlimited possibilities coaching affords. I have not presented any new theories or approaches, but I believe I have brought together all of the corners of the coaching world to help human services and health care professionals, or anyone wanting to make a difference for others, see coaching in a new and expanded light. We have yet to solve the critical issue—one that is more urgent than ever in a down economy—of finding solid sources of funding for all of the arenas in which coaching can make a difference. Coaching, nonetheless, continues to expand its reach and knowledge base, and it is beginning to coalesce as a mature profession that has a significant contribution to make. However you decide you use coaching for yourself, I hope I have expanded your world.

—Marilyn Edelson, LICSW, MCC, CPCC, Newton, Massachusetts

What lies behind you and what lies in front of you, pales in comparison to what lies inside of you.

—Ralph Waldo Emerson

References

Adams, E. (1994). Growing your business plan. *Home Office Computing, 13*(5), 43–47.

American Psychiatric Association. (1994). *Diagnostic and statistical manual of mental disorders* (4th ed.). Washington, DC: Author.

Asperger syndrome. (n.d.). Retrieved from Wikipedia: http://en.wikipedia.org/wiki/Asperger_syndrome

Awakening the Dreamer. (n.d.). *Our story.* Retrieved from http://awakeningthedreamer.org/content/view/85/134/

Bandler, R. (2008). *Get the life you want: The secrets to quick and lasting life change with Neuro-Linguistic Programming.* Deerfield Beach, FL: Health Communications, Inc.

Bandler, R., & Grinder, J. (1979). *Frogs into princes: Neuro Linguistic Programming.* Boulder, CO: Real People Press.

Beck, J. (Producer), & Koster, H. (Director). (1950). *Harvey* [Motion picture]. United States: Universal Pictures.

Bennis, W. (1994). *An invented life: Reflections on leadership and change.* New York: Basic Books.

Berglas, S. (2002, June). The very real dangers of executive coaching. *Harvard Business Review, 80*(6), 86–92.

Blanchard, K., & Johnson, S. (1983). *The one minute manager.* New York: Wm. Morrow.

Blanchard, K., & Shula, D. (1995). *Everyone's a coach: Five business secrets for high performance coaching.* New York: HarperCollins.

Bluckert, P. (2004). *The similarities and differences between coaching and therapy.* Retrieved from http://www.pbcoaching.com/article-coaching-and-therapy.php

Brain training exercises and coaching for senior leaders and managers. (n.d.). Retrieved from http://www.coachinglogic.com/Research_Studies.htm

Budd, M., & Rothstein, L. (2000). *You are what you say: A Harvard doctor's six-step proven program for transforming stress through the power of language.* New York: Crown Books.

Burns, D. D. (1989). *The feeling good handbook.* New York: Wm. Morrow.

Burns, D. D. (1999). *Feeling good: The new mood therapy* (Rev. ed). New York: HarperCollins.

Butterworth, S., Linden, A., McClay, W., & Leo, M. C. (2006). Effect of motivational interviewing–based health coaching on employees' physical and mental health status. *Journal of Occupational Health, 11,* 358–365.

Cahill, V. (2008, October 10). *Hearts of Fire rolls through California.* Retrieved from http://www.landmarkeducationnews.info/2008/10/10/hearts-of-fire-rolls-through-california/

Cameron, J. (1992). *The artist's way: A spiritual path to higher creativity.* New York: Jeremy P. Tarcher/Putnam.

Carson, R. (1983). *Taming your gremlin: A guide to enjoying yourself.* New York: Harper & Row.

Center for Right Relationship. (n.d.). *Center for Right Relationship.* Retrieved from http://crrglobalalliance.com/

Center for Right Relationship. (2009). *What we believe about relationship systems.* Retrieved from http://www.centerforrightrelationship.com/professionals/thought-leadership/74-what-we-believe-about-relationship-systems

Chopra, D. (1993). *Ageless body, timeless mind: The quantum alternative to growing old.* New York: Harmony Books.

Chopra, D. (1994). *The seven spiritual laws of success: A practical guide to the fulfillment of your dreams.* San Rafael, CA: Amber-Allen Publishing.

Coaches Training Institute. (n.d.). *The Coaches Training Institute (CTI).* Retrieved from http://www.thecoaches.com/

Cooperrider, D. (2005). *Appreciative inquiry: A positive revolution in change.* San Francisco: Berrett-Kohler.

Coutu, D., & Kauffman, C. (2009, January 1). What can coaches do for you? *Harvard Business Review, 87*(1), 91–97.

Covey, S. (1989). *The seven habits of highly effective people: Powerful lessons in personal change.* New York: Fireside Books.

De Bono, E. (1990). *Lateral thinking: Creativity step-by-step.* New York: Harper Colophon.

Dembkowski, S., & Eldridge, F. (2003). *Measuring snowflakes? Calculating the return on investment of executive coaching.* Retrieved from http://www.coachfederation.org/includes/docs/048HowtoCalulateCoachingROIEuropeanStudy2003.doc

Ditzler, J. S. (2000). *Your best year yet! Ten questions for making the next twelve months your most successful ever.* New York: Warner Books.

Drucker, P. F. (1966). *The effective executive.* New York: HarperCollins.

Dyer, W. (1976). *Your erroneous zones.* New York: Funk & Wagnalls.

Dyer, W. (2005). *The power of intention.* Carlsbad, CA: Hay House.

Echeverria, R. (1990). *The basic linguistic acts.* San Francisco: Newfield Group.

Edelson, M. (2002a). *Family business: Move ahead together in uncertain times.* Retrieved from http://www.coachlink.net/resources/move_ahead.htm

Edelson, M. (2002b, June). *The universal language of coaching.* Paper presented at the International Conference for the Advancement of Private Practice Social Work, Lisbon, Portugal.

Elaine, K. (n.d.). *The Asperger advantage: About Kristina Elaine.* Retrieved from http://www.coachingasperger.com/kristina.htm

Flores, F., & Winograd, T. (1989). *Understanding computers and cognition: A new vision for design.* Norwood, NJ: Ablex.

Ford, D. (1999). *The dark side of light chasers: Reclaiming your power, creativity, brilliance, and dreams.* New York: Riverhead Books.

Fortgang, L. B. (1998). *Take yourself to the top: The secrets of America's #1 career coach.* New York: Warner Books.

Frankl, V. E. (1984). *Man's search for meaning.* New York: Washington Square Press.

Friedman, S., & Fanger, M. (1991). *Expanding therapeutic possibilities: Getting results in brief therapy.* Lexington, MA: Lexington Books.

Fritz, R. (1984). *The path of least resistance: Learning to become the creative force in your own life.* New York: Fawcett Columbine.

Gallwey, T. (1974). *The inner game of tennis.* New York: Random House.

Gardner, H. (1993). *Frames of mind: The theory of multiple intelligences.* New York: Basic Books.

Garfield, C. (1984). *Peak performance.* Boston: Houghton.

Gendlin, E. T. (1982). *Focusing.* New York: Bantam Books.

Gerber, M. E. (1995). *The e-myth revisited: Why most small businesses don't work and what to do about it.* New York: HarperCollins.

Goldsmith, M., & Lyons, L. (Eds.) (2006). *Coaching for leadership: The practice of leadership coaching from the world's greatest coaches.* San Francisco: Pfeiffer.

Goleman, D. (1995). *Emotional intelligence: Why it can matter more than IQ.* New York: Bantam Books.

Goleman, D. (2000). *Working with emotional intelligence.* New York: Bantam Books.

Goleman, D. (2006). *Social intelligence: The new science of human relationships.* New York: Bantam/Dell.

Gottman, J. (1994). *Why marriages succeed or fail: What you can learn from the breakthrough research to make your marriage last.* New York: Simon & Schuster.

Gottman, J., & Silver, N. (1999). *The seven principles for making marriage work.* new York: Crown.

Greene, J., & Grant, A. (2003). *Solution-focused coaching: Managing people in a complex world.* Upper Saddle River, NJ: Pearson Education.

Greenleaf, R. H. (2002). *Servant leadership: A journey into the nature of legitimate power and greatness* (25th anniversary ed.). New York: Paulist Press.

Hallowell, E. M., & Ratey, J. J. (1994). *Driven to distraction: Recognizing and coping with attention deficit disorder from childhood through adulthood.* New York: Touchstone.

Hargrove, R. (1995). *Masterful coaching: Extraordinary results by impacting people and the way they think and work together.* San Francisco: Jossey-Bass/Pfeiffer.

Harvard Medical School. (2009). *Positive psychology: Harnessing the power of happiness, personal strength, and mindfulness.* Cambridge, MA: Harvard Health Publications.

Hay, L. L. (1984). *You can heal your life.* Carlsbad, CA: Hay House.

Hayes, E., & Kalmakis, K. A. (2007). From the sidelines: Coaching as a nurse practitioner strategy for improving health outcomes. *Journal of the American Academy of Nurse Practitioners, 11,* 555–562.

Hayes, E., McCahon, C., Panahi, M. R., Hamre, T., & Pohlman, K. (2008). Alliance not compliance: Coaching strategies to improve type 2 diabetes outcomes *Journal of the American Academy of Nurse Practitioners, 20,* 155–162.

Hearts of Fire. (n.d.). *Hearts of Fire project.* Retrieved from http://www.globalgiving.org/pfil/2982/projdoc.pdf

Hesse, H. (1956). *Journey to the east.* New York: Farrar, Straus and Giroux. (Original work published 1932)

Hill, N. (1982). *Think and grow rich.* Meriden, CT: The Ralston Society.

Hudson, F. (n.d.). *Career coaching.* Retrieved from http://www.careertrainer.com/Request.jsp?lView=ViewArticle&Article=OID%3A121631&Page=OID%3A121632

Hudson, F. (1991). *The adult years: Mastering the art of self-renewal.* San Francisco: Jossey-Bass.

Hudson, F. (1999). *The handbook of coaching.* San Francisco: Jossey-Bass.

Hudson, F., & McLean, P (1995). *Life launch: A passionate guide to the rest of your life.* Santa Barbara, CA: Hudson Institute Press.

Hudson Institute. (n.d.-a). *Co-founder, Frederic Hudson.* Retrieved from http://www.hudsoninstitute.com/aboutus/frederichudson.php

Hudson Institute. (n.d.-b). *ThirdLaunch: Passion and purpose beyond career.* Retrieved from https://www.hudsoninstitute.com/transition/thirdlaunch/

Hunt, J., & Weintraub, J. (2002). *The coaching manager: Developing top talent in business.* Thousand Oaks, CA: Sage Publications.

Integrity. (2004). In *Merriam-Webster's collegiate dictionary* (11th ed., p. 650). Springfield, MA: Merriam-Webster.

International Coach Federation. (n.d.). *What is coaching?* Retrieved from http://www.miamicoach-federation.org/Whatis.html

International Coach Federation. (2008). *Global coaching study.* Retrieved from http://www.coach-federation.org/includes/docs/064GlobalCoachingStudyExecutiveSummary2008.pdf

International Coach Federation. (2009). *Code of ethics.* Retrieved from www.coachfederation.org/about-icf/ethics-%26-regulation/icf-code-of-ethics/

Jaworski, J. (1996). *Synchronicity: The inner path of leadership.* San Francisco: Berrett-Koehler.

Jung, C. G. (1960). Synchronicity: An acausal connecting principle. In *The collected works of C. G. Jung, Vol. 8: The structure and dynamics of the psyche.* (R.F C. Hull, Trans.) (pp. 5–146). Princeton, NJ: Princeton University Press.

Kelly, K., & Ramundo, P. (1995). *You mean I'm not lazy, stupid or crazy?! A self-help book for adults with attention deficit disorder.* New York: Scribner.

Kitaj, K. (2002). *Women who could . . . and did: Lives of 26 exemplary artists and scientists.* Chestnut Hill, MA: Huckle Hill Press.

Knowles, M. S. (1950). *Informal adult education.* New York: Association Press.

Knowles, M. S. (1990). *The adult learner: A neglected species* (4th ed.). Houston, TX: Gulf Publicating Company.

Kofman, F., & Senge, P. M. (1995). Communities of commitment: The heart of learning organizations. In S. Chawla & J. Renesch (Eds.), *Learning organizations: Developing cultures for tomorrow's workplace* (pp. 14–43). Portland, OR: Productivity Press.

Korin, E. H. (2006). *Asperger syndrome: An owner's manual—What you, your parents and your teachers need to know.* Shawnee Mission, KS: Autism Asperger Publishing.

Korin, E. H. (2007). *Asperger syndrome: An owner's manual for older adolescents and adults—What you, your parents and friends, and your employer need to know.* Shawnee Mission, KS: Autism Asperger Publishing.

Leonard, T. J. (2007). *The 28 laws of attraction: Stop chasing success and let it chase you.* New York: Scribner.

Leonard, T. J., & Larson, B. (1998). *The portable coach: 28 surefire strategies for business and personal success.* New York: Scribner.

List of therapies. (n.d.). Retrieved from http://en.wikipedia.org/wiki/List_of_therapies

Loehr, J., & Schwartz, T. (2003). *The power of full engagement: Managing energy, not time, is the key to high performance and personal renewal.* New York: Simon & Schuster.

Maslow, A. H. (1968). *Toward a psychology of being.* New York: John Wiley & Sons.

May, R. (1981). *Freedom and destiny.* New York: W. W. Norton.

McLean Hospital/Harvard Medical School 2nd Annual Coaching Conference launched. (2009, August 11). Press release retrieved from http://www.mclean.harvard.edu/news/press/current.php?kw=mclean-harvard-medical-school-second-annual-coaching-conference&id=144

Meinke, L. F. (n.d.). *Top ten indicators to refer to a mental health professional.* Retrieved from http://www.omneclinic.com/TenIndicators.htm

Miller, W. R., & Rollnick, S. (2002). *Motivational interviewing: Preparing people to change.* New York: Guilford Press.

Mindell, A. (1992). *The leader as martial artist: An introduction to deep democracy.* San Francisco: Harper San Francisco.

Moore. M. (n.d.). *DNA of well-beings.* Retrieved from http://www.coachmeg.com/index.cfm?page=dna

Murphy, J. S., & Hudson, F. (1995). *The joy of old: A guide to successful elderhood.* Balcelona, Spain: Geode Press.

Neurotypical. (n.d.). Retrieved from Wikipedia: http://en.wikipedia.org/wiki/Neurotypical

Nevis, E. C. (1987). *Organizational consulting: A Gestalt approach.* New York: Gardner Press.

Noonan, E. (2006, September 10). "Emotional intelligence" a new hiring criterion. *Boston Globe.* Retrieved from http://www.boston.com/jobs/news/articles/2006/09/10/emotional_intelligence_a_new_hiring_criteria/

Norcross, J. C., & Guy, J. D., Jr. (2007). *Leaving it at the office: A guide to psychotherapist self-care.* New York: Guilford Press.

O'Connor, J., & Seymor, J. (1993). Introducing Neuro-Linguistic Programming: Psychological skills for understanding and influencing people (2nd ed.). New York: Thorsons/Element.

O'Hanlon, W. H. (1999). *Do one thing different.* New York: HarperCollins.

Olalla, J. (2004). *What is ontological coaching?* Retrieved from http://www.newfieldasia.com/CoachTraining/AdditionalResources/OntologicalCoachingWhitePaper/index.htm.

Peale, N. V. (1952). *The power of positive thinking.* Engleside Cliffs, NJ: Prentice-Hall.

Peck, M. S. (1978). *The road less traveled: A new psychology of love, traditional values and spiritual growth.* New York: Touchstone.

Peddy, S. (2002). *The art of mentoring: Lead, follow and get out of the way.* Houston: Bullion Books.

Peterson, C., & Seligman, M.E.P. (2004). *Character strengths and virtues: A handbook and classification.* Oxford, England: Oxford University Press.

Possibility. (2004). In *Merriam-Webster's collegiate dictionary* (11th ed., p. 968). Springfield, MA: Merriam-Webster.

Prochaska, J. O., Norcross, J. C., & DiClemente, C. C. (1995). *Changing for good.* New York: Avon Books.

Ratey, N. (2002). Life coaching for adult ADHD. In S. Goldstein & A. T. Ellison (Eds.), *Clinicians guide to adult ADHD: Assessment and intervention* (pp. 261–279). London: Academic Press.

Richardson, C. (1998). *Take time for your life: A personal coach's seven-step program for creating the life you want.* New York: Broadway Books.

Robbins, A. (1991). *Awaken the giant within: How to take immediate control of your mental, emotional, physical and financial destiny!* New York: Simon & Schuster.

Robbins, A., & Wilner, A. (2001). *Quarterlife crisis: The unique challenges of life in your twenties.* New York: Tarcher.

Rock, D. (2006). *Quiet leadership: Six steps to transforming performance at work.* New York: HarperCollins.

Rock, D., & Schwartz, J. (2006). *The neuroscience of leadership.* Retrieved http://www.strategy-business.com/press/freearticle/06207?gko=498f4-12656449-15832258

Root Cause. (n.d.). *Social Innovation Forum.* Retrieved from http://www.rootcause.org/social_enterprises/social_innovation_forum

Rubin, H. (2007, December 18). *The power of words.* Retrieved from http://www.fastcompany.com/node/36313/print

Ruiz, M. A. (1997). *The four agreements: A practical guide to personal freedom.* San Rafael, CA: Allen Amber.

Schein, E. H. (2006). Coaching and consultation revisited: Are they the same? In M. Goldsmith & L Lyons (Eds.), *Coaching for leadership: The practice of leadership coaching from the world's greatest coaches* (2nd ed., pp. 17–25). San Francisco: Pfeiffer.

Schwartz, J., Stapp, H. P., & Beauregard, M. (2005). Quantum physics in neuroscience and psychology: A neurophysical model of mind–brain interaction. *Philosophical Transactions. Of the Royal Society, 360,* 1309–1327.

Searle, J. R. (1970). *Speech acts.* Cambridge, England: Cambridge University Press.

Seligman, M.E.P. (1994). *Learned optimism: How to change your mind and your life.* New York: Knopf.

Seligman, M.E.P. (2002). *Authentic happiness: Using the new positive psychology to realize your potential for lasting fulfillemnt.* New York: Free Press.

Spinelli, E. (2005). *The interpreted world.* London: Sage Publications.

Stober, D., & Grant, A. M. (Eds.). (2006). *Evidence-based coaching: Putting best practices to work for your clients.* Hoboken, NJ: John Wiley & Sons.

Twist, L. (2006). *The soul of money: Reclaiming the wealth of our inner resources.* New York: W. W. Norton.

Vergano, D. (2006, August 6). Study: Emotion rules the brain's decisions. *USA Today.* Retrieved from http://usatoday.com/tech/science/discoveries/2006-08-06-brain-study_x.htm

Wheatley, M. J. (2002). *Turning to one another: Simple conversations to restore hope to the future.* San Francisco: Berrett-Koehler.

White, D. (1998, February 23). Coach for life. *Boston Globe.* Retrieved from http://www.jerriudelson.com/articles/coach_for_life.html

White, M. (2007). *Maps of narrative practice.* New York: W. W. Norton.

White, M., & Eptson, D. (1990). *Narrative means to therapeutic ends.* New York: W. W. Norton.

Whitworth, L., Kimsey-House , H., & Sandahl, P. (1998). *Co-active coaching: New skills for coaching people toward success in work and life.* Palo Alto, CA: Davies-Black.

Williams, P., & Anderson, S. (2006). *Law and ethics in coaching: How to solve and avoid difficult problems in your practice.* Hoboken, NJ: John Wiley & Sons.

Williams, P., & Davis, D. (2002). *Therapist as life coach: Transforming your practice.* New York: W. W. Norton .

Winograd, T., & Flores, F. (1986). *Understanding computers and cognition: A new vision for design.* Norwood, NJ: Ablex.

Yancey, S. (2006). *Relationship networking: the art of turning contacts into connections.* Dallas: eWomenPublishing Network.

Zander, R. S., & Zander, B. (2000). *The art of possibility: Transforming professional and personal life.* Cambridge , MA: Harvard University Press.

Resources

BOOKS

Business and Consulting

Albrecht, K., & Zemke, R. (1985). *Service America*. New York: Warner Books.

Arkebauer, J. (1995). *A guide to writing a high impact business plan*. New York: McGraw-Hill.

Edwards, P., & Edwards, S. (1994). *Working from home: Everything you need to know about living and working under the same roof*. New York: Tarcher/Putnam.

Gerber, M. E. (1995). *The e-myth revisited: Why most small businesses don't work and what to do about it*. New York: HarperCollins.

Kamoroff, B. B. (2008). *Small time business operator: How to start your own business, keep your books, pay your taxes & stay out of trouble* (10th ed.). Willits, CA: Bell Springs Press.

Perrott, L. A. (1999). *Reinventing your practice as a business psychologist: A step-by-step guide*. San Francisco: Jossey-Bass.

Port, M., & Sanders, T. (2006). *Book yourself solid: The fastest, easiest, and most reliable system for getting more clients than you can handle even if you hate marketing and selling*. Hoboken, NJ: John Wiley & Sons.

Sohnen-Moe, C. (1996). *Business mastery: A business planning guide for creating a fulfilling, thriving business and keeping it successful*. Tucson, AZ: Sohnen-Moe Associates.

Leadership

Arbinger Institute. (2002). *Leadership and self-deception: Getting out of the box*. San Francisco: Berrett-Koehler.

Arbinger Institute. (2008). *The anatomy of peace: Resolving the heart of conflict*. San Francisco: Berrett-Koehler.

Collins, J. (2001). *Good to great: Why some companies make the leap . . . and others don't*. New York: HarperCollins.

Goldsmith, M., & Lyons, L. (Eds.) (2006). *Coaching for leadership: The practice of leadership coaching from the world's greatest coaches*. San Francisco: Pfeiffer.

Hadikin, R., & Butterworth, H. (2003). *Effective coaching in healthcare practice*. Hale, Chesire, England: Books for Midwives Press.

Jaworski, J. (1996). *Synchronicity: The inner path of leadership*. San Francisco: Berrett-Koehler.

Raelin, J. A. (2003). *Creating leaderful organizations: How to bring out leadership in everyone*. San Francisco: Berrett-Koehler.

Ruiz, M. A. (1997). *The four agreements: A practical guide to personal freedom.* San Rafael, CA: Allen Amber.

Senge, P., Scharmer, C. O., Jaworski, J., & Flowers, B. S. (2005). *Presence: Human purpose and the field of the future.* New York: Currency Books.

Sincock, P. F. (2000). *Inner path leadership. Exploring the spiritual demands of a new century* Victoria, British Columbia, Canada: Trafford.

Wheatley, M. J. (2006). *Leadership and the new science: Discovering order in a chaotic world* (3rd ed.). San Francisco: Berrett-Koehler.

Wheatley, M. J. (2009). *Turning to one another: Simple conversations to restore hope to the future* (2nd ed.). San Francisco: Berrett-Koehler.

Money and Prosperity

Boldt, L. G. (1993). *Zen and the art of making a living: A practical guide to creative career design.* New York: Penguin Books.

Chopra, D. (1993). *Creating affluence: Wealth consciousness in the field of all possibilities.* New York: Amber-Allen Publishing and New World Library.

Dominguez, J., & Robin, V. (1992). *Your money or your life: Transforming your relationship with money and achieving financial independence.* New York: Penguin Books.

Mundis, G. (1989). *Earn what you deserve: How to stop underearning and start thriving.* New York: Bantam Books.

Orman, S. (1997). *The 9 steps to financial freedom: Practical spiritual steps so you can stop worrying.* New York: Crown.

Orman, S. (1999). *The courage to be rich: Creating a life of material and spiritual abundance.* New York: Riverhead Books.

Orman, S. (1997). *You've earned it, don't lose it: Mistakes you can't afford to make when you retire* (Rev. ed.). New York: Newmarket Press.

Twist, L. (2006). *The soul of money: Reclaiming the wealth of our inner resources.* New York: W. W. Norton.

Organizational Skills

Allen, D. (2001). *Getting things done: The art of stress-free productivity.* New York: Penguin Books.

Franklin, L. (2003). *How to get organized without resorting to arson: A step-by-step guide to clearing your desk without panic or the use of open flame.* Granite Bay, CA: Clara Fyer Books.

Sales, Marketing, and Publicity

Beckwith, H. (1997). *Selling the invisible: A field guide to modern marketing.* New York: Warner Books.

Eades, K. M. (2004). *The new solution selling: The revolutionary sales process that is changing the way people sell.* New York: McGraw-Hill.

Fox, J. (2002). *How to become a rainmaker: The rules for getting and keeping customers and clients.* New York: Hyperion.

Hayden, C. J. (1999). *Get clients now! A 28-day marketing program for professionals and consultants.* New York: AMACOM.

Klauser, H. (2000). *Write it down, make it happen: Knowing what you want and getting it.* New York: Fireside Books.

Levinson, J., & Godin, S. (1995). *Guerilla marketing for home-based businesses.* New York: Houghton Mifflin.

Port, M., & Sanders, T. (2006). *Book yourself solid: The fastest, easiest, and most reliable system for getting more clients than you can handle even if you hate marketing and selling.* Hoboken, NJ: John Wiley & Sons.

Ries, L., & Ries, A. (1998). *The 22 immutable laws of branding: How to build a product or service into a world class brand.* New York: HarperCollins.

Schloff, L., & Yudkin, M. (1991). *Smart speaking: 60-second strategies for more than 100 speaking problems and fears.* New York: Henry Holt.

Stephens, N. (1998). *Streetwise customer-focused selling: Understanding customer needs, building trust, and delivering solutions . . . the smarter path to sales success.* Holbrook, MA: Adams Media.

Yudkin, M. (1994). *Six steps to free publicity and dozens of other ways to win free media attention for your business.* New York: Penguin Books.

Yudkin, M. (1995). *Marketing online: Low-cost, high-yield strategies for small businesses and professionals.* New York: Penguin Books.

Assessments Used in Personal and Business Coaching (those marked with an asterisk require certification)

Authentic Happiness (Martin E. P. Seligman, University of Pennsylvania): http://www.authentic happiness.sas.upenn.edu/Default.aspx

> Emotion Questionnaires
> *Authentic Happiness Inventory Questionnaire* (overall happiness)
> *CES-D Questionnaire* (depression symptoms)
> *Fordyce Emotions Questionnaire* (current happiness)
> *General Happiness Questionnaire* (enduring happiness)
> *PANAS Questionnaire* (positive and negative affect)
>
> Engagement Questionnaires
> *Brief Strengths Test* (24 character strengths)
> *Gratitude Questionnaire* (appreciation about the past)
> *Grit Survey* (perseverence)
> *Optimism Test* (optimism about the future)
> *Transgression Motivations Questionnaire* (forgiveness)
> *VIA Signature Strengths Questionnaire* (24 character strengths)
> *VIA Strength Survey for Children* (24 character strengths for children)
> *Work–Life Questionnaire* (work–life satisfaction)
>
> Meaning Questionnaires
> *Close Relationships Questionnaire* (attachment style)
> *Compassionate Love Scale* (tendency to support, help, and understand other people)
> *Meaning in Life Questionnaire* (meaningfulness)
>
> Life Satisfaction Questionnaires
> *Approaches to Happiness Questionnaire* (three routes to happiness)
> *Satisfaction with Life Scale* (life satisfaction)

Birkman Method (facilitates team building, executive coaching, leadership development, and career management): http://www.birkman.com/index.php

Buckingham, M., & Cliftyen, D. O. (2001). *Now, discover your strengths.* New York: Free Press. (includes two free strengths assessments)

Energy Director Assessment. A Guide to Determining Your Energy Profile (Crout Performance, Inc.)

*FIRO-B *[Fundamental Interpersonal Relations Orientation–Behavior]* (Consulting Psychologists Press): http://www.cpp-db.com, http://www.discoveryourpersonality.com; 1-800-624-1765

Hartman Color Code: http://www.thecolorcode.com/personality/personalityassessment/personalityassessment.htmll

Highlands Ability Battery (provides a 33-page report on 18 different natural abilities that contribute to career choice and success): http://www.highlandsco.com/battery.php

Hogan Assessment Systems: http://www.hoganassessments.com

Keirsay Character Sorter and Temperament Sorter (James Keirsay): http://keirsay.com; 1-800-754-0039

Life Planning and Purpose Cards (Hudson Institute): e-mail: info@hudsoninstitute.com; 1-800-582-4401

*LIFO (Stuart Atkins and Allan Katcher)

*Myers–Briggs Type Indicator (Isabel Briggs Meyers): http://www.knowyourtype.com

Predictive Index (the only Equal Employment Opportunity Commision–approved, work-related assessment on the market; used to profile positions as well as the fit of candidates and in consulting on leadership development, teamwork, onboarding, and other management issues): http://www.PIWorldwide.com

Seven Habits Profile and Action Planning Guide [a.k.a. the "Covey 360"] (Covey Leadership Center)

Stress Map (Essi Systems, Inc.): http://www.essisystems.com; 1-800-252-3774

Team Diagnostic Assessment: http://teamdiagnosticassessment.com

The Universal Language: DISC (Bill Bonnstetter, Judy Suiter, and Randy Widrick; Target Training International): http://www.ttidisc.com

Values-Driven Work (Career Action Center): http://www.careers.com

Coaching-Related Journals and Magazines

AC Bulletin (Association for Coaching): http://www.associationforcoaching.com/pub/pub02.htm

Business Coaching Worldwide (WABC): http://www.wabccoaches.com/bcw/

Choice: The Magazine of Professional Coaching: http://www.choice-online.com/

The Coach Connection Blog: http://findyourcoach.blogharbor.com/

Coaching: An International Journal of Theory, Research and Practice

Coaching at Work (CIPD): http://www.cipd.co.uk/coachingatwork/presales.htm

Coaching Magazine: Desarrollo Personal y Organizacional (Spanish): http://www.coachingmagazine.net

Coaching Psychologist (British Psychological Society): http://www.sgcp.org.uk/publications/the-coachingpsychologist.cfm

Consulting Psychology Journal (American Psychological Association): http://www.apa.org/journals/cpb/homepage.html

Industrial & Commercial Training: http://www.business-magazines.com/product.php

International Coaching Psychology Review (British Psychological Society): http://www.bps.org.uk/coachingpsy/publications.cfm

International Journal of Coaching in Organizations (IJCO): http://www.ijco.info/publications/subscriptions.php

International Journal of Evidence-Based Coaching and Mentoring (Oxford Brookes University): http://www.brookes.ac.uk/schools/education/ijebcm/home.html

International Journal of Management Development (IJMD): http://www.inderscience.com/browse/index.php?journalID=251

Journal of Applied Behavioral Science: http://www.sagepub.com/journalsProdDesc.nav?prodId=Journal200967

Journal of Applied Behavioral Science: http://jab.sagepub.com/archive

Journal of Management Development: http://www.ingentaconnect.com/content/mcb/026

Journal of Organizational Change Management: http://business.nmsu.edu/~dboje/jocm.html

Journal of Positive Psychology: http://www.informaworld.com/smpp/title~content=t724921263

Leadership Excellence: http://www.eep.com/merchant/newsite/eeindex.htm

The Peer Bulletin (Peer Resources): http://www.peer.ca/

Peer Resources (coaching directory): http://www.peer.ca/coaching.html

People Management Magazine: http://www.peoplemanagement.co.uk/pm/contactus/subscribe.htm

Personal Success (The Academy Club): http://www.theacademyclub.com/

Psychologies (French): http://www.psychologies.com/

Society for Human Resource Management HR Magazine (SHRM): https://sapphire.shrm.org/subscriptions/subscriptionsform.cfm

Websites and Online Resources

Coaching Industry Resources

Association for Coach Training Organizations (ACTO): http://www.acto1.com/

Bath Consultancy Group: http://www.bathconsultancygroup.com/

Chartered Institute for Personnel and Development (CIPD): http://www.cipd.co.uk/default.cipd

Coaching Commons (a noncommercial, coach-driven site regarding the industry and work of coaching): http://www.coachingcommons.org

CoachVille: http://www.coachville.com

Consortium for Research on Emotional Intelligence in Organizations: http://www.eiconsortium.org/

European Mentoring & Coaching Council (EMCC): http://www.emccouncil.org/

Foundation of Coaching (Research Division): http://repository.thefoundationofcoaching.org/research/

Graduate School Alliance for Executive Coaching (research and scholarship): http://www.gsaec.org/links.html

Harvard Medical School/McLean Hospital, Coaching and Positive Psychology Initiative: http://www.harvardcppi.org

Institute for Life Coach Training: http://www.lifecoachtraining.com/resources/index.shtml

International Coach Federation (ICF): http://www.coachfederation.org; e-mail: info@coachfederation.org; membership information: 1-888-423-3131

International Coach Federation–New England (my ICF chapter): http://www.icfne.org; 1-617-264-2888 or 1-877-NE-COACH

International Consortium for Coaching in Organizations (ICCO): http://www.coaching
    consortium.org/
Lore International Institute: http://www.lorenet.com/LIB-Library.asp
Medical Research Council: http://www.mrc.ac.uk/index.htm
Peer Resources Library: http://www.peer.ca/articles/index.php?mode=results&keyword=&journal
    =&author=&year=&perpage=10&submit=Search+the+Library
Worldwide Association of Business Coaches (WABC): http://www.wabccoaches.com/

Practice Building and Marketing

Action Plan Marketing: http://www.actionplan.com
Coaching Blog Catalogue: http://www.blogcatalog.com/directory/coaching
Constant Contact (for creating online newsletters): http://www.constantcontact.com
Get Clients Now!: http://www.getclientsnow.com
WebFlexor (Web site design for coaches): http://webflexor.com

Teleclasses and Webinars

Planet Teleclass: http://www.planetteleclass.com
Teleclass.com: http://www.teleclass.net
Teleclass4U (teleclass training): http://www.teleclass4u.com/solutions/index.html
Teleclass International: http://www.teleclassinternational.com

Client-Tracking/Goal-Setting Software

Best Year Yet Online: http://www.bestyearyet.com (to login to Best Year Yet Online); https://www.
    bestyearyet.com/BYYO/Start.html# (use code #197 and I will receive notification your have
    completed your program and offer a complimentary half-hour follow-up coaching session)
Client Compass: http://www.wiley.com/WileyCDA/Section/id-290930.html
Coaches Consol: http://coachesconsole.com
Llamagraphics Life Balance Software: http://www.llamagraphics.com

Links to Institutional Research on Coaching

Babson College (research center): http://www3.babson.edu/ESHIP/research-publications/
    publications.cfm
College of Executive Coaching (research): http://www.executivecoachcollege.com/executive
    coachingresearch.htm
Fielding Graduate University (The Research Community): http://www.fielding.edu/research/index.htm
Kennesaw State University/Coles College of Business (research and development): http://coles.
    kennesaw.edu/KSUColes/FacultyAndDepartments/
New York University/Division of Graduate Programs in Business (faculty and research): http://
    w4.stern.nyu.edu/faculty/research/
Sheffield Hallam University (research): http://www.shu.ac.uk/research/
Special Group in Coaching Psychology (research articles): http://www.sgcp.org.uk/articles/articles_
    home.cfm
University of Sydney, School of Psychology/Coaching Psychology Unit (research): http://www.
    psych.usyd.edu.au/research/

Training Institutes
(those marked with an asterisk are ICF accredited [ACTP] and prepare individuals for ACC-level certification; those bolded are the best known)

ADD Coach Academy (Advanced Professional ADHD Coach Training Program; PCACG Program—PCACG, ACSTH): http://www.ADDCoachAcademy.com; 518-482-3458

CCI Creative Consciousness International (Diploma in Professional Consciousness Coaching, ACTP)

Center for Right Relationship (Organization and Systems Relationship Coaching Program, ACSTH, ACTP pending)

Coach 21 Co., Ltd. (Coach Training Program, ACTP)

Coach For Life (Certified Life Coach Program, Master Certified Life Coach Program, ACTP)

Coach Training Alliance (Certified Coach Program, ACSTH)

Coach University (Advanced Coaching Program, ACT): http://www.coachinc.com; 800-482-6224

Coaches Training Institute (Co-Active Coach Training Program and Certification, ACTP): http://www.thecoaches.com; 800-691-6008

CoachVille (Center for Coaching Mastery, Graduate School of Coaching, ACTP): http://www.coachville.com

College of Executive Coaching (Certified Personal and Executive Coach, ACTP): http://www.executivecoachcollege.com

Corporate Coach U International (Advanced Corporate Coaching Program, ACTP). http://www.ccui.com; 888-391-2740

Corporate Coach Academy (Certified Professional Coach Program, ACSTH)

Duquesne University (Professional Coaching Certification Program, ACTP Pending)

Erickson College (The Art and Science of Coaching, ACTP)

Executive Career Coach Institute(Certified Executive Career Coach, ACSTH); http://www.ocp.gwu.edu; 202-496-8380

Fielding Graduate University (Evidence-Based Coaching Certificate Program, ACTP): http://www.fielding.edu/programs/hod/omd

Gardner Institute (Mindset for Success Coach Training Program, ACSTH)

Georgetown University Center for Continuing and Professional Education (Leadership Coaching Certificate Program, ACTP): http://www12.georgetown.edu/scs/ccpe/ccpe_cert_coaching.cfm

Gestalt Center for Organization and Systems Development (International Gestalt Coaching Program, ACTP): http://www.gestaltosd.org/igcp/index.php

Hudson Institute of Santa Barbara (Coaching Certification Program, ACTP): http:// www.Hudson Institute.com; 800-582-4401

Institute for Life Coach Training (Life Coach Certification Program, ACTP): http://www.life coachtraining.com

Institute of Executive Coaching (Accreditation in Executive Coaching,ACTP)

Integral Coaching Canada (Integral Coaching Certification Program, ACTP)

International Coach Academy (Professional Certified Coach Program, ACTP)

International Teaching Seminars (European Coaching Certification Programme, ACTP)

inviteCHANGE (formerly Academy for Coach Training): http://www.coachtraining.com or http://www.invitechange.com; 1-800-897-8707

iPEC Coaching (iPEC's Core Energy Coach Certification and Coaching Mastery Curriculum, ACTP)

Leadership Coach Academy (Certified Leadership & Talent Management Coach, ACSTH)

Life Coaching Academy (Certificate IV in Life Coaching, ACTP)

Life Purpose Institute (Life Coach Training Certification, Advanced Life Coach Training, ACSTH)

MentorCoach LLC (The MentorCoach Coach Training Program, ACTP): http://www.mentor coach.com; 301-986-5688

New Ventures West (Professional Coaching Course, ACTP): http://www.newventureswest. com; 800-332-4618

Newfield Network (Newfield's Certified Coach Training Program, ACTP): http://www.newfield network.com; 301-570-6680

OnTrack Coaching and Consulting (for social workers and other helping professionals): http://www.ontrackcoaching.com; 617-964-3202

Success Unlimited Network (Coach Training and Certification Program, ACTP): http://www. successunlimited.net; 703-716-8374

Therapist U (for helping professionals only, ACTP): http://www.TherapistU.com; 888-267-1206

Universidad de Puerto Rico (Recinto de Río Piedras-División de Educación y Estudios Profesio-nalesCertificado Profesional en Coaching, ACSTH)

University of Texas at Dallas (Executive and Professional Coaching Program, ACTP)

Coaching Organizations

American Coaching Association: http://www.americoach.org

Association for Professional Executive Coaching & Supervision: http://www.apecs.org/

European Coaching Institute: http://www.europeancoachinginstitute.org/

European Mentoring and Coaching Council: http://www.europeancoachinginstitute.org/

International Association of Coaches: http://www.certifiedcoach.org/

International Business Coach Institute: http://www.businesscoachinstitute.org/

International Coach Federation: http://coachfederation.org

International Consortium for Coaching in Organizations: http://www.coachingconsortium.org/

Organizational Development Network: http://www.odnetwork.org/

Professional Coaches and Mentors Association: http://pcmaonline.com/

Society for Human Resource Management: http://www.shrm.org/

Worldwide Association of Business Coaches: http://www.wabccoaches.com/

Appendix A

International Coach Federation (ICF) Code of Ethics

Part One: Definition of Coaching

Section 1: Definitions

- **Coaching:** Coaching is partnering with clients in a thought-provoking and creative process that inspires them to maximize their personal and professional potential.
- **A professional coaching relationship:** A professional coaching relationship exists when coaching includes a business agreement or contract that defines the responsibilities of each party.
- **An ICF Professional Coach:** An ICF Professional Coach also agrees to practice the ICF Professional Core Competencies and pledges accountability to the ICF Code of Ethics.

In order to clarify roles in the coaching relationship, it is often necessary to distinguish between the client and the sponsor. In most cases, the client and sponsor are the same person and therefore jointly referred to as the client. For purposes of identification, however, the International Coach Federation defines these roles as follows:

- **Client:** The "client" is the person(s) being coached.
- **Sponsor:** The "sponsor" is the entity (including its representatives) paying for and/or arranging for coaching services to be provided. In all cases, coaching engagement contracts or agreements should clearly establish the rights, roles, and responsibilities for both the client and sponsor if they are not the same persons.

Part Two: The ICF Standards of Ethical Conduct

Preamble: ICF Professional Coaches aspire to conduct themselves in a manner that reflects positively upon the coaching profession; are respectful of different approaches to coaching; and recognize that they are also bound by applicable laws and regulations.

Section 1: Professional Conduct At Large

As a coach:

1. I will not knowingly make any public statement that is untrue or misleading about what I offer as a coach, or make false claims in any written documents relating to the coaching profession or my credentials or the ICF.

2. I will accurately identify my coaching qualifications, expertise, experience, certifications and ICF Credentials.

3. I will recognize and honor the efforts and contributions of others and not misrepresent them as my own. I understand that violating this standard may leave me subject to legal remedy by a third party.

4. I will, at all times, strive to recognize personal issues that may impair, conflict, or interfere with my coaching performance or my professional coaching relationships. Whenever the facts and circumstances necessitate, I will promptly seek professional assistance and determine the action to be taken, including whether it is appropriate to suspend or terminate my coaching relationship(s).

5. I will conduct myself in accordance with the ICF Code of Ethics in all coach training, coach mentoring, and coach supervisory activities.

6. I will conduct and report research with competence, honesty, and within recognized scientific standards and applicable subject guidelines. My research will be carried out with the necessary consent and approval of those involved, and with an approach that will protect participants from any potential harm. All research efforts will be performed in a manner that complies with all the applicable laws of the country in which the research is conducted.

7. I will maintain, store, and dispose of any records created during my coaching business in a manner that promotes confidentiality, security, and privacy, and complies with any applicable laws and agreements

8. I will use ICF member contact information (e-mail addresses, telephone numbers, etc.) only in the manner and to the extent authorized by the ICF.

Section 2: Conflicts of Interest

As a coach:

9. I will seek to avoid conflicts of interest and potential conflicts of interest and openly disclose any such conflicts. I will offer to remove myself when such a conflict arises.

10. I will disclose to my client and his or her sponsor all anticipated compensation from third parties that I may pay or receive for referrals of that client.

11. I will only barter for services, goods or other non-monetary remuneration when it will not impair the coaching relationship.

12. I will not knowingly take any personal, professional, or monetary advantage or benefit of the coach-client relationship, except by a form of compensation as agreed in the agreement or contract.

Section 3: Professional Conduct with Clients

As a coach:

13. I will not knowingly mislead or make false claims about what my client or sponsor will receive from the coaching process or from me as the coach.
14. I will not give my prospective clients or sponsors information or advice I know or believe to be misleading or false.
15. I will have clear agreements or contracts with my clients and sponsor(s). I will honor all agreements or contracts made in the context of professional coaching relationships.
16. I will carefully explain and strive to ensure that, prior to or at the initial meeting, my coaching client and sponsor(s) understand the nature of coaching, the nature and limits of confidentiality, financial arrangements, and any other terms of the coaching agreement or contract.
17. I will be responsible for setting clear, appropriate, and culturally sensitive boundaries that govern any physical contact I may have with my clients or sponsors.
18. I will not become sexually intimate with any of my current clients or sponsors.
19. I will respect the client's right to terminate the coaching relationship at any point during the process, subject to the provisions of the agreement or contract. I will be alert to indications that the client is no longer benefiting from our coaching relationship.
20. I will encourage the client or sponsor to make a change if I believe the client or sponsor would be better served by another coach or by another resource.
21. I will suggest my client seek the services of other professionals when deemed necessary or appropriate.

Section 4: Confidentiality/Privacy

As a coach:

22. I will maintain the strictest levels of confidentiality with all client and sponsor information. I will have a clear agreement or contract before releasing information to another person, unless required by law.
23. I will have a clear agreement upon how coaching information will be exchanged among coach, client, and sponsor.
24. When acting as a trainer of student coaches, I will clarify confidentiality policies with the students.
25. I will have associated coaches and other persons whom I manage in service of my clients and their sponsors in a paid or volunteer capacity make clear agreements or contracts to adhere to the ICF Code of Ethics Part 2, Section 4: Confidentiality/Privacy standards and the entire ICF Code of Ethics to the extent applicable.

Part Three: The ICF Pledge of Ethics

As an ICF Professional Coach, I acknowledge and agree to honor my ethical and legal obligations to my coaching clients and sponsors, colleagues, and to the public at large.

I pledge to comply with the ICF Code of Ethics, and to practice these standards with those whom I coach.

If I breach this Pledge of Ethics or any part of the ICF Code of Ethics, I agree that the ICF in its sole discretion may hold me accountable for so doing. I further agree that my accountability to the ICF for any breach may include sanctions, such as loss of my ICF membership and/or my ICF Credentials.

Approved by the Ethics and Standards Committee on October 30, 2008.

Approved by the ICF Board of Directors on December 18, 2008.

Source: International Coach Federation: http://www.coachfederation.org/ethics/; http://www.coachfederation.org/includes/media/docs/Ethics-2009.pdf. Because documents of this sort are subject to periodic revision, *always* consult the source itself to be certain what you are reading is the most up-to-date version.

Appendix B

International Coach Federation (ICF) Core Competencies

The following eleven core coaching competencies were developed to support greater understanding about the skills and approaches used within today's coaching profession as defined by the ICF. They will also support you in calibrating the level of alignment between the coach-specific training expected and the training you have experienced.

These competencies were used as the foundation for the ICF Credentialing process examination. The core competencies are grouped into four clusters according to those that fit together logically based on common ways of looking at the competencies in each group. The groupings and individual competencies are not weighted—they do not represent any kind of priority in that they are all core or critical for any competent coach to demonstrate.

A. Setting the Foundation

1. Meeting Ethical Guidelines and Professional Standards—Understanding of coaching ethics and standards and ability to apply them appropriately in all coaching situations

1. Understands and exhibits in own behaviors the ICF Standards of Conduct (see list, Part III of ICF Code of Ethics),
2. Understands and follows all ICF Ethical Guidelines (see list),
3. Clearly communicates the distinctions between coaching, consulting, psychotherapy and other support professions,
4. Refers client to another support professional as needed, knowing when this is needed and the available resources.

2. Establishing the Coaching Agreement—Ability to understand what is required in the specific coaching interaction and to come to agreement with the prospective and new client about the coaching process and relationship

1. Understands and effectively discusses with the client the guidelines and specific parameters of the coaching relationship (e.g., logistics, fees, scheduling, inclusion of others if appropriate),

2.   Reaches agreement about what is appropriate in the relationship and what is not, what is and is not being offered, and about the client's and coach's responsibilities,

3.   Determines whether there is an effective match between his/her coaching method and the needs of the prospective client.

B. Co-Creating the Relationship

3. Establishing Trust and Intimacy with the Client—Ability to create a safe, supportive environment that produces ongoing mutual respect and trust

1.   Shows genuine concern for the client's welfare and future,
2.   Continuously demonstrates personal integrity, honesty and sincerity,
3.   Establishes clear agreements and keeps promises,
4.   Demonstrates respect for client's perceptions, learning style, personal being,
5.   Provides ongoing support for and champions new behaviors and actions, including those involving risk taking and fear of failure,
6.   Asks permission to coach client in sensitive, new areas.

4. Coaching Presence—Ability to be fully conscious and create spontaneous relationship with the client, employing a style that is open, flexible and confident

1.   Is present and flexible during the coaching process, dancing in the moment,
2.   Accesses own intuition and trusts one's inner knowing - "goes with the gut",
3.   Is open to not knowing and takes risks,
4.   Sees many ways to work with the client, and chooses in the moment what is most effective,
5.   Uses humor effectively to create lightness and energy,
6.   Confidently shifts perspectives and experiments with new possibilities for own action,
7.   Demonstrates confidence in working with strong emotions, and can self-manage and not be overpowered or enmeshed by client's emotions.

C. Communicating Effectively

5. Active Listening—Ability to focus completely on what the client is saying and is not saying, to understand the meaning of what is said in the context of the client's desires, and to support client self-expression

1.   Attends to the client and the client's agenda, and not to the coach's agenda for the client,
2.   Hears the client's concerns, goals, values and beliefs about what is and is not possible,
3.   Distinguishes between the words, the tone of voice, and the body language,

4. Summarizes, paraphrases, reiterates, mirrors back what client has said to ensure clarity and understanding,

5. Encourages, accepts, explores and reinforces the client's expression of feelings, perceptions, concerns, beliefs, suggestions, etc.,

6. Integrates and builds on client's ideas and suggestions,

7. "Bottom-lines" or understands the essence of the client's communication and helps the client get there rather than engaging in long descriptive stories,

8. Allows the client to vent or "clear" the situation without judgment or attachment in order to move on to next steps.

6. Powerful Questioning—Ability to ask questions that reveal the information needed for maximum benefit to the coaching relationship and the client

1. Asks questions that reflect active listening and an understanding of the client's perspective,

2. Asks questions that evoke discovery, insight, commitment or action (e.g., those that challenge the client's assumptions),

3. Asks open-ended questions that create greater clarity, possibility or new learning

4. Asks questions that move the client towards what they desire, not questions that ask for the client to justify or look backwards.

7. Direct Communication—Ability to communicate effectively during coaching sessions, and to use language that has the greatest positive impact on the client

1. Is clear, articulate and direct in sharing and providing feedback,

2. Reframes and articulates to help the client understand from another perspective what he/she wants or is uncertain about,

3. Clearly states coaching objectives, meeting agenda, purpose of techniques or exercises,

4. Uses language appropriate and respectful to the client (e.g., non-sexist, non-racist, non-technical, non-jargon),

5. Uses metaphor and analogy to help to illustrate a point or paint a verbal picture.

D. Facilitating Learning and Results

8. Creating Awareness—Ability to integrate and accurately evaluate multiple sources of information, and to make interpretations that help the client to gain awareness and thereby achieve agreed-upon results

1. Goes beyond what is said in assessing client's concerns, not getting hooked by the client's description,

2. Invokes inquiry for greater understanding, awareness and clarity,

3. Identifies for the client his/her underlying concerns, typical and fixed ways of

perceiving himself/herself and the world, differences between the facts and the interpretation, disparities between thoughts, feelings and action,

4. Helps clients to discover for themselves the new thoughts, beliefs, perceptions, emotions, moods, etc. that strengthen their ability to take action and achieve what is important to them,

5. Communicates broader perspectives to clients and inspires commitment to shift their viewpoints and find new possibilities for action,

6. Helps clients to see the different, interrelated factors that affect them and their behaviors (e.g., thoughts, emotions, body, background),

7. Expresses insights to clients in ways that are useful and meaningful for the client,

8. Identifies major strengths vs. major areas for learning and growth, and what is most important to address during coaching,

9. Asks the client to distinguish between trivial and significant issues, situational vs. recurring behaviors, when detecting a separation between what is being stated and what is being done.

9. Designing Actions—Ability to create with the client opportunities for ongoing learning, during coaching and in work/life situations, and for taking new actions that will most effectively lead to agreed-upon coaching results

1. Brainstorms and assists the client to define actions that will enable the client to demonstrate, practice and deepen new learning,

2. Helps the client to focus on and systematically explore specific concerns and opportunities that are central to agreed-upon coaching goals,

3. Engages the client to explore alternative ideas and solutions, to evaluate options, and to make related decisions,

4. Promotes active experimentation and self-discovery, where the client applies what has been discussed and learned during sessions immediately afterwards in his/her work or life setting,

5. Celebrates client successes and capabilities for future growth,

6. Challenges client's assumptions and perspectives to provoke new ideas and find new possibilities for action,

7. Advocates or brings forward points of view that are aligned with client goals and, without attachment, engages the client to consider them,

8. Helps the client "Do It Now" during the coaching session, providing immediate support,

9. Encourages stretches and challenges but also a comfortable pace of learning.

10. Planning and Goal Setting—Ability to develop and maintain an effective coaching plan with the client

1. Consolidates collected information and establishes a coaching plan and development goals with the client that address concerns and major areas for learning and development,

2. Creates a plan with results that are attainable, measurable, specific and have target dates,

3. Makes plan adjustments as warranted by the coaching process and by changes in the situation,

4. Helps the client identify and access different resources for learning (e.g., books, other professionals),

5. Identifies and targets early successes that are important to the client.

11. Managing Progress and Accountability—Ability to hold attention on what is important for the client, and to leave responsibility with the client to take action

1. Clearly requests of the client actions that will move the client toward their stated goals,

2. Demonstrates follow through by asking the client about those actions that the client committed to during the previous session(s),

3. Acknowledges the client for what they have done, not done, learned or become aware of since the previous coaching session(s),

4. Effectively prepares, organizes and reviews with client information obtained during sessions,

5. Keeps the client on track between sessions by holding attention on the coaching plan and outcomes, agreed-upon courses of action, and topics for future session(s),

6. Focuses on the coaching plan but is also open to adjusting behaviors and actions based on the coaching process and shifts in direction during sessions,

7. Is able to move back and forth between the big picture of where the client is heading, setting a context for what is being discussed and where the client wishes to go,

8. Promotes client's self-discipline and holds the client accountable for what they say they are going to do, for the results of an intended action, or for a specific plan with related time frames,

9. Develops the client's ability to make decisions, address key concerns, and develop himself/herself (to get feedback, to determine priorities and set the pace of learning, to reflect on and learn from experiences),

10. Positively confronts the client with the fact that he/she did not take agreed-upon actions.

Source: International Coach Federation: http://www.coachfederation.org/research-education/icf-credentials/core-competencies/; http://www.coachfederation.org/includes/media/docs/CoreCompEnglish.pdf. Because documents of this sort are subject to periodic revision, *always* consult the source itself to be certain what you are reading is the most up-to-date version.

Appendix C

Top Ten Indicators to Refer a Client to a Mental Health Professional (Meinke, n.d.)

Your Client:

1. Is exhibiting a decline in his/her ability to experience pleasure and/or an increase in being sad, hopeless and helpless

- As a coach you may notice that your client is not as upbeat as usual.
- He/she may talk much more frequently about how awful life/the world is and that nothing can be done about it.
- The client may make comments about "why bother" or "what's the use."
- There will be a decline in talking about things that are enjoyable.
- He/she may stop doing things they like to do (examples: going to the movies, visiting with friends, participating in athletic events or being a spectator of sporting events).
- The client begins to talk about being unable to do anything that forwards their dreams or desires.

2. Has intrusive thoughts or is unable to concentrate or focus

- As a coach you may notice that your client is not able to focus on their goals or the topic of conversation.
- The client is unable to complete their action steps and isn't aware of what got in the way.
- You notice that your client begins talking about unpleasant events during the course of talking about themselves and their goals.
- The client tells you that unpleasant thoughts keep popping into their minds at inopportune moments or when they are thinking about or doing other things and that they can't seem to get away from these thoughts.
- Your client tells you about recurring scary dreams that they didn't have before.
- Your client reports that they have so many thoughts swirling in their heads and that they can't get them to slow down.

3. Is unable to get to sleep or awakens during the night and is unable to get back to sleep or sleeps excessively

- Your client comes to his/her coaching sessions tired and exhausted.
- Your client begins talking about not being able to get to sleep or how he/she just wants to sleep all the time.
- Your client may report to you how he/she gets to sleep and then wakes up and can't get back to sleep.
- Your client tells you how he/she needs to take naps during the day, something they have not done before.
- Your client reports that they fell asleep at an inopportune time or place.

4. Has a change in appetite: decrease in appetite or increase in appetite

- Your client reports that he/she isn't hungry and just doesn't want to eat.
- Your client reports that he/she is eating all the time, usually sweets or junk food, whether or not they are hungry.
- Your client says he/she doesn't get any enjoyment from eating when they did in the past.
- Your client reports that he/she is not sitting down to eat with friends or family when he/she did in the past.

5. Is feeling guilty because others have suffered or died

- Your client reports that he/she feels guilty because they are alive or have not been injured.
- Your client states that he/she doesn't understand why he/she is still here/alive when others have had to suffer/die.
- Your client doesn't want to move forward with his/her goals because he/she doesn't deserve to have the life he/she chose, especially when other people have had to suffer/die.
- Your client questions his/her right to have a fulfilling life/career in the face of all that has happened.
- Your client expresses the belief that he/she is unworthy of having a satisfying life.

6. Has feelings of despair or hopelessness

- According to your client nothing in life is OK.
- Your client misses session times or says he/she wants to quit coaching because life is not worth living or he/she doesn't deserve to get what they want.
- Your client moves into excessive negative thinking.
- Your client says that he/she can't make a difference or that whatever he/she does doesn't matter.
- Your client has the attitude of "Why bother?"

7. Is being hyper alert and/or excessively tired

- Your client reports that he/she can't relax.
- Your client states that he/she is jumping at the slightest noise.
- Your client reports that it feels like she/he always has to be on guard.
- Your client states that they are listening for any little sound that is out of the ordinary.
- Your client reports that he/she has no energy.
- Your client states that he/she can't do their usual chores because he/she is so tired.
- Your client states that it takes too much energy to do things he/she normally did in the past.

8. Has increased irritability or outbursts of anger

- Your client becomes increasingly belligerent or argumentative with you or other people.
- Your client reports that everyone or everything annoys them.
- Your client starts making comments about how miserable everyone and everything is.
- Your client reports that other people in their life are telling them how miserable/angry they have become.
- Your client reports getting into arguments with people.
- Your client states that they get so upset they don't know what to do with themselves.
- Your client reports that they feel like a "pressure cooker" or are "ready to burst."
- Your client increasingly tells you about wanting to do or doing things that would harm themselves or others (examples: wanting to put their fist through a window; wanting to punch someone; wanting to hit someone/something with their car).

9. Has impulsive and risk-taking behavior

- Your client reports doing things, such as going on a buying spree, without thinking about the consequences of their behavior.
- Your client tells you that something came to their mind so they went and did it without thinking about the outcome.
- Your client reports an increase in doing things that could be detrimental to themselves or others (examples: increase in promiscuous sexual behavior; increase in alcohol/drug consumption; deciding to get married after knowing someone an unusually short period of time).

10. Has thoughts of death and/or suicide

- Your client begins talking a lot about death, not just a fear of dying.
- Your client alludes to the fact that dying would be appropriate for them.
- Your client makes comments that to die right now would be OK with them.
- Your client becomes fascinated with what dying would be like.
- Your client talks about ways to die.

- Your client talks about going to a better place and how wonderful it would be and seems to be carried away by the thought.
- Your client tells you they know how they would kill themselves if they wanted to/ had the chance.
- Your client alludes to having a plan or way they would die/go to a better place/leave the planet/leave the situation/get out of here.
- Whereas previously your client was engaging, personable and warm and now they present to you as cold, distant and aloof tell them what you are observing and ask them what has changed for them. This is often a signal that they have disengaged from living and are silently thinking or planning to suicide.
- Some questions you might ask your client if you are unclear about what is going on with them or their intentions: "Are you wanting to die?" "How would you die if you decided to?" "Are you planning on dying?" "When are you planning on dying?"
- If you have any inclination or indication that your client is planning on dying or committing suicide immediately refer them to an emergency room or call 911.
- Tell your client that you care about them, are concerned for them, that you are taking what they say seriously and that they must get help immediately.
- If the client balks at what you are saying, gets belligerent or even more distant AND you become even more concerned about them, you may need to tell them you will break confidentiality because of your concern for their well-being and that you will call 911 (You can call your local 911 and give them the address and phone number of your client, even if it is in another state, and they can contact the client's local 911 dispatcher).

If is important to note that the appearance of any one of these indicators, except for #10 which must be referred and followed up on immediately, does not indicate the immediate need for a referral to a psychotherapist or community mental health agency; everyone can experience a very brief episode of any of the indicators. However, if you see that several indicators are emerging and that the client is not presenting as whole, competent and capable then it is time for a referral to a mental health professional

Coaching Vocabulary

Accountability—What are you going to do? By when? How will you let me know?

Acknowledgment—expressing your deep knowledge of the other and who they had to be in order to produce the result (for example, "I want to acknowledge you for . . . your courage . . .").

Asking permission—"Can I coach you on this" "Can I tell you exactly what I see?"

Assertions—statements about our observations.

Bottom-lining—getting to the essential in the communication, cutting through the client's "story" and details that can obscure the issue.

Breakthrough/Breakdown—when change occurs; when we are confronted with the limits of change. Breakdowns often precede breakthroughs. Breakthroughs can lead to breakdowns or "bigger and better problems."

Celebrating—deepens the clients appreciation of both their successes and failures. Failures can be celebrated as well as they are valuable in the clients process (for example, "You didn't do your 10 calls this week. I celebrate your courage to fail").

Challenging—requesting the client to go beyond their self-imposed limits.

Championing—encouraging clients to continue when they are doubtful of their ability. It's like being ahead of the client on the track, saying, "Come on, you can do it."

Clearing—allowing for emotional release of discharge of complaints in order to have an effective session without baggage in the way. It is often useful for the coach to clear to be wholly present to the client.

Coachability—the client's receptivity to the coaching process; willingness, if asked, to "run through the tires."

Compelling way—"pulls" the client into action by providing a future marker for fulfillment that represents what they want. The compelling way also sustains clients on days when they become frustrated. Having a visual image or mantra often helps remind the client of what they are going towards in their lives.

Completion—what is needed to put something in the past. Successful "completions" leave a sense of satisfaction. Emotions of sadness and loss may be present but regret and longing for the past is resolved if only by declaration.

Contribution—state of being. When we are "making a contribution," our actions may be said to be guided by something bigger than our individual lives and concerns.

Declarations—powerful statements that can immediately alter a reality, depending on the authority behind them. Examples are the Declaration of Independence, wedding vows, and a jury finding of "guilty." Personal declarations such as "I'm a success" can also generate a whole new world for ourselves.

Designing the alliance—asking the client to give power to the coaching alliance so they will be coachable.

Distinctions—concepts that distinguish what we previously "knew" as the same.

Forwarding the action—visibly moving the client closer to their goal; it is most powerful when it occurs during the coaching session.

Goal setting and planning—defining the outcome the client would like to achieve. Goals should be specific and measurable in time, distance, and form.

The Gremlin—the internal self-saboteur. Most of us have several but usually there is one that causes us the most grief.

Holding the client agenda—the ability to hold the big picture for the client, especially when the client is discouraged.

Inquiry—a thought-provoking question, often is the form of homework given at the end of the session (for example, "What are you tolerating?" "What's the lie in your life?").

Possiblity—what exists when we move outside of the box of our normal, everyday thinking and paradigms of reality— new life, new ideas, generativity.

Powerful questions—questions that are direct, to the point, and get right to the heart of the client's concerns (for example, "What do you really want?" "What does that cost you?").

Promises—commitments to action, the results of which can be seen in time, distance, and form.

Requests/Requesting—asking client's permission (for example, "Are you ready for an assignment that will move you ahead in giant steps?").

Self-management—the ability of the coach to be invisible in holding the client's agenda; it involves the complete absence of ego on the coach's part.

Structures—reminders of the actions the client plans to take (for example, calendars, collages, e-mail notes).

Synchronicity—first written about by Carl Jung, this is a state in which there is flow around us and things just seem to happen (for example, coincidences, reduced effort, natural attraction of what we want).

Transformation—also known as "second-order change" (that is, when something changes form as opposed to becoming a better version of its previous form).

Visioning—a vivid, often sensuous, exciting, magnetic, future-oriented picture of where the client is going, compelling the client to bring that image to fruition; it can be created in guided visualization.

Appendix E

Psychotherapy and Coaching Compared

The following shows some distinctions between coaching and psychotherapy. For the sake of comparison, I have used a psychodynamic model of therapy. None of the distinctions are absolute. There is much "gray area" in coaching and therapy as every clinician practices in their own unique way. The comparison below is for teaching purposes only.

Coaching Model	Therapy Model
Follows a business/sports training model	Follows a medical model
Clients are already functional and healthy but are dissatisfied with their current situation and want to improve it	Deals with quantifiable dysfunctions or conditions
Aims to move the client functional to "extraordinary"	Moves the person from dysfunctional to functional
Future driven	Past driven: Therapy is present and future oriented. It uses the past to understand the dynamics.
Focused on empowerment	Focused on understanding and acceptance
Works with the conscious mind	Works with the conscious and unconscious— depending on therapeutic orientation.
Focus on actions	Primary focus on feelings
High value on self-responsibility	Based on notion of illness and lack
Meetings by phone, Internet, or in person	Face-to-face sessions and are mandatory for insurance reimbursement.
Focus on values, needs, blocks as clues for getting client into action	Focus on feelings, conflicts, symptoms
Client may talk about feelings.	Patient may talk about feelings to avoid actions.

Coaching Model	Therapy Model
A relationship of peers: mentoring, partnering, "co-active"	Tends to be more hierarchical—an "expert" model
The relationship itself is not a subject of discussion; how well the process is working may be asked	"Transference" is used as a way to explore and understand the patient's conflicts and work toward their resolution
Nonhierarchical	Hierarchically organized by degree or professional status
May be deducted as a business expense	Often deducted as a medical expense
Rapid growth possible	A slower process, with psychological issues brought to light gradually over time
Vacations are not an issue.	Vacations are viewed as traumatic and as a subject for discussion
Can be very spiritual as it brings goals and desires in line with people's values	Spirituality has often been viewed as being in conflict with therapy

Appendix F

Coaching and Consulting Compared

Coaching Model	Consulting Model
Whole company/organization's development	Immediate or circumscribed problem solving
Focus on skills training and empowerment	Focus on problem, finding and giving answers
Large requests made, and the coach works along with the client to realize goals	Recommendations given, and they may or may not be implemented
Client reports to the coach regularly.	Consultant comes and goes, leaving individuals to figure out how to do it for themselves.
Relationship-based	Information-based
Coach is a partner	Consultant is an expert

Appendix G

The Coaching Intake

1. Sample Client Contracts and Disclosure Forms

1.1: Disclosure Statement

The following is a sample disclosure statement I use in my initial client agreement (please check with an attorney before using it or anything similar in your own practice):

> The services to be provided by ONTRACK COACHING & CONSULTING, INC. to the client are coaching or tele-coaching as designed jointly with the client. Coaching, which is not psychotherapy, is not intended to treat mental disorders or nervous conditions. Coaching may address specific personal projects, life balance, business achievements or general conditions in the client's life, business or profession. Other coaching services or activities include personal strategic planning, values clarification, brainstorming, and examination various modes of operating in life.

1.2: Draft Coaching Agreement for Therapists Who Coach by Eric Harris, JD (used with permission)

Background Notes:

- This particular contract is the "top end" agreement for use with clients who are closest to *DSM* territory. It focuses in detail on the distinctions between coaching and psychotherapy.
- For other coaching niches, less language about the Coaching–Psychotherapy dimension is needed. For example, executive coaching or small business coaching would need relatively little emphasis on this dimension since clients are not likely to have confusion about this distinction.
- This is a *draft* coaching agreement. It is not carved in stone. There may be portions of this agreement—for example, the definition of coaching—that you would change to fit your own practice.

- This contract represents the work of Eric Harris. If you are insured by the American Psychological Association Insurance Trust (APAIT), you can schedule free phone consultations with Eric by calling 1-800-477-1200. If you are not insured by APAIT and would like to tailor a coaching agreement to your own needs or for any other reason, you can contact Eric at 1-781-259-3363.
- *Please note that at the time of this writing, revisions are still being made to this agreement. Please do not use it or anything similar without consulting an attorney.*

THE COACHING AGREEMENT

Welcome to [name of practice], a professional Coaching practice. This document and attachments constitute a contract between us (the "Agreement"). You should read it carefully and raise any questions and concerns that you have before you sign it.

Services:

The services provided by _____ include Coaching or TeleCoaching on topics decided jointly with you, the client. The purpose of coaching is to develop and implement strategies to help the you reach personally identified goals of enhanced performance and personal satisfaction. Coaching may address a wide variety of goals including specific personal projects, life balance, job performance and satisfaction, or general conditions in the client's life, business, or profession.

Payment Procedure:

Coaching fees are described on the attachment, "Coaching Fee Plan." Please choose the plan that best fits your needs and your schedule, sign the Plan, and include it with this Agreement. The Coach is paid in advance of each series of coaching calls. The first coaching session will begin after this agreement is signed and faxed to the Coach and the first payment is received by credit/debit card (Visa, MC, Amex) or check. Services must be paid for in advance, or they cannot be provided. Services requested by the Client, in addition to coaching calls, will be billed at a prorated hourly rate (agreed in advance) and will be paid within 30 days of service. Any changes to this procedure must be mutually agreed upon in writing.

Feedback:

If, at any time, you feel that your needs are not being met or you are not getting what you want out of the coaching or training group, please tell me, so we can discuss your needs and adjust your coaching program, as needed. We will continue to work on the goals that you define unless you want to stop, which we will do whenever you ask.

Session Time:

Coaching is scheduled at the mutual convenience of the Coach and the Client. The day and time for the next call will be scheduled at the close of each coaching session.

Call Procedure:

The Client will call the Coach at the pre-arranged time and telephone number as scheduled, and pays the telephone charges for the call. For group coaching calls and classes, the Coach will pay for the teleconference line, and the Clients will pay for the call into the conference line.

Cancellations:

Please remember that you must give 24 hours prior notice if you need to cancel or change the time of an appointment, otherwise you will be charged for the session in full. The Coach will make reasonable efforts to reschedule sessions which are cancelled in a timely manner.

Termination:

Either party may end the coaching relationship by providing the other party with a one-week written notice, which may be transmitted by email or fax.

Confidentiality:

As a licensed therapist, I protect the confidentiality of the communications with my clients, including my coaching clients. I will only release information about our work to others with your written permission, or if I am required to do so by a court order. There are some situations in which I am legally obligated to breach your confidentiality in order to protect others from harm, including (1) if I have information that indicates that a child or elderly or disabled person is being abused, I must report that to the appropriate state agency and (2) if a client is an imminent risk to him/herself or makes threats of imminent violence against another person, I am required to take protective actions. These situations rarely occur in coaching practices, but if such a situation does occur,

I will make every effort to discuss it with you before taking any action.

Some sessions are conducted in groups, including teleconference groups. You agree to maintain the confidentiality of all information communicated to you by other coaching clients and by your Coach. We also understand that progress is often enhanced when clients discuss their coaching relationship with trusted colleagues and friends. You can have these discussions, but you are expected to be very careful not to share any information which would allow others in the group to be identified. One way to decide how and what to discuss is to think about how you would feel if someone else in the group was discussing you.

As you are probably aware, it is impossible to protect the confidentiality of information which is transmitted electronically. This is particularly true of E-mail and information stored on computers connected to the internet (unless you use encryption and other forms of security protection), and if you use a cordless or cell phone, someone with a scanner could hear you talk.

Coaching and Psychotherapy:

The staff of _____ includes licensed mental health professionals who are trained to help people learn new skills and make significant behavior changes. We are here to offer our skills in the areas of communication, problem-solving, and behavior change. We do this through a service called "Coaching", in which you come to us for help in making decisions and implementing them, in order to achieve goals that you decide for yourself.

In addition to being a Coach, I am also a licensed therapist in [state], with training and experience in diagnosing and treating emotional and psychological problems. Although there are some similarities between Coaching and psychotherapy, I will not conduct psychotherapy with my coaching clients. These are different activities, and it is important that you understand the differences between them. Although both Coaching and psychotherapy use knowledge of human behavior, motivation, behavioral change, and interactive counseling techniques, there are major differences in the goals, focus, and level of professional responsibility.

As your Coach, my job is to help you to take information and skills that you already have and (1) to make decisions about which changes you would like to make (including [list of coaching targets/goals]) (2) to develop a personal "action plan" in order to make those changes, (3) to implement your action plan and make the behavioral changes, and (4) to develop strategies to maintain the changes you have made. I will support, encourage, teach, and help you stay "on track" toward your goals.

You, as the Client, set the agenda for your coaching, and your success will depend on your willingness to define and take risks and try new approaches. You can expect your Coach to be honest and direct, asking straightforward questions and using challenging techniques to help you move forward. You are expected to evaluate your own progress, and if the coaching is not working as you wish, you should immediately inform your Coach so we can both take steps to correct the problem. Like any human endeavor, coaching can involve feelings of distress and frustration which accompany the process of change. Coaching does not offer any guarantee of success.

Psychotherapy, on the other hand, is a health care service. Its primary focus is to identify, diagnose, and treat nervous and mental disorders. The goals include alleviating symptoms, understanding the underlying personality dynamics which create symptoms, changing the dysfunctional behaviors which are the result of these disorders, and developing helping patients to cope with their psychological problems. It is usually reimbursable through health insurance policies (while coaching is not, at present).

Psychotherapy patients are often emotionally vulnerable. This vulnerability is increased by the expectation that they will discuss very intimate personal information and will expose feelings about themselves that are understandably sensitive about. The past life experiences of psychotherapy patients have often made trust difficult to achieve. These factors give psychotherapists greatly disproportionate power that creates a fiduciary responsibility to protect the safety of their clients. The coaching relationship is designed to avoid this power differential.

Because of these differences, the roles of Coach and psychotherapist are often in potential conflict, so I believe that it is ethically inappropriate, under most circumstances, for me to play both roles with a client. If I am your Coach, I cannot be your therapist. This means that if either of us recognizes that you have a problem that would benefit from psychotherapy, I will refer or direct you to appropriate resources. In some situations, I may insist that you enter psychotherapy and that I have access to your psychotherapist, as a condition of my continuing as your Coach.

It is also important to understand that Coaching is a professional relationship. While it may feel at times like a close personal relationship, it is not one that can extend beyond professional boundaries, either during and after our work together. Considerable experience shows that when boundaries blur, the hard-won benefits gained from the coaching relationship are endangered.

Mutual Nondisclosure

The Coach and Client mutually recognize that they may discuss future plans, business affairs, customer lists, financial information, job information, goals, personal information, and other private information. The Coach will not voluntarily communicate the Client's information to a third party. In order to honor and protect the Coach's intellectual property, the Client likewise agrees not to disclose or communicate information about the Coach's practice, materials, or methods to any third parties.

Dispute Resolution

Any controversy or claim arising out of or relating to this agreement, or the breach of this agreement, shall be settled by arbitration, which will occur via telephone by an arbitrator that we mutually agree upon. The costs of the arbitration shall be [shared equally] [borne by the losing party] .

Your signature below indicates that you have read the information in this document ("Coaching Agreement and Informed Consent) and any Attachments, such as the Coaching Fee Plan, and agree to abide by its terms during our professional Coaching relationship.

Client _____ Date_____

Coach _____ Date_____

1.3: Model Coaching Agreement (Connie Adkins)

The following coaching agreement has been provided by Connie Adkins ("The Transitions Coach"; http://www.thetransitioncoach.com/). Connie is an LICSW who also maintains a clinical practice. She was trained at both Coach University and Coaches Training Institute and has been coaching for over 10 years. (For a *New York Times* article featuring Connie, see http://www.thetransitioncoach.com/article2.html.)

Coaching Agreement

The Coaching Relationship. The coaching process encourages two critical components: (1) reflection, an opportunity to think about and clarify ones values, vision, goals, and personal hurdles; and (2) action, a commitment to take self-defined steps to move toward one's goals. The coach's role is to be a partner in this process, providing appropriate exploration, supports and structure to guide and enhance the coaching process. Coaching is neither therapy nor consultation.

Length of Coaching Agreement. The coaching process is dependent upon the interests and goals of each client and is therefore highly individualized. The length of time in coaching, consequently, varies.

Clients usually obtain maximum benefit by making a commitment to coaching for a minimum of three months.

It is requested that ending coaching should be discussed at least one month (three calls) in advance. This allows the coach and client to review accomplishments and provide mutual feedback.

Confidentiality. It is essential that the coaching relationship be built on trust. As a result, all information disclosed during the course of coaching will remain confidential.

Rescheduling Policy. A minimum 24-hour notice is requested for rescheduling. When notice is not provided, the appointment will be considered cancelled. This policy does not pertain to emergencies.

Coaching Fees. The monthly coaching fee is _____. This includes a minimum of three 30-minute phone calls plus supplementary emails and spot calls.

The coaching fee is payable in advance and due by the 5th of each month. Please send payment to the above address.

I have read this agreement and agree to the above terms.

_____   _____

_____   _____

1.4: Model Coaching Agreement (Claudette Rowley)

The following agreement is provided by Claudette Rowley, LICSW (Metavoice Coaching; http://www.metavoice.org):

Coaching Agreement

I, _____, am committed to creating a coaching alliance with Claudette Rowley. Claudette agrees to hold all content of our sessions completely confidential and to create a place for me to stay clear, focused, and in action. I commit to creating a successful alliance that supports me in reaching my goals and living the life I want.

I agree to coaching for a minimum of three months.   yes   no

I agree to shape the coaching relationship to best meet my needs by:
- Sharing what I know about my own motivation   yes   no
- Co-designing structures that will support me   yes   no
- Asking for changes if the coaching relationship is not working   yes   no

I give Claudette permission to:
- Challenge me with powerful questions   yes   no
- Make requests that I take action when I identify things
  that are important to me   yes   no
- Hold me accountable for taking actions I commit to   yes   no
- Provide inquiries for me to think about   yes   no

I agree to the following business arrangements:
- Fee of $___ per month   yes   no
- Fee paid at the beginning of the month   yes   no
- Fee for the initial intake session of $ yes   no
- Fee covers four ___ hour sessions per month with unlimited e-mail   yes   no
- In months with five weeks, one week is off   yes   no

I agree to the following scheduling items:
- If I am late for an appointment, my session will be shortened   yes   no
- I will re-schedule any appointments 24 hours in advance
  or forfeit the appointment and pay the fee   yes   no
- If I want to take a break, I will give 2 weeks notice   yes   no
- I will give 2 weeks notice when I decide to complete
  the coaching relationship.   yes   no

_____   _____
Client's signature   Date

_____   _____
Claudette Rowley   Date

2. OnTrack Coaching Personal Information Fact Sheet

Date _____

CLIENT INFORMATION

Full name _____

Name you like to be called _____

Address_____

_____

Mailing address, if different _____

_____

TELEPHONE NUMBERS

Home phone _____ Work phone _____

Pager# _____ Fax # _____

Email _____ Work email _____

Cellular phone _____

EMPLOYMENT INFORMATION

Occupation (what you do to earn a living): _____

_____

Profession/degree/training: _____

_____

Employer name: _____

Employer address: _____

_____

Special Accomplishments (Books, awards):

_____

_____

_____

PERSONAL INFORMATION

Date of birth _____   Age _____   Your sex _____

Marital status _____   Number of children _____

Significant other's name _____

Wedding or special anniversary date _____

Name(s) of child(ren) and ages. Include stepchildren. Indicate where if not living with you: _____

_____

_____

_____

3. Sample Client Questionnaires

3.1: OnTrack Coaching New Client Questionnaire

Do the best you can to complete these questions. Do it as quickly as possible so your answers reflect your initial, intuitive responses. There are no right or wrong answers.

1. What accomplishments or measurable events must occur in your life for you to feel satisfied?
2. What would you like your life to look like in 5 years? What changes would you see are needed to make that happen?
3. What's missing in your life that, were it present, would make your life more fulfilling?
4. What do you think people are afraid to tell you about yourself?
5. Do you have a sense of your life purpose? If so, how do you know it's the right one for you? How does it impact your day to day? Do others know it or is it something you keep to yourself?
6. If there were a passion in your life which you could freely express without regard to money, fear, obligations to or the thoughts and opinions of others, what would that be?
7. What do you see your role as being in your community and on a global level? Do you see yourself as making a difference? How?
8. If you had only a short time to live and could live that time exactly the way you wanted to, what changes would those closest to you see in you?
9. If you had total and complete trust in your coach, what advice would you give her about how to best coach you?
10. What else would you like your coach to know about you?

3.2: Coaching Profile by Claudette Rowley, LICSW (used with permission)

Name: _____   Phone : (h) _____

                                     Phone: (w) _____

Address: _____   Fax: _____

_____

Place of Work: _____   Email: _____

Work Address: _____   Birthdate: _____

_____

1. Where do you want your primary focus to be right now? What is most important for you to accomplish? Please be specific and personal.

    a. _____

    b. _____

    c. _____

    d. _____

2. What changes/actions are needed for these to be accomplished?

3. What do you need to drop, simplify, or let go in order to move forward in these areas? What are your typical obstacles?

4. How can I, as your coach, be of most help to you?

5. What are your ten top intentions? Be *sure* to feel excitement for each of these. Be careful that they are not "shoulds" or things others want for you.

6. What are 20 things you tolerating, e.g., putting up with in your life—at home, in relationships, at work, or with yourself?

7. What are your greatest pleasures?

8. Where/when do you feel the most fulfilled? When are you at your best?

9. What are your greatest strengths?

10. What do you consider your greatest accomplishments?

11. If you could change/add one thing in your life that would make a big difference to you, what would it be?

You have a choice here. Either write a short biography, including the main accomplishments, milestones, and events—both positive and negative—that have influenced you and shaped your life.

and/or

Write an imagined letter to a friend, pretending it is a year from now. You are looking back over the past year with a sense of satisfaction and accomplishment. It has been a great year for you—both personally and professionally. You feel very good about yourself and all that has transpired in the last 12 months.

You sit down to write a letter to your best friend, describing the year. There has been an underlying theme for the whole year—the thread that weaves through it all.

The letter starts with: "This has been a most extraordinary year for me . . ."

- What were the highlights?
- What were the obstacles you had to overcome?
- Who did you have to *be* to get to that place?

4. Questions to Determine the Client's Agenda

4.1: Ten Desires You Would Like to Focus on Over the Next 90 Days in Your Personal and Business Life

1. _____
2. _____
3. _____
4. _____
5. _____
6. _____
7. _____
8. _____
9. _____
10. _____

or

4.2: Primary Focus—What Do You Want?

Identify five areas you would like to have as your main focus for the coaching process. For each area fgive a simple heading and underneath write a description of specific, measurable results(s) you would like to see.

EXAMPLE: Be more organized

I write everything down. I can find what I need when I need it. I am on time with both appointments and deadlines. I have a budget I follow. I follow through on commitments. I'm not overwhelmed.

1. _____
2. _____
3. _____
4. _____
5. _____

5. Tolerations

"Tolerations" are events, people, situations you put up with that drain your energy . . . that keep you from being yourself and enjoying life to the fullest. Tolerations are found in all aspects of our life: home /office, relationships/family, clients/customers, pets, car/ appliances/equipment, body/appearance, and so forth. To discover your tolerations, write down everything you can think of that you would no longer like to have to put up with in your life. You easily be able to come up with a list of ten and can probably keep going.

Please list below 10 areas you are tolerating in your personal and business life

1. _____
2. _____
3. _____
4. _____
5. _____
6. _____
7. _____
8. _____
9. _____
10. _____

6. Wheels of Life and Business

6.1: Wheel of Life

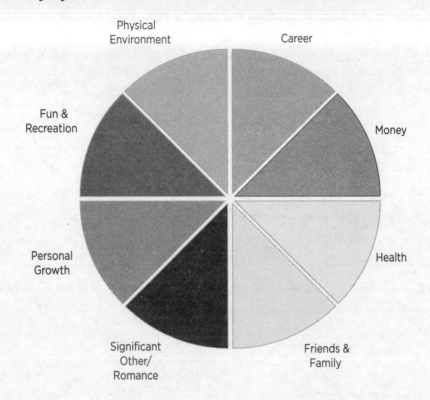

Directions:

The eight sections in the Wheel of Life represent balance. Regarding the center of the wheel as 0 and the outer edge as 10, rank your level of satisfaction with each area by drawing a straight or curved line to create a new outer edge (see example). The new perimeter of the circle represents the Wheel of Life. How bumpy would the ride be if this were a real wheel?

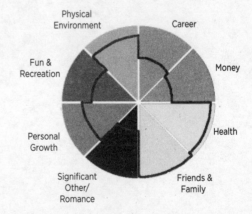

6.2: Wheel of Business

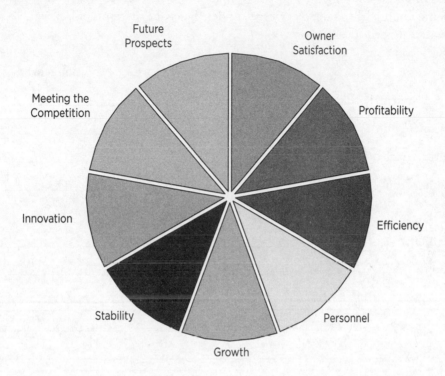

Directions:

The nine sections in the Wheel of Business represent the balance of your business or career. Regarding the center of the wheel as 0 and the outer edge as 10, rank your level of satisfaction with each area by drawing a straight or curved line to create a new outer edge (see example). The new perimeter of the circle represents your Wheel of Business. How bumpy would the ride be if this were a real wheel? What areas do you immediately see where you could make some changes?

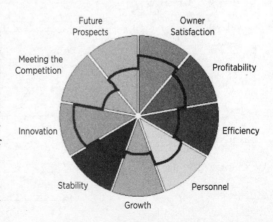

7. Rankings

7.1: Values Clarification

Choose 10 of the following (or add your own). Rank them in order of their importance to you (left column). Then rank *the same ten* under "behavior" in terms of how you actually live. Notice if both are aligned.

Value	Importance	Behavior
Accomplishment/Results	_____	_____
Achievement	_____	_____
Adventure/Excitement	_____	_____
Aesthetics/Beauty	_____	_____
Altruism	_____	_____
Authenticity	_____	_____
Autonomy	_____	_____
Clarity	_____	_____
Commitment	_____	_____
Community	_____	_____
Compassion	_____	_____
Connection/Bonding	_____	_____
Creativity	_____	_____
Ease	_____	_____
Emotional health	_____	_____
Environment	_____	_____
Family/Family first	_____	_____
Financial freedom/Wealth	_____	_____
Fitness	_____	_____
Freedom/Independence	_____	_____
Fun	_____	_____
Health/Well-being	_____	_____
Honesty	_____	_____

Value	Importance	Behavior
Humor/Integrity	_____	_____
Intimacy	_____	_____
Joy	_____	_____
Leadership	_____	_____
Loyalty	_____	_____
Making a difference	_____	_____
Mastery/Excellence	_____	_____
Moving things forward	_____	_____
Openness	_____	_____
Orderliness/Accuracy	_____	_____
Partnership	_____	_____
Philanthropy	_____	_____
Power	_____	_____
Privacy/Solitude	_____	_____
Recognition/Acknowledgment	_____	_____
Religion	_____	_____
Risk taking	_____	_____
Romance	_____	_____
Security	_____	_____
Self-expression	_____	_____
Sensuality	_____	_____
Service/Contribution	_____	_____
Spirituality	_____	_____
Success	_____	_____
Trust	_____	_____
Vitality	_____	_____
Wisdom	_____	_____
Other	_____	_____

7.2: *"Sophie's Choice" Method*

Rank order your 10 by comparing the first and second and choosing as if you could only have one but not the other. Take that choice and continue down the list until the order of choices becomes clear. I use this method to show clients that sometimes, in a pinch, two values compete very closely. If in doubt, this method provides a way to make decisions and stay truest to one's core values. For the example, I am using only five.

Original order:
Accomplishment – 1
Fun
Honesty
Openness
Security

Accomplishment – 2
Honesty – 1
Openness
Security
Fun

Honesty – 2
Openness – 1
Security
Fun
Accomplishment – 3

Openness – 1
Security – 4
Fun
Honesty – 2
Accomplishment – 3

Security – 4
Fun
Openness – 1
Honesty – 2
Accomplishment – 3

Final order:
Openness – 1
Honesty – 2
Accomplishment – 3
Security – 4
Fun – 5

What difference does the new order make? What might this person have learned about him- or herself?

8. Strengths Inventory

A – Strongly agree, B – Agree, C – Disagree

	Health
	My life is full of only healthy stress.
	I have lots of energy, vim, and vigor.
	I look great physically.
	My body is healthy and well taken care of.
	I recover well from illnesses.
	Financial
	I am financially independent or on track.
	I am free of credit cards, debt.
	I can count of monthly income.
	I have extra money in safe place.
	Money (or lack of it) doesn't hold me back.
	Career
	I like, get what I need, from the work I do.
	I have the training, education to advance.
	I am respected at work.
	I get paid well for the work I perform.
	Relationships
	My friends love me more than I need.
	My family loves me more than I need.
	I feel a special connection with certain people.
	I have a best friend.
	People are there when I need them to be.
	Outlook
	I am optimistic about myself and my future.
	I trust in a higher power.
	I recover well from challenges and difficulties.
	I am actively engaged in creating my future.

	Self-Care
	I readily put myself when I need to.
	I am free from addiction to substances, food.
	I get help quickly, and appropriately, when I need it.
	Communication
	I get my point across, powerfully, and consistently.
	People listen and respond to me and what I say.
	I hear beyond what people are saying
	I often and willingly share my thoughts and ideas.
	I can articulate what is really happening.
	Social
	I attract great people to/around me.
	I am graceful in social situations.
	I make people feel great about themselves.
	I deliver parties that others love.
	My social calendar is full/nearly full.
	Professional
	I lead a group/staff well.
	I am a great people manager.
	I handle myself well in business situations/meetings.
	I know my "stuff" (technical, info, procedures).
	I meet and exceed my targets and goals at work.
	Challenges
	I recover well from disappointments and problems.
	I anticipate problems and handle them early.
	I don't mind risk; I use it to get what I want.
	I adapt and make the most of changes around me.
	I can count on myself to survive the worst.

	Style
	People can count on me to be on time and keep my word.
	I am organized, neat.
	I ask for, and get, what I need.
	I don't gossip; I keep confidences, am trustworthy.
	Proaction
	I have, and honor, my personal standards
	I make and follow through on my commitments.

9. Homework and Feedback Forms

9.1: How to Get the Most Out of Your Coaching

I want you to get the most from the time we have together each week and from the time in-between our sessions. This brief guide describes what most of my clients do to get full value from their coaching time with me.

Make a List of What You Really Want in Life

Coaching works best when you have clear desires, which are based on your needs and values. I will help you define what you need, but you probably already have a pretty good idea.

Come to the Coaching session with an Agenda

We have a relatively short time together, and I suggest that you prepare a written list of topics for us to discuss. This may include the following:

- successes from the week;
- problems you've faced and how you handled them;
- what you're currently working on and how that's going;
- insights, new information and any new awareness which excite you;
- "homework" you completed;
- specific coaching you want from me;
- new skills you want to develop; and
- strategies you wish to develop for a client or for your business.

Having an agenda helps you get what you want from the meeting. I recommend you also keep a separate journal to make notes in during the week as important issues arise.

There Will Be Fieldwork

These are tasks, actions, results, or changes that you are telling yourself and your coach you want to complete before the next session.

9.2: The Coaching Prep Form (ask client to e-mail before each session)

Before our next coaching session, please think through the following questions, choosing those that are most relevant and important to you now. Please always include 7. Having this information ready helps you—and me—make the most of our calls.

1. Any important feedback about our last call?
2. What have I accomplished since our last call?
3. What didn't I get done that I intended to do?
4. What opportunities do I have?
5. What challenges am I facing now?
6. What have I learned?
7. How can I best use my coach during our call?
8. What actions will I take next?
9. Anything else?

10. Completion Form

This is similar to the session form but also designed to give the coach helpful feedback on their coaching:

- What have I accomplished during our coaching?
- What didn't I get done that I intended to do?
- What opportunities do I have now that I didn't have before?
- What challenges am I facing going forward?
- What have I learned?
- What didn't I learn or get that I hoped to?
- What actions will I take next to keep growing and moving forward?
- How can I best use coaching in the future?
- I would return to my present coach? _____Yes/No
- _____ to a different coach? Yes/No
- Feedback for my coach about the coaching?
- Anything else?

11. "Future Self" Letter

To put clients into a future mindset, some coaches use the future self either as a guided visualization or as a letter to oneself. Ben Zander (see Zander & Zander, 2000, p. 26) uses this technique with his music students at the New England Conservatory of Music. At the beginning of each semester, he tells them they each have an "A." All they need to do is write him a letter from the end of the semester, telling him what they accomplished to deserve it. Needless to say, the majority of students do outstanding work. Zander has stated that the A "is not an expectation to live up to, but a possibility to live into."

Here is an "A" exercise anyone can do: Write a letter from your future self (five years from now) to your current self:

- Describe where you are, what you are doing, what you have gone through to get there, and so on.
- Tell yourself the crucial things you realized or did to get there.
- Give yourself some sage and compassionate advice from the future.
- Give yourself that "A."

Checklist for Going into Business
(adapted by Cherie Sohnen-Moe from U.S. Small Business Administration [SBA] Checklist MP-12)

Under each question, check the answer that says what you feel or comes closest to it. Be honest with yourself.

Are you a self-starter?

_____   I do things on my own, nobody has to tell me to get going.

_____   If someone gets me started, I keep going all right.

_____   Easy does it. I don't put myself out until I have to.

How do you feel about other people?

_____   I like people. I can get along with just about anybody.

_____   I have plenty of friends—I don't need anyone else.

_____   Most people irritate me.

Can you lead others?

_____   I can get most people to go along when I start something.

_____   I can give orders if someone tells me what we should do.

_____   I let someone else get things moving. Then I go along if I feel like it.

Can you take responsibility?

_____   I like to take charge of things and see them through.

_____   I'll take over if I have to, but rather let someone else be responsible.

_____   There's always some eager beaver around wanting to show how smart s/he is.

How good an organizer are you?

_____ I like to have a plan before I start. I'm usually the one to get things lined up when the group wants to do something.

_____ I do all right unless things get too confused. Then I quit.

_____ I get all set and then something comes along and presents too many problems. So I just take things as they are.

How good worker are you?

_____ I can keep going as long as I need to. I don't mind working hard for something I want.

_____ I'll work hard for a while, but when I've had enough, that's it.

_____ I can't see that hard work gets you anywhere.

Can you make decisions?

_____ I can make up my mind in a hurry if I have to. It usually turns out okay, too.

_____ I can if I have plenty of time. If I make up my mind fast, I think later I should have decided the other way.

_____ I don't like to be the one who decides things.

Can people trust what you say?

_____ You bet they can. I don't say things I don't mean.

_____ I try to be on the level most of the time, but sometimes I just say what 's easiest.

_____ Why bother if they other person doesn't know the difference?

Can you stick with it?

_____ If I make up my mind to do something, I don't let anything stop me.

_____ I usually finish what I start— if it goes well.

_____ If it doesn't go right away, I quit. Why beat your brains out?

How good is your health?

_____ I never run down!

_____ I have enough energy for most things I want to do.

_____ I run out of energy sooner than most of my friends seem to.

Now count the checks you made beside each question.

How many checks are beside the first answer?   _____

How many checks are beside the second answer?   _____

How many checks are beside the third answer?   _____

If most of your checks are the first answers, you probably have what it takes to run a business. If not, you are likely to be have more difficulty than you can handle by yourself. It would be best to find a partner who is strong on some points in which you're weak.

According to the SBA, if many checks are beside the third answer, it's possible not even a good partner could shore you up. If, however, you are highly motivated, these answers will point to the areas in which you need to develop yourself. Make sure to get good coaching and to pay particular attention to self-care and self-development issues. For example, attending to your health and well-being might increase your energy for getting things done, organizational and time-management skills can be learned and decision-making can be shared with a partner.

Appendix I

Starting Up a Business Checklist

This checklist is designed to help you meet the needs of business planning. Because every business is different, no attempt has been made to prioritize these items, many of which can be done simultaneously. Print the list, and assign completion dates to each item or place a check mark on the line as you complete each task. Some of the items listed may not be applicable to your business or may only apply if you are starting a business in the United States. Cross off items that do not apply to your business.

Start-up issues

_____ Determine whether you're ready to start this business.

_____ Do a feasibility study to assess the viability of this particular business.

_____ Decide whether to operate as a sole proprietorship, partnership, or corporation.

_____ Begin writing out your business idea in the form of a business plan.

_____ Begin lining up sources to finance your venture. You will have start-up expenses.

_____ Decide if you need an office or will work from home.

_____ Decide if you will do it all or hire an assistant, use a bookkeeper, or virtual assistant.

Business registration and forms

_____ Contact the City Tax Collector to determine if you must register your business.

_____ File a Fictitious Business Name Statement (d/b/a) with the County Clerk.

_____ Contact the Secretary of State's office to determine if your business name is valid. (This only applies if you're going to engage in business outside your country or form a corporation.)

_____ If you are going to operate your business as a corporation, prepare and file incorporation papers with the State Department of Corporations. You will also have to draw up Articles of Incorporation and Corporate By-laws as part of the incorporation process.

_____ Apply for a Taxpayer's Identification Number from the IRS and check to see which tax forms you'll need.

Business permits and licenses

_____ Check with City and State Licensing Divisions to see if a license or permit is needed to conduct your business. Obtain any required licenses.

_____ Check with the local Zoning Department to determine if you can legally operate your business at your intended location.

_____ Apply for a building permit if you plan to make structural improvements to your facility.

_____ Check with the State Tax Board to see if you need a Seller's Permit. Obtain a Seller's Permit, if required (for example, if you plan to sell books or tapes).

Sales and marketing

_____ Set long-term and short-term goals for your business.

_____ Develop a marketing strategy to achieve your business goals.

_____ Determine your niche and who your customers and competitors are.

_____ Develop pricing and compute your break-even point.

_____ Design and order stationery and business cards.

_____ Design and have a website and or blog built.

_____ Plan your sales and marketing approach.

_____ Plan your advertising, sales promotion, and publicity activities.

Operations

_____ Acquire the necessary equipment and machinery—computer, headset.

_____ Choose a business location and negotiate and secure the lease.

_____ Determine the appropriate insurance coverage needed to cover the risks inherent in your business and select an insurance agent or broker.

_____ Apply for the appropriate copyrights, trademarks, or patents necessary to protect your intellectual property.

Recordkeeping, Finance, and Accounting

_____ Set up files and other recordkeeping systems.

_____ Set up accounting and bookkeeping procedures.

_____ Familiarize yourself with financial statements and their use.

_____ Choose a bank and open a business account.

_____ Familiarize yourself with local, state, and federal tax requirements and submit the required documents.

_____ Set up cash management procedures for conserving cash.

_____ Set up expense and income forecasts.

Miscellaneous

_____ Attend meetings of your local International Coach Federation chapter and consider membership.

_____ Attend other networking events in your area. Choose one that is related to your niche area if possible.

Appendix J

Business Plan Basics (based on Adams, 1994)

Introduction
Cover sheet; Plan objective; Executive summary; Table of contents

Part One—The Business
Business Profile or Company Analysis—name, brief description of the business, long-term goals and objectives
Product or Service Analysis—product benefits, special technology or design, future products
Marketing and Sales—marketing strategy, product distribution, sales, promotion, sales forecast
Location and Facilities
Management Profile—organizational structure, personnel profiles, resumes

Part Two—Financial Analysis
Start-up expenses
Capital equipment list
Income projection—first year by month
Cash-flow projections—first year by month
Balance sheet—at start of business
Income projections—years 2 and 3 by quarter
Break-even analysis

Part Three—Supporting Documents
Personal financial statement

Business Resources
U.S. Small Business Administration Web site:
http://www.sba.gov/smallbusinessplanner/index.html

Marketing Communications

1. The Marketing Communications Checklist

This checklist is designed to help you create effective marketing materials for your business. Copy this checklist, and assign completion dates to each item or place a check mark on the line as you complete each task.

Business name

_____ Select a name that let prospects know what your business does.

_____ Imply a benefit, such as economical, dependable, or quality-driven.

_____ Avoid words that have negative or offensive connotations.

Logo

_____ Create a logo that is different enough not to be confused with those of other firms.

_____ Select a design that projects the identity you want for your company.

_____ Make sure that it looks professional.

Business cards

_____ Make that your business cards look professional.

_____ Match your cards to your other business stationery.

_____ Include your name, business name, and business address.

_____ Include your business telephone number, fax number, and other appropriate ways of contacting you (home telephone number, modem, and so forth).

_____ Design the card so that it advertises your business. To do this, you may want to add a motto, tagline or slogan on the front of it.

_____ Use the back of your business card as a miniadvertisement to promote your products or services or to provide a map to your location.

Business stationery

_____ Print your letterheads and envelopes on good quality paper.

_____ Create a professional looking design.

_____ Make sure the type face is easy to read.

_____ Include your telephone number and make sure it is clearly visible on your letterhead.

_____ Make sure that the size of and printing on your envelopes comply with postal regulations.

Brochures

_____ Create a brochure that will fit into a #10 standard business envelope.

_____ Make sure it looks like it comes from an established, quality-conscious business.

_____ Use heavy, good quality paper stock.

_____ Develop content, especially the main points, that is easy to understand even if a person spends less than a minute looking at it.

_____ Use type that is large enough to be read easily (no smaller than 10 point).

_____ Write the copy from the audience's point of view and in their words.

2. Marketing Materials Questionnaire

Questions

Who is your target market?

In your experience, what are the top overall challenges facing these people or businesses? List three to five. *Examples:*

- succession issues, divorce, intergenerational conflict for family businesses;
- work–life balance, how much to grow the business for entrepreneurial women; and
- the challenge of running an organization true to its values, organizer wearing too many hats, finding and managing the right staff, generating leadership for nonprofits.

Why do you think coaching really works for people in this group? *Examples:*

- It's practical approach for practical people.
- Family businesses are motivated to succeed and tend especially to thrive with the support of a nurturing and open communications program.
- It's practical approach for human services—results oriented and fast.
- It's a fresh, dynamic, innovative approach that can invigorate professionals in a challenging field.

What in your background or experience gives you special insight or talents for successfully coaching people in this market? *Example:* Education, work experience, personal life path, 30 years of experience in human services, certified as a coach and a licensed and board certified MSW, training in systems dynamics and organizational development, teach and train post graduate social workers, psychologists and other therapists; have consulted with physicians and other health care providers.

Give an example of a specific problem that you coached someone in this group through. What were the major obstacles they faced and how did you work together to overcome them? What was the result? *Get a testimonial!*

Why do you love working with people in this group? *Examples:*

- Because it is so rewarding to see the results?
- Because you love applying therapeutic skills to resolve complex business problems?
- Because you have great empathy for folks like this and want to share your wisdom?

Template for Questions for Brochure Development
Part 1

• What image of [your business] do you want people to take away from all your direct marketing?	
• Is there an established corporate identity (that is, colors, typefaces) we need to tie into?	
• How would you describe [your business]'s culture?	
• Please provide a positioning statement on [your business].	
• Please define your services in one sentence.	
• What differentiates your services from competitive or substitute products? (Rank major differences in order of importance)	
• What is the key claim we can make about your services ?	
• What is the single most essential point of your services you want people to take away from all your direct marketing?	
• How do you substantiate your claims on accuracy, ease of use and overall quality?	
• What would the most influential critic/cynic say about your services, and how would you respond?	
• Please provide complete information on payment options.	
• Please explain relevant trends we should know about.	
• Please describe the audience for this mailing	
• What is the #1 benefit of your services?	
• What is the #1 problem your services solve?	

Part 2

Please rank the features and corresponding benefits of your services for this audience, in order of importance.

Features	Benefits
•	•
•	•
•	•
•	•
•	•
•	•

Please supply a ranking of the top questions/objections relating to your service prospects raise most often—with appropriate responses.

Question/Objection	Response
•	•
•	•
•	•
•	•
•	•
•	•
•	•
•	•
•	•

Appendix L

Sample Marketing Materials

1. Family Business: Move Ahead Together in Uncertain Times (adapted from Edelson, 2002a)

In these uncertain times, preserving a family business and strengthening it for the next generat\ion are crucial undertakings. Many once-thriving businesses are at serious risk of failing as the result of "funnel vision" or by being driven apart by seemingly irreconcilable conflicts.

The passion to keep a legacy going gives closely held businesses a great incentive to survive economic downturns. Yet, half or less of all family-owned businesses make it to the third generation. In fact, these businesses face unique challenges. Divorce of a key family business member, conflict between married principals or between generations, handing over leadership to a generation yet unprepared to take the reins or getting the current generation to let go can rock, even destroy, ongoing concerns.

The will to try a new way of relating, however, can make a huge bottom-line impact for family businesses under stress. Working with a business coach with a background in family systems work can help families safely and intelligently negotiate their unique and complex issues so they can work on the technical issues of running a business while developing behaviors that lead to desired results.

The issues seen most frequently are those related to succession planning, family conflict and divorce. Each business has its own specific issues. It isn't uncommon, for instance, to see the owner/parent wanting to control everything about the business despite the children being capable of running it more than adequately. While the younger generation feels like they are being treated like small children, the older generation often feels no longer valued for their knowledge and experience by "ungrateful" children. The younger generation may receive coaching on using the parent as an inside consultant, while the older generation may be helped to get perspective on their achievements, rebalance their lives and find a meaningful next step.

Succession planning is a complex process primarily involving considerable legal and tax planning, but emotions can derail the process. A typical example is when one child is successfully engaged in the business, but siblings are not. The parent/business owner wants to be fair to all children but the child who has sacrificed and stayed in the business feels she deserves more for giving herself to the family. Openly discussing what is fair can not only lead to more creative approaches to estate and succession plans but also to equalizing the other siblings shares of their parents' overall estate.

In a business impacted by painful divorce, the spouse leaving the family business might be guided to see his or her self-interest in behaving mindfully of the business, while other family members might be guided on getting back to business, rebuilding and planning for the future.

In all situations, the consultant plays an important role in defusing emotions and keeping everyone's eyes on the prize. Participants are asked to acknowledge and take responsibility for the results they produce, progressive and regressive. Clients already have the answers within. The family business coach's role is to help them organize and surface that knowledge in order to move beyond the issues that block—or threaten to block—progress.

Given the regressive pull of families, the biggest task is freeing from those ties that bind so they can make good choices— individually, for the business and for the family.

2. Emotional Intelligence (excerpted from Noonan, 2006)

This is the age of emotional intelligence, often called EQ, and today's hiring managers want proof you've got it. Do you have the maturity and independence to follow a project to completion? Can you motivate and lead a group of your peers? Do you genuinely care about the company's values and goals? Are you the type to be sensitive to the needs of a troubled co-worker? Can you control your anger when a supervisor is rude to you?

"Employers are looking for better-rounded workers these days," said Marilyn Edelson, founder and chief executive of Newton-based OnTrack Coaching and Consulting Inc. "If you're just a grabber, looking for what you can get for yourself, you might be seen as a bright spark in the beginning, but it won't carry you through a career."

EQ comprises a collection of so-called "soft" skills, including self-awareness, an understanding of how your mood and behavior affect others; impulse control, including how you manage stress on the job; initiative, whether you can be counted on to report to work on time, manage your own time, and meet expectations; and the ability to motivate and lead others.

Some EQ tips from the experts:

- Know yourself, and learn everything possible about the values and culture of the company you hope to work for. "It's not emotionally intelligent to force yourself into an office culture where you won't be happy," said Edelson.
- Demonstrate reliability and trustworthiness. One of Edelson's favorite stories is about a 23-year-old woman who wrecked her car en route to an interview for a sales position at a pharmaceutical company. Instead of being a no-show, she called and explained the situation, and got a ride to the interview. "She was determined to show them she was reliable and would show up when she said she would," said Edelson. (Impressed, the firm hired her on the spot.)

Testimonials

Marilyn, has been a mentor and guide supreme for me, as a coach and as a professional. She brings great integrity, love, creativity and passion to her work with clients. I continue to work with her and would recommend her to anyone interested in challenging themselves to be their finest, as a professional and as a person. She is a rare and wonderful person, colleague and coach.

—Deirdre Danahar, MSW, MPH, In Motion Coaching and Consulting

Marilyn is an intelligent, articulate and dynamic entrepreneur as well as a gifted business coach. A brief conversation with Marilyn is like holding a brainstorming session with a mastermind group. You come away refreshed and full of actionable ideas to improve your professional and personal development.

—Cenmar Fuertes, founder and CEO, CoachLink, Costa Mesa, CA

Marilyn's training was invaluable to me personally and also gave me a new paradigm to bring to my agency where we work with HIV+ teens. Guiding the kids to look ahead to a future they could design according to what's important to them not only instilled new hope in their lives but directly led to increased medication compliance, and inspired all of us.

—Bea Fulton, LICSW, Philadelphia, PA

Marilyn is an engaging and experienced coach and teacher. In her seminar, she instructs attendees on the differences between coaching and consulting, explains personal and professional coaching, and describes how to build a coaching business. I found the sessions very worthwhile and recommend them for anyone who thinks coaching may be of professional interest.

—Mike Oleksak, CMC, president, Trek Consulting, Milton, MA

Beyond excellent.

—Debra Lefkovic-Abrams, LICSW, Boston, MA

A very powerful combination of psychological expertise and great business talent.

—Judy Silverstein, PhD, Needham, MA

I attended three coach-related workshops, listened to approximately twenty-five hours of coach-related tapes, read many articles, spent hours on the internet "checking out" coaching websites, newsletters, and various general philosophies of coaching. I was "turned-off" by "hard sell" approaches I encountered. In contrast, your conference had many refreshing, practical aspects that could be beneficial to [any] professional transitioning into coaching. A day well spent. Thank you.

—Anne Gooding, PhD, LICSW, New York, NY

Recently, Marilyn accepted a high profile coach training assignment with the Epilepsy Foundation Massachusetts & Rhode Island. The focus of Marilyn's work will have significant impact in New England as well as other Epilepsy Affiliates through out the United States. Marilyn's professional yet relaxed training style left the EFMRI employees energized and motivated to build a successful employment program. The knowledge that was gained affects both the employees' personal and professional lives in a positive manner. Her humor and engaging personality created a safe haven to explore potential roadblocks and to enhance insight into successful goal planning. Marilyn is an exceptional ambassador for the coaching profession bringing credit to women in business in Boston and beyond.

—Leslie G. Brody, PhD, MSW, president and CEO,
Epilepsy Foundation Massachusetts & Rhode Island, Boston, MA

Marilyn's mix of coaching, teaching and writing keep her at the cutting edge of her field. Her positive approach brings out the best that people need to discover about themselves and others.

—Rev. Stephen C. Washburn, Marshfield, MA

About the Author

Marilyn Edelson is an International Coach Federation master certified coach as well as a certified co-active coach. Her career as a business and leadership development coach is a natural evolution of 30 years' experience in human services, 15 spent in private practice. In 1996, having achieved success in business as a real estate broker, Marilyn shifted her career path from family systems counseling to coaching. Over the past seven years, she has worked with entrepreneurs, executives, professionals, and family business owners who are committed to their own personal and professional success. Her focus is on helping clients create powerful mindsets and actions that maximize their results. A graduate of the Coaches Training Institute, Edelson holds an MS in social services from Boston University. She received advanced training in organizational development and family business consulting at the Cambridge Center for Creative Enterprise. She is an active member of the International Coach Federation–New England Chapter and belongs to the New England Women's Business Owners.

Index